21世纪高等院校财经类专业
实训教材

国际贸易单证

实训教程

（第二版）

沈 生 主编

张 帆 黄 玮 副主编

东北财经大学出版社
Dongbei University of Finance & Economics Press
大连

图书在版编目（CIP）数据

国际贸易单证实训教程／沈生主编．—2版．—大连：东北财经大学出版社，2014.9（2015.8重印）
（21世纪高等院校财经类专业实训教材）
ISBN 978-7-5654-1689-7

Ⅰ．国…　Ⅱ．沈…　Ⅲ．国际贸易-原始凭证-高等学校-教材
Ⅳ．F740.44

中国版本图书馆 CIP 数据核字（2014）第 204461 号

东北财经大学出版社出版
（大连市黑石礁尖山街217号　邮政编码　116025）
教学支持：（0411）84710309
营销部：（0411）84710711
总编室：（0411）84710523
网　址：http：//www.dufep.cn
读者信箱：dufep@dufe.edu.cn

大连美跃彩色印刷有限公司印刷　　　　　东北财经大学出版社发行

幅面尺寸：170mm×240mm　　　　字数：388千字　　　　印张：20
2014年9月第2版　　　　　　　　2015年8月第4次印刷

责任编辑：李　彬　王芃南　王　丽　　　　责任校对：贺　力
　　　　　吉　扬　时　博
封面设计：张智波　　　　　　　　　　　　版式设计：钟福建

ISBN 978-7-5654-1689-7
定价：32.00元

总　序

　　20 世纪 90 年代末以来，我国高等教育取得了跨越式的发展，开始由"精英教育"向"大众化教育"转变。在高等教育大众化的背景下，培养学生的实践能力和创新能力逐步成为各高等院校提高本科教学质量的重要目标。财经类专业作为当前经济社会中最具发展性和时代活力的专业之一，本身就具有极强的实践性和应用性特点。随着经济社会形势的发展，大学生就业形势日益严峻，用人单位对财经类专业毕业生的实际操作能力的要求也越来越高。学生不但要有比较坚实的理论功底，更要有较强的实践能力和创新能力。

　　在财经类应用型人才的培养过程中，实践教学具有不可或缺的作用。高等教育的教学过程主要由理论教学和实践教学两部分组成。理论教学以教师讲授为主，主要任务是传授知识；实践教学包括军训、社会实践、实习、实验、实训、毕业论文（设计）等内容，主要任务在于培养学生的能力与素质。为实现人才培养过程中传授知识、培养能力和提高素质的协调统一，学校在注重理论教学的同时，也必须高度重视实践教学。在理论教学中传授的知识需要在实践教学中验证、消化与巩固，同时，实践教学还发挥着培养学生的动手能力、形成专业素养、启发学生创新思维、增强创新意识、提升创新能力的重要作用。可以说，没有高质量的实践教学，培养高素质的财经类应用型人才这一目标就难以实现。

　　随着大众化教育的推行，高校的学生规模急剧扩大，实习资源日益紧缺，实训作为实践教学的重要组成部分，在培养学生的实践能力方面起着越来越重要的作用。与实习相比，实训的地点和形式更为灵活，可以在校内进行，也可以在校外进行，克服了实习过程中实习单位、实习岗位等因素的限制，可以较好地解决目前学生实习难的问题。实训在教师的指导下，按照人才培养规律与目标，通过全真的角色模拟、岗位轮换，让学生亲身体验，从而切实达到提高其动手能力和训练职业技能的目的。实训不仅具有巩固学生所学的理论知识，使学生获得实践知识和管理知识，培养学生的实际工作能力，完成实践教学目标的功能，还具有引导学生了解社会、接触实际，增强学生的职业道德意识、团队精神和社会责任感的育人功能。

　　目前，很多财经类院校已经意识到实训教学的重要性，开始建立实训中心或基地，开设相关实训课程。要真正搞好实训教学，必须遵循实训教学的规律，创立一个目的明确、层次分明、系统完整的实训教学体系。作为教学过程中一个不可缺少的重要环节，实训教学有其自身的科学性、系统性和衔接性，与理论教学平行而又相互协调、相辅相成。为更好地推动实训教学的发展，高校除了建立良好的实训条件、创造较为逼真的实训情境和环境外，还必须有切实可行、可操作性强的实训教程，并以此为基础逐步形成以学生为主体、教师为主导，多层次、系列化、模块化、开放式的实训教学体系。因此，在理论教材的基础上结合社会需求，编写出要求一致、规范统一的实训配套教材成为推动实训教学发展的关键。

为更加有效地开展实训教学，我们组织编写了这套"21世纪高等院校财经类专业实训教材"，具体包括《旅游管理实训教程》、《市场营销实训教程》、《人力资源管理实训教程》、《成本会计实训教程》、《财务管理实训教程》、《审计实训教程》、《电算化会计实训教程》、《国际贸易实务实训教程》、《国际贸易单证实训教程》、《经济法实训教程》等10本书，涉及旅游管理、人力资源管理、市场营销、会计学、财务管理、国际经济与贸易等专业。本套教材注重实训教学与理论教学的衔接，突出实训教材的实用性、适用性、仿真性、可操作性等特点，适用于高等院校经济管理类专业本科生的实训教学，也可作为相关从业人员的学习、培训用书。

在本系列教材的编写过程中，我们力求精益求精，但由于经验不足、时间有限，教材中难免存在不妥之处，恳请读者给予指正。

"21世纪高等院校财经类专业实训教材"编审委员会

第二版前言

国际贸易实务课程的实务性及贸易实践的复杂性决定了该课程必然涉及很多的单证操作训练问题。然而很长时间以来，由于受教学时间和教学手段所限，很多学校在该课程的课堂教学中都无法开展这项训练，导致学生毕业后虽然具备了较高的理论水平，却缺乏业务操作能力。

近些年来，各个学校都对国际货物贸易操作课程给予了不同程度的重视，为了方便教学和指导学生熟悉国际货物买卖的全过程，在理论课和理论基础的指导下，我们决定编写一本实训教程，以适应学校和社会对国际经济与贸易专业人才的要求。

第二版教材的编写目的是为国际货物贸易操作的教与学提供规范性指导，使教材的使用者在仿真的国际货物买卖商业环境中，切身体会货物进出口交易的全过程，全面系统地掌握规范的交易操作技能。本书以货物出口交易的基本过程为主线，以设定的具体出口商品交易为背景，设定了十四个实训环节，涉及建立出口业务关系、出口报价及还价核算、交易磋商、贸易合同拟订、信用证审核及修改、出口订舱、出口报检、出口报关、出口保险、贸易单证制作及审核、退税等内容。在介绍信用证开立、审核、修改及结汇单证、官方单证的制作的同时，也详细介绍了进出口贸易的整个业务流程，集外贸单证实务与进出口贸易实务于一身。

第二版教材具有以下特点：第一，适用性强。本书的编写自成体系，内容编排完全按照国际货物买卖的一般过程进行，不依赖于某一具体的国际贸易实务教材。本书通过案例教学，在对案例进行分析的过程中，让学生把所学的基础知识融入到对案例的分析应用中，使没有实践经验的学生通过对案例数据的操作，为适应今后工作岗位上的真实数据和现实工作环节的需要奠定基础。第二，实训环节设计科学。本书的实训环节完全按照实际业务步骤进行编排，一气贯通，能帮助学生全面掌握业务操作流程。第三，实训指导全面、具体、规范。对各业务环节的操作都做了全面细致的规范指导，从而保证了学生能够科学地进行正规训练，培养实际业务操作能力。最后一章是综合实训，并配有参考答案，可让学生熟悉国际货物买卖的整个流程。第四，融入了信息化教学理念，在相关章节中设置了"网络链接"项目，介绍了商务部、海关总署等官方网站资源，培养学生自主学习、拓展学习的能力。

为方便教学，本书配有网络教辅资料，请任课教师登录东北财经大学出版社网站（www.dufep.cn）查询和下载。

本书由沈生任主编，张帆、黄玮担任副主编，具体分工如下：沈生负责编写模块一、三、八、九；张帆负责编写模块二、四、五；蔡锦晖负责编写模块六、七；陈茹负责编写模块十、十一；李虹负责编写模块十二；黄玮负责编写模块十三；张洁璇负责编写模块十四；王得加、张智荣协助教材的电脑编辑工作。在编写过程中，作者参考了相关文献，在此对相关作者表示衷心感谢。

由于编者经验、水平、时间有限，书中难免存在不足之处，恳请专家及读者给予指正。

编　者
2014 年 6 月

目　录

模块一　信用证在国际贸易结算中的运用

一、实训目的

（一）学生能依据进口合同填制信用证开证申请书

（二）学生能依据出口合同审核信用证

（三）学生能根据信用证的相关要求正确缮制相关单据

二、理论知识点

（一）填制开证申请书

在以信用证方式支付的进口货物交易中，开立信用证是履行进口合同的第一步，也是进口商的一项重要履约行为，因为根据法律规定，及时申请开立信用证是买方的一项重要义务。

开证申请书是申请人与开证行之间法律关系的书面契约，进口方应根据银行的开证申请书的格式填制开证申请书，一式三份，业务部门、财务部门各自留一份，另一份连同保证金、开证手续费等一并送交开证行。

开证申请书是银行开出信用证的依据。由于信用证与合同是相互独立的，原则上就应将合同的主要条款列入申请书中，但合同项下的货物与信用证项下的单据彼此是分离的，银行只依据单据的表面内容（而非商品的本质和单据的真实性）决定付汇与否，因此，信用证对于保障出口商严格履行交易合同的作用是有限的，关键还是在于出口商的信誉。为方便银行审单，避免卷入商务合同纠纷，信用证中的有关条款，尤其是关于商品的规定应适当简化。为确保信用证内容与合同相符，申请人一般会将合同副本一并提交给银行以供参考和核对。

填制开证申请书，必须按合同条款的具体规定，写明对信用证的各项要求，内容要明确、完整，表述要准确、清楚。

开证申请书的内容及填制要求如下：

1. 正面内容

（1）DATE（申请开证日期）。在申请书右上角填写实际申请日期。

（2）TO（致）。银行印制的申请书上事先都会印就开证银行的名称、地址，银行的 SWIFT CODE、TELEX NO. 等也可同时显示。

（3）PLEASE ISSUE ON OUR BEHALF AND/OR FOR OUR ACCOUNT THE FOLLOWING IRREVOCABLE LETTER OF CREDIT（请开立以下不可撤销信用证）。如果信用证是保兑或可转让的，应在此加注有关字样。开证方式多为电开（BY TELEX），也可以是信开、快递或简电开立。

（4）L/C NUMBER（信用证号码）。此栏由银行填写。

（5）APPLICANT（申请人）。填写申请人的全称及详细地址，有的要求注明联系电话、传真号码等。

（6）BENEFICIARY（受益人）。填写受益人的全称及详细地址。

（7）ADVISING BANK（通知行）。由开证行填写。

（8）AMOUNT（信用证金额）。分别用数字和文字两种形式表示，并且表明币制。如果允许有一定比率的上下浮动，要在信用证中明确表示出来。

（9）EXPIRY DATE AND PLACE（到期日期和地点）。填写信用证的有效期及到期地点。

（10）PARTIAL SHIPMENT（分批装运）、TRANSSHIPMENT（转运）。根据合同的实际规定打"×"进行选择。

（11）LOADING IN CHARGE、FOR TRANSPORT TO、LATEST DATE OF SHIPMENT（装运地/港、目的地/港的名称、最迟装运日期）。按实际填写，如允许有转运地/港，也应清楚标明。

（12）CREDIT AVAILABLE WITH/BY（付款方式）。在所提供的即期、承兑、议付和延期付款四种信用证有效兑付方式中选择与合同要求一致的类型。

（13）BENEFICIARY'S DRAFT（汇票要求）。金额应根据合同规定填写为：发票金额的一定百分比；发票金额的 100%（全部货款都用信用证支付）；如部分信用证、部分托收时按信用证下的金额比例填写。付款期限可根据实际填写即期或远期，如属后者必须填写具体的天数。信用证条件下的付款人通常是开证行，也可能是开证行指定的另外一家银行。

（14）DOCUMENTS REQUIRED（单据条款）。各银行提供的申请书中已印就的单据条款通常为十几条，从上至下一般为发票、运输单据（提单、空运单、铁路运输单据及运输备忘录等）、保险单、装箱单、质量证书、装运通知和受益人证明等, 最后一条是 OTHER DOCUMENTS, IF ANY (其他单据), 如要求提交超过上述所列范围的单据就可以在此栏填写, 比如有的合同要求 CERTIFICATE OF NO SOLID WOOD PACKING MATERIAL (无实木包装材料证明)、CERTIFICATE OF FREE SALE (自由销售证明书)、CERTIFICATE OF CONFORMITY (合格证明书) 等。申请人填制这部分内容时应依据合同规定, 不能随意增加或减少。选中某单据后对该单据的具体要求 (如一式几份、要否签字、正副本的份数、单据中应标明的内容等) 也应如实填写, 如申请书印制好的要求不完整应在其后予以补足。

(15) COVERING/EVIDENCING SHIPMENT OF (商品描述)。所有内容 (品名、规格、包装、单价、唛头) 都必须与合同内容相一致, 价格条款里附带 "AS PER INCOTERMS 2000"、数量条款中规定 "MORE OR LESS" 或 "ABOUT"、使用某种特定包装物等特殊要求必须清楚列明。

(16) ADDITIONAL INSTRUCTIONS (附加指示)。该栏通常体现为以下一些印就的条款:

+ALL DOCUMENTS MUST INDICATE CONTRACT NUMBER (所有单据加列合同号码)。

+ ALL BANKING CHARGES OUTSIDE THE OPENING BANK ARE FOR BENEFICIARY'S ACCOUNT (所有开证行以外的银行费用都由受益人承担)。

+ BOTH QUANTITY AND AMOUNT FOR EACH ITEM % MORE OR LESS ALLOWED (每项数量与金额允许 % 增减)。

+THIRD PARTY AS SHIPPER IS NOT ACCEPTABLE (第三方作为托运人是不能接受的)。

+DOCUMENTS MUST BE PRESENTED WITHIN ××× DAYS AFTER THE DATE OF ISSUANCE OF THE TRANSPORT DOCUMENTS BUT WITHIN THE VALIDITY OF THIS CREDIT (单据必须在提单日后×××天送达银行并且不超过信用证有效期)。

+ SHORT FORM/BLANK BACK/CLAUSED/CHARTER PARTY B/L IS UNACCEPTABLE (银行不接受略式/不清洁/租船提单)。

+ ALL DOCUMENTS TO BE FORWARDED IN ONE COVER, UNLESS OTHERWISE STATED ABOVE (除非有相反规定, 所有单据应一次提交)。

+PREPAID FREIGHT DRAWN IN EXCESS OF L/C AMOUNT IS ACCEPTABLE AGAINST PRESENTATION OF ORIGINAL CHARGES VOUCHER ISSUED BY SHIPPING CO. /AIR LINE OR ITS AGENT (银行接受凭船公司/航空公司或其代理人签发的正本运费收据索要超过信用证金额的预付运费)。

+DOCUMENT ISSUED PRIOR TO THE DATE OF ISSUANCE OF CREDIT NOT ACCEPTABLE (不接受早于开证日出具的单据)。

如需要已印就的上述条款, 可在条款前打 "×", 对合同涉及但未印就的条款还可以做补充填写。

（17） NAME，SIGNATURE OF AUTHORISED PERSON，TEL NO.，FAX，ACCOUNT NO. （授权人名称、签字、电话、传真、账号等内容）。

2. 背面内容

申请书的背面通常是申请人对开证行的声明，用来明确双方的责任和义务，主要内容有：

（1）声明申请人同意按照有关国际惯例办理该信用证项下的一切事宜，并承担由此产生的一切责任。

（2）声明委托银行开立信用证，并保证按时向银行支付信用证项下的货款、手续费、利息及其他一切费用。

（3）明确收到单据后，申请人在若干个工作日内复审单据，并在规定期限内通知银行接受与否。

（4）声明该信用证及其项下的业务往来函电及单据，如因邮电或其他方式传递过程中发生遗失、延误、错漏等，银行一概不负责。

（5）声明若信用证需要修改，应由申请人及时通知银行，并及时核对信用证副本或修改副本是否与原申请书相符。

（6）声明因申请书字迹不清或词义含混所引起的后果由申请人负责。

开证申请书的具体格式见表 1-1。

表 1-1   **开证申请书**

不可撤销跟单信用证申请书
APPLICATION FOR IRREVOCABLE DOCUMENTARY CREDIT

To：   Place/Date：

Beneficiary (fullname and address)		Date and place of expiry of credit
Partial shipments ☐allowed ☐not allowed	Transshipment ☐allowed ☐not allowed	☐Issue by airmail ☐Issue by teletransmission
Loading on board/dispatch/taking in charge at/from		Amount (both in figures and words)
Description of goods：	Credit available with ☐by sight payment ☐by acceptance ☐by negotiation ☐by deferred payment at against the documents detailed herein ☐and beneficiary's draft for 100% of the invoice value ☐FOB ☐C&F ☐CIF	

Documents required：（marked with ×）

1. （ ） Signed Commercial Invoice in 4 copies indicating L/C No. and Contract No.

2. （ ） Full set of clean on board ocean Bills of Lading made out to the order and blank endorsed，marked "freight ［ ］ to collect/ ［×］ prepaid ［ ］ showing freight amount" notifying CRYSTAL KOBE LTD. 1410 BROADWAY，ROOM 300 NY 10018 U. S. A.

3. (　) Air Waybills showing "freight [　] to collect/ [　] prepaid [　] indicating freight amount" and consigned to _____ .

4. (　) Memorandum issued by (　) consigned to _____ .

5. (　) Insurance Policy/Certificate in 2 copies for 110% of the invoice value showing claims payable in China in currency of the draft. Blank endorsed, covering (［×］ Ocean Marine Transportation All Risks, War Risks.

6. (　) Packing List/Weight Memo in 3 copies indicating quantity/gross and net weights of each package and packing condition as called for by the L/C.

7. (　) Beneficiary's certified copy of cable/telex dispatched to the accountees within 24 hours after shipment advising ［×］ name of vessel/ [　] No. / [　] wagon No. , date, quantity, weight and value of shipment.

8. (　) Beneficiary's Certificate certifying that extra copies of the documents have been dispatched according to the contract terms.

9. (　) Other documents, if any：

Additional instructions：

1. (　) All banking charges outside the opening bank are for beneficiary's account.

2. (　) Documents must be presented within 15 days after the date of issuance of the transport documents but within the validity this credit.

3. (　) Third party as shipper is not acceptable. Short form/Blank back B/L is not acceptable.

4. (　) Both quantity and amount ____% more or less are allowed.

5. (　) All documents to be forwarded in one cover, unless otherwise stated above.

Your correspondences to advise beneficiary are □adding their confirmation ⊠ without adding their confirmation.

Payments should be debited to our _____ amount no _____ .

Signature：_____

（二）关于 SWIFT 信用证

1. SWIFT 介绍

SWIFT 是 "Society for Worldwide Interbank Financial Telecommunication"（环球同业银行金融电讯协会）的缩写。它是一个国际银行同业间非营利性的国际合作组织，其总部设在比利时的布鲁塞尔。该组织成立于 1973 年 5 月，由北美和西欧 5 个国家的 239 家银行发起，董事会为最高权力机构。

SWIFT 专门从事传递各国之间的非公开性的国际金融电讯业务，其中包括外汇买卖、证券交易、开立信用证、办理信用证项下的汇票业务及托收等，同时还承担国际间账务清算及银行间的资金调拨等业务。目前，SWIFT 在全世界拥有会员国 200 多个，会员银行近 8 000 家，其环球计算机数据通讯网在荷兰的阿姆斯特丹和美国的纽约设有运行中心，在各会员国设有地区处理站，为 SWIFT 会员提供安全、可靠、快捷、标准化、自动化的通讯服务。

2. SWIFT 的特点

（1）SWIFT 需要会员资格。我国的大多数专业银行都是其成员。

（2）SWIFT 的费用较低。同样多的内容，SWIFT 的费用只有 TELEX（电传）的 18% 左右、CABLE（电报）的 2.5% 左右。

（3）SWIFT 的安全性较高。SWIFT 的密押比电传的密押可靠性强、保密性高，并且具有较高的自动化。

（4）SWIFT 的格式标准化。对于 SWIFT 电文，SWIFT 组织有着统一的要求和格式。

3. SWIFT 信用证的结构

SWIFT 信用证可分为五部分：

（1）基本报头（Basic Header Block）：显示通知行信息。

（2）应用报头（Application Header Block）：显示开证行信息。

（3）用户报头（User Header Block）：传送电码格式，表示系统开始。

（4）电文正文（Text Block）：这是进出口应重点阅读和审核的部分。

（5）报尾（Trailer Block）：传送电码格式，表示系统结束。

4. SWIFT 电文表示方式

（1）项目表示方式。SWIFT 由项目（FIELD）组成，项目由两位数字的代号（Tag）组成或由两位数字代号加上字母组成，如"44C LATEST DATE OF SHIPMENT（最后装船期）"。

SWIFT 的项目分为必选项目（MANDATORY FIELD）和可选项目（OPTIONAL FIELD）两种类型。项目代号前加了"＊"的为必选项目，即只要是 SWIFT 信用证都必有的项目。没有"＊"的为可选项目，是开证行选择的。

（2）日期表示方式。SWIFT 电文的日期表示为：YYMMDD（年月日）。如：2014 年 5 月 12 日，表示为：140512；2014 年 12 月 9 日，表示为：141209。

（3）货币表示方式。在 SWIFT 信用证中出现的货币名称，要使用国际标准的货币代码。

澳大利亚元：AUD	奥地利元：ATS	比利时法郎：BEF
加拿大元：CAD	人民币：CNY	丹麦克朗：DKK
港元：HKD	日元：JPY	英镑：GBP
瑞典克朗：SEK	美元：USD	欧元：EUR

（4）数字表示方式。在 SWIFT 电文中，数字不使用分格号，小数点用逗号"，"来表示。例如，8，152，286.36 表示为 8152286,36；4/5 表示为 0，8；5% 表示为 5 PERCENT。

5. SWIFT 代码介绍

目前，开立 SWIFT 信用证的格式代码为 MT700（参见表 1-2）和 MT701（参见表 1-3）。

表 1-2 MT700 Issue of a Documentary Credit

M/O	Tag 代码	Field Name 栏位名称	Contents/Options 内容
M	27	Sequence of Total 合计次序	1n/1n 1 个数字/1 个数字
M	40A	Form of Documentary Credit 跟单信用证形式	24x 24 个字
M	20	Documentary Credit Number 跟单信用证号码	16x 16 个字
O	23	Reference to Pre-Advice 预通知的编号	16x 16 个字
O	31C	Date of Issue 开证日期	6n 6 个数字
M	31D	Date and Place of Expiry 到期日及地点	6n/29x 6 个数字/29 个字
O	51a	Applicant Bank 申请人银行	A or D A 或 D
M	50	Applicant 申请人	4 * 35x 4 行×35 个字
M	59	Beneficiary 受益人	[134x] 4 * 35x [134 个字] 4 行×35 个字
M	32B	Currency Code, Amount 币别代号、金额	3a, 15n 3 个字母, 15 个数字
O	39A	Percentage Credit Amount Tolerance 信用证金额加减百分比	2n/2n 2 个数字/2 个数字
O	39B	Maximum Credit Amount 最高信用证金额	13x 13 个字
O	39C	Additional Amounts Covered 可附加金额	4 * 35x 4 行×35 个字
M	41A	Available with…by… 向……银行押汇，押汇方式为……	A or D A 或 D
O	42C	Drafts at… 汇票期限	3 * 35x 3 行×35 个字
O	42A	Drawee 付款人	A or D A 或 D
O	42M	Mixed Payment Details 混合付款条款	4 * 35x 4 行×35 个字

续表

M/O	Tag 代码	Field Name 栏位名称	Contents/Options 内容
O	42P	Deferred Payment Details 延迟付款条款	4 * 35x 4 行×35 个字
O	43P	Partial Shipments 分批装运	1 * 35x 1 行×35 个字
O	43T	Transshipment 转运	1 * 35x 1 行×35 个字
O	44A	Loading on Board/Dispatch/Taking in Charge at/from… 由……装船/发运/接管地点	1 * 65x 1 行×65 个字
O	44B	For Transportation to… 转运至……	1 * 65x 1 行×65 个字
O	44C	Latest Date of Shipment 最晚装运日	6n 6 个字
O	44D	Shipment Period 装运期间	6 * 65x 6 行×65 个字
O	45A	Description of Goods and/or Services 货物及/或服务描述	50 * 65x 50 行×65 个字
O	46A	Documents Required 应具备的单据	50 * 65x 50 行×65 个字
O	47A	Additional Conditions 附加条件	50 * 65x 50 行×65 个字
O	71B	Charges 费用	6 * 35x 6 行×35 个字
O	48	Period for Presentation 提示期间	4 * 35x 4 行×35 个字
O	49	Confirmation Instructions 保兑指示	7x 7 个字
O	53A	Reimbursement Bank 清算银行	A or D A 或 D
O	78	Instructions to the Paying /Accepting/ Negotiation Bank 对付款/承兑/议付银行的指示	12 * 65x 12 行×65 个字
O	57A	"Advising through" Bank 收讯银行以外的通知银行	A, B or D A, B 或 D
O	72	Sender to Receiver Information 银行间的通知	6 * 35x 6 行×35 个字

注：①M/O 为 Mandatory 与 Optional 的缩写，前者是指必要项目，后者为任意项目。

②合计次序是指本证的页次，共两个数字，前后各一。如"1/2"，其中"2"指本证共 2 页，"1"指本页为第 1 页。

表 1-3　　　　　　　　　　　MT701 Issue of a Documentary Credit

M/O	Tag 代码	Field Name 栏位名称	Contents/Options 内容
M	27	Sequence of Total 合计次序	1n/1n 1 个数字/1 个数字
M	20	Documentary Credit Number 信用证编号	16x 16 个字
O	45B	Description of Goods and/or Services 货物及/或服务描述	50 * 65x 50 行×65 个字
O	46B	Documents Required 应具备的单据	50 * 65x 50 行×65 个字
O	47B	Additional Conditions 附加条件	50 * 65x 50 行×65 个字

注：①M/O 为 Mandatory 与 Optional 的缩写，前者是指必要项目，后者为任意项目。

②合计次序是指本证的页次，共两个数字，前后各一。如"1/2"，其中"2"指本证共 2 页，"1"指本页为第 1 页。

（三）审核信用证

信用证是出口商制单的依据，为确保收汇安全和合同顺利履行，出口商必须对信用证进行认真的审核。一般来说，国外来证后，受益人和通知行都要进行审核，但两者审核的侧重点又会不同。银行侧重于议付、收汇方面，如对开证行、保兑行的资信、态度和作风的审查以及对付款办法、使用货币、汇率、利率等条款的审核；出口商应侧重于交货、履约方面，如对货运单据、价格条件、运输方式、装运期等条款进行审查，并特别要与有关的合约函电进行核对，以确保货物如期出运与安全收汇。

1. 信用证审核的依据

（1）贸易合同。信用证是申请人根据销售合同申请开立的，所以其条款应与合同条款相符。

（2）国际商会的《跟单信用证统一惯例》（《UCP600》）。

（3）国际商会的《关于审核跟单信用证项下单据的国际标准银行实务》（ISBP681）。

（4）结合实际业务情况。对于合同中没有规定又无法根据《UCP600》来判断的信用证条款，外贸单证员应根据业务实际情况来审核。例如，信用证要求提供由进口商签字的商业发票，这对于出口商来说是很被动的。如果进口商不签字，出口商就不能获得符合信用证的单据，将会遭到银行的拒付。

2. 信用证审核的要点

（1）来证背景。信用证是开证行对出口商作出的付款保证，开证行的资信状况直接影响出口商是否能顺利地收回货款，所以出口商应该对来证的政治背景、开证行的资信和信用等级进行了解。若开证行的资信差，出口商可以要求申请人找另一家资信状况较好的银行对信用证加以保兑，或者要求申请人找一家可靠的银行重开信用证。

（2）信用证的类型。不论是即期、远期、保兑、可转让、循环还是备用的信用证，都应该有"Irrevocable"字样。若信用证没有明示是否可撤销，根据《UCP600》的规定，应理解为不可撤销。当合同规定开出的是保兑信用证或可转让信用证时，应检查信用证内是否有注明"Confirmed"字样或"Transferable"字样。

（3）信用证中的几个日期。信用证中一般会出现开证日、到期日、装运期和议付有效期等几个日期。开证日一般是在合同签订日之后的；信用证的到期日不能早于开证日；装运期应在信用证的开证日与到期日之间；若合同中明确规定议付有效期，则信用证中的议付有效期要与合同中规定一致，若合同没有规定，则信用证中规定的议付有效期至少不能早于装运期，且不能迟于信用证的到期日。

（4）有效地点。若合同的支付条款中明确规定了信用证的有效地点，则信用证应与其保持一致。若合同中并未规定信用证的有效地点，一般而言，有效地点在受益人所在国，以便做到及时交单。

（5）申请人与受益人。受益人应特别注意信用证上的受益人、申请人名称和地址应与其印就好的文件上的名称和地址内容相一致。如果受益人的名称不正确，将会给今后的收汇带来不便。例如，出口商的名称为 HONG KONG GRACIOUS CO., LIMITED，而 L/C 上显示的是 HONG KONG GRACIOUS CO. LTD.，应提出修改。

（6）信用证的金额。信用证金额的币别与数额都必须与合同一致。若合同中规定了商品数量的溢短装条款时，信用证金额也应相应规定在支付金额时允许有一定幅度的伸缩。若信用证中的金额有大小写，则大写与小写要保持一致。

（7）汇票条款。汇票条款主要包括汇票的付款期限和付款人。一般情况下，这两项内容会在合同的支付条款中明确规定，那么，信用证中的汇票条款应与合同规定一致。若合同中未说明汇票的有关情况时，出口商最好不要接受信用证中将汇票的付款人规定为申请人的条款。

（8）装运条款。信用证中的装运条款包括装运港（地）、目的港（地）、装运期、分批装运与转运。一般情况下，这些内容会在合同中规定。如果信用证中规定了每一批货物出运的确切时间，则必须按此照办；如办不到，必须提出修改。

（9）货物描述。信用证中关于货物的描述是来自于合同的，所以信用证中提及的货物的情况，应与合同中相应的内容完全一致。需要提醒注意的是，若信用证没有提到合同中货物描述的一些内容，不需要修改。例如，信用证只是提到货物的名称、货号、规格等内容，并没有提及货物的包装，则不需要修改，即信用证中货物描述有哪些内容，就审哪些内容。

（10）单据条款。要仔细审核信用证中的单据条款，注意单据由谁出具、能否出具、信用证对单据是否有特殊要求、单据的规定是否与合同条款一致。

（11）信用证软条款。信用证软条款是指开证申请人（进口商）申请开立信用证时，通过故意制造一些限制性或隐蔽性的条款，使得受益人很难制作或获得相符单据，从而无法顺利结汇。常见的信用证软条款大致可归纳为以下四种：

①变相可撤销信用证条款。根据这类条款，在某种需要（条件）得不到满足时（如未收到对方的汇款、信用证或保函等），开证银行可随时单方面解除其保证付款的责任。

②暂不生效条款。这类条款通常规定信用证开出后并不生效，要待开证行另行通知或以修改书通知后方可生效。带有未生效条款的软条款信用证，如果遇到开证行不通知生效，不发修改书，开证申请人不出具证书或收据，不来验货，不通知船公司、船名等情况，该信用证的开证行保证付款的责任就形同虚设。如果出口商再根据买卖合同提前支付一定金额的履约金，就有被诈骗的可能。

③开证申请人控制条款。信用证中规定一些非经开证申请人指示不能按正常程序进行的条款，如发货需等申请人通知，运输工具和起运港或目的港需由申请人确认等。

④无金额信用证。信用证开出时无金额，通过修改增额或只能记账，而不发生实际现汇支付。

（12）费用条款。对于信用证中规定的有关费用，比如运费或检验费等，应事先协商一致；否则，对于额外的费用，原则上不应承担。对于银行费用，如事先未商定，一般情况下，出口方银行费用由受益人承担，进口方银行的费用由开证申请人承担。

（13）交单期。若合同的支付条款明确规定交单期，则信用证中的交单期应与合同中的一致。若合同中没有提及交单期，一般为货物装运后的 15 天或者 21 天，以便有充裕的时间来制单结汇。

（14）保险条款。若信用证要求的投保险别或加成超出了合同的规定，除非信用证上表明由此产生的超保费由开证申请人承担并允许在信用证项下支取，否则应予以修改。若加成过高，还需征得保险公司的同意，否则应予以修改。

（15）信用证的批注。对信用证上用铅字印好的文句内容和规定，特别是信用证空白处、边缘处加注的打字、缮写或橡皮戳记加注字句应特别注意。

（16）信用证是否受约束。明确信用证受《UCP600》的约束，可以使出口商在具体处理信用证业务中有一个公认的解释和理解，避免因对某一规定的不同理解而产生争议。

（四）信用证修改

受益人在收到进口人开来的信用证后，在审核信用证时，如发现己方不能接受的条款和要求，应及时向对方提出修改要求。有时，进口方也可能由于形势的变化而要求修改信用证。

1. 修改的原则

在任何情况下，不可撤销信用证的修改应由开证申请人提出，由开证行修改，并经开证行、保兑行（如已保兑）和受益人的同意，才能生效。对出口方不利，不改会严重影响安全结汇的条款，应坚决要求修改；对于介于可修改与可不修改之间的条款，在不影响合同实质履行的情况下可以考虑不做修改。

2. 关于信用证修改的有关规定

信用证修改涉及开证申请人、开证行、受益人和通知行，修改有时要经过几次才能完成，因此我们需要了解相关的规定。

（1）原信用证的效力。信用证是开证行与受益人之间的金融协议，一个已生效的信用证，未经双方同意，任何一方对其做出变更都是无效的。事实上，信用证的全部内容通知到受益人之后，受益人无须立即对其表示接受。《UCP600》第十条第（一）款规定："除本惯例第三十八条另有规定外，凡未经开证行、保兑行（如有）以及受益人同意，信用证既不能修改也不能撤销。"可见，信用证开立之后，开证行即受其约束。如果受益人对该证的条款无异议，日后的交单议付行为即其接受的意思表示。

如果受益人对信用证的某些条款提出修改，未被修改的部分仍然有效；修改未被开证行同意并做出修改通知，原证被提出修改的部分亦仍然有效。《UCP600》第十条第（三）款规定："在受益人向通知修改的银行表示接受该修改内容之前，原信用证（或包含先前已被接受修改的信用证）的条款和条件对受益人仍然有效。"因此，受益人对信用证提出修改，并不必然导致信用证被修改，只有修改建议被开证行接受并通过修改通知表示出来，该修改建议才发生效力，原证被修改部分才失去效力。

（2）开证行修改书的效力。开证行的修改通知一经发出即发生效力，不论该修改通知是否已经到达受益人。《UCP600》第十条第（二）款规定："自发出信用证修改书之时起，开证行就不可撤销地受其发出修改的约束。保兑行可将其保兑承诺扩展至修改内容，且自其通知该修改之时起，即不可撤销地受到该修改的约束。然而，保兑行可选择仅将修改通知受益人而不对其加具保兑，但必须不延误地将此情况通知开证行和受益人。"

（3）受益人对开证行修改的接受。受益人对开证行的修改应当做出书面或行为表示，未经此种表示，该项修改对受益人不发生效力。《UCP600》第十条第（三）款规定："受益人应发出接受或拒绝接受修改的通知。如受益人未提供上述通知，当其提交至被指定银行或开证行的单据与信用证以及尚未表示接受的修改的要求一致时，则该事实即视为受益人已做出接受修改的通知，并从此时起，该信用证已被修改。"

同时，《UCP600》第十条第（五）款规定："不允许部分接受修改，部分接受修改将被视为拒绝接受修改的通知。"因此，当对开证行修改书提出部分修改时，受益人应当要求开证行对其修改书的全部内容重新做出确认。

此外，根据《UCP600》第十一条的规定，经证实的修改的电讯文件将被视为有效的修改，任何随后的邮寄证实书将被不予置理。若该电讯文件声明"详情后告"（或类似词语）或声明随后寄出的邮寄证实书将是有效的修改，则该电讯文件将被视为无效的修改。开证行，也只有开证行，必须随即不延误地开出有效的修改，且条款不能与电讯文件相矛盾。

3. 信用证修改通知的路径

信用证修改通知的路径涉及受益人要求修改的路径和开证行通知修改的路径。

受益人要求修改应当按照以下路径进行：受益人将修改要求通知开证申请人，由开证申请人向开证行申请进行修改，开证行再将修改内容通知给受益人。

开证行的修改通知应当通过以下路径进行：开证行将修改通知发给通知行（一般情况下，会通过原信用证的通知行），由通知行转发给受益人。有时，根据银行业务关系，可能存在两个以上的通知行。当然，从法律角度上说，开证行可以将修改通知直接发给受益人，但这样做第一不符合银行实务习惯，第二不便于受益人识别修改书的真伪，因此实务中很少出现这种情况。

4. 受益人信用证修改函的基本内容

受益人信用证修改函应当包括以下三个方面的内容：

（1）确认收到信用证。该项确认应当包括感谢对方诚信守约开来信用证和通过提及开证行、信用证编号、开证日期或合同编号指出要修改信用证。

（2）提出不符点和修改意见。不符点应当逐条列出，并指出具体修改要求。

（3）希望。希望包括感谢合作和激励对方及早做出修改两项主要内容。

5. 受益人信用证修改函的写作要领

除商业信函的一般写作要求外，受益人信用证修改函的写作应当把握以下几点：

（1）态度和蔼。尽管导致信用证修改的主要责任可能在于对方，修改本身又费时、费力、费财，但信用证不修改可能有损己方利益，同时，修改又需要对方支出时间成本和现金成本，因此，只有保持良好的合作关系，才有利于信用证修改的顺利进行。这就要求我们放弃不悦心情，用和蔼的态度与对方沟通。

（2）条理清楚。信用证修改函结构虽然简单，但核心部分可能较为复杂，这部分写作尤其要求条理清楚。较好的方法是按照原证的顺序，从前至后，逐条指出不符点。对于 SWIFT MT700 格式的信用证，应当首先提及栏位名称（也称场名），然后列出原文，紧接着提出具体修改意见。

（3）用词准确，言简意赅。修改应使词句准确表达修改意见，避免笼统和模棱两可。同时，也应当锻炼言简意赅的用词能力，用最简单、最少量的词语准确、全面地表达修改意见。

6. 受益人修改信用证应当注意的问题

受益人修改信用证应当注意以下问题：

（1）信用证修改书必须经原通知行传递才有效，受益人必须在收到通知银行的"修改通知书"后，才能办理装运事宜，绝不可仅凭买方通知"证已改妥"或其他类似的通知就发货装船。

（2）避免多次改证。不符点应当一次性提出，改正意见应符合合同规定。

（3）对于开证行的改证书，如有不可接受部分，除要求改正该部分外，还应要求对其余部分作重新确认。

（4）敦促对方按时改证。如果有必要，应要求买方延展信用证装运期和有效期。

（5）为方便议付，应将原证相关规定和改证书的相关规定及时添加到信用证分析表中。

（6）修改手续费一般由提出修改的一方负担。国内银行按修改次数计算修改费用，不按信用证金额的大小来计算。

7. SWIFT 信用证修改标准格式 MT707（参见表 1-4）

表 1-4 　　　　　　　　　　　　**MT707 格式代号说明**

代码（Tag）	栏位名称 （Field Name）
20	送讯银行的编号 （Sender's Reference）
21	收讯银行的编号 （Receiver's Reference）
23	开证银行的编号 （Issuing Bank's Reference）
52a	开证银行 （Issuing Bank）
31c	开证日期 （Date of Issue）
30	修改日期 （Date of Amendment）
26E	修改序号 （Number of Amendment）
59	受益人（修改以前的）（Beneficiary（before this amendment））
31E	新的到期日 （New Date of Expiry）
32B	跟单信用证金额的增加 （Increase of Documentary Credit Amount）
33B	跟单信用证金额的减少 （Decrease of Documentary Credit Amount）
34B	修改后新的跟单信用证金额 （New Documentary Credit Amount after Amendment）
39A	信用证金额加减百分率 （Percentage Credit Amount Tolerance）
39B	最高信用证金额 （Maximum Credit Amount）
39C	可附加金额 （Additional Amount Covered）
44A	由……装船/发送/接管 （Loading on Board/Dispatch/Taking in Charge at /from…）
44B	装运至…… （For Transportation to…）
44C	最晚装船日 （Latest Date of Shipment）
44D	装船期间 （Shipment Period）
79	叙述 （Narrative）
72	银行间的备注 （Sender to Receiver Information）

三、实训内容与要求

（一）通读 SWIFT MT700/701 格式说明，掌握格式中各代码的含义和项目内容

（二）归纳买卖合同中信用证开立的有关约定

（三）掌握信用证修改的有关惯例规定

（四）根据实训指导的审核依据，逐条审核信用证

（五）完成信用证预审单的填写，标明信用证与买卖合同相关约定的不同之处和需要修改之处

四、实训单证填制

（一）出口商根据进出口合同审核信用证

1. 销售合同实例（见表 1-5）

表 1-5　　　　　　　　　　销售合同实例

SALES CONTRACT

S/C No.：KH-SPTSC38

Date：30-Jul-13

The Seller：JINZHE IMP. & EXP. CO. LTD.	The Buyer：GLOBAL TRADING UM GMBH
Address：ROOM 302, WORLD TRADE CENTER, 277 WU XING ROAD, SHANGHAI, CHINA	Address：MOOSFELDSTRABE 96 D - 746 BALINGEN, W-GERMANY

Item No. G6610	Commodity & Specifications	Unit	Quantity	Unit Price (USD)	Amount (USD)
	Dumbbell　　　　10kgs/set	Set	1 700	10.67	18 139.00

TOTAL：SAY US DOLLAR EIGHTEEN THOUSAND ONE HUNDRED AND THIRTY NINE ONLY.

PRICE TERM：CIF Hamburg, Germany

PACKING：to be packed in cartons of 1 set each, 20 cartons to a plate, total 1 700 cartons to one 20′ container

PORT OF LOADING: Shanghai

PORT OF DESTINATION: Hamburg

TIME OF SHIPMENT: within 30 days after receipt of the relevant L/C

TERMS OF PAYMENT: by irrevocable L/C at 30 days sight through a bank acceptable to the seller. The buyer shall open the L/C to the seller before August 4, 2013. The L/C shall be valid for negotiation in China until the 15th day after the date of shipment.

INSURANCE: to be covered by the seller for 110% of invoice value against All Risks and War Risk as per CIC.

OTHER TERMS AND CONDITIONS:

1. The buyer shall have the covering letter of credit reach the Seller 30 days before shipment, failing which the Seller reserves the right to rescind without further notice, or to regard as still valid whole or any part of this contract not fulfilled by the Buyer, or to lodge a claim for losses thus sustained, if any.

2. In case of any discrepancy in Quality/Quantity, claim should be filed by the Buyer within 130 days after the arrival of the goods at port of destination; while for quantity discrepancy, claim should be filed by the Buyer within 150 days after the arrival of the goods at port of destination.

3. For transactions concluded on C. I. F. basis, it is understood that the insurance amount will be for 110% of the invoice value against the risks specified in the Sales Contract. If additional insurance amount or coverage required, the Buyer must have the consent of the Seller before shipment, and the additional premium is to be borne by the Buyer.

4. The Seller shall not hold liable for non-delivery or delay in delivery of the entire lot or a portion of the goods hereunder by reason of natural disasters, war or other causes of Force Majeure, However, the Seller shall notify the Buyer as soon as possible and furnish the Buyer within 15 days by registered airmail with a certificate issued by the China Council for the Promotion of International Trade attesting such event (s).

5. All deputies arising out of the performance of, or relating to this contract, shall be settled through negotiation. In case no settlement can be reached through negotiation, the case shall then be submitted to the China International Economic and Trade Arbitration Commission for arbitration in accordance with its arbitral rules. The arbitration shall take place in Shanghai. The arbitral award is final and binding upon both parties.

6. The Buyer is requested to sign and return one copy of this contract immediately after receipt of the same. Objection, if any, should be raised by the Buyer within 3 working days, otherwise it is understood that the Buyer has accepted the terms and conditions of this contract.

7. Special conditions: (These shall prevail over all printed terms in case of any conflict.)

THE SELLER	THE BUYER
JINZHE IMP. & EXP. CO. LTD	GLOBAL TRADING UM GMBH
×××_____	Horgen F. Nissen LL. M.
(signature)	(signature)

2. 信用证实例（见表1-6）

表1-6 信用证实例

```
****** RECEIVED MESSAGE ****        3-AUG-2013 08：30        page no.：5294
Status  ： MESSAGE DELIVERED
Station  ：  1                    BEGINNING OF MESSAGE

RCVD    * FIN/Session/OSN    : F01    6036      942305

RCVD    * Own Address        : COMMONSHADLN   BANK OF CHINA SHANGHAI

RCVD    *                                     BRANCH 50 HUQIU RD. , SHANGHAI

RCVD    *                                     CHINA

RCVD    * Output Message Type  : 700          ISSUE OF A DOCUMENTARY CREDIT

RCVD    * Input Time          : 1401

RCVD    * MIR                 : 130802DEUTGEBKAXXX5737638647

RCVD    * Sent by            : AYUDTHBKAXXX   DEUTSCHE BANK

RCVD    *                                     FILIALE HANNOVER

RCVD    * Output Date/Time    : 130802/1002

RCVD    * Priority            : Normal

RCVD    *

RCVD    *27 /  SEQUENCE OF TOTAL

RCVD    *      1/1

RCVD    *40A/ FORM OF DOCUMENTARY CREDIT

RCVD    *      IRREVOCABLE

RCVD    *20 /  DOCUMENTARY CREDIT NUMBER

RCVD    *      384010021947

RCVD    *31C/ DATE OF ISSUE

RCVD    *      130802

RCVD    *      02-AUG-2013

RCVD    *31D/ DATE AND PLACE OF EXPIRY

RCVD    *      130905 CHINA
```

RCVD	*	05-SEP-2013
RCVD	*50 /	APPLICANT
RCVD	*	GLOBAL TRADING UM GMBH
RCVD	*	MOOSFELDSTRABE 96
RCVD	*	D-746 BALINGEN, W, GERMANY
RCVD	*59 /	BENEFICIARY-NAME & ADDRESS
RCVD	*	JINZHE IMP. AND EXP. CO. LTD.
RCVD	*	JIN DU BUILDING,
RCVD	*	277 WU XING ROAD,
RCVD	*	SHANGHAI, CHINA
RCVD	*32B/	CURRENCY CODE, AMOUNT
RCVD	*	USD18 139.00
RCVD	*	US Dollar
RCVD	*	18 139.00
RCVD	*41D/	AVAILABLE WITH…BY-NAME & ADDR
RCVD	*	ANY BANK, IN CHINA
RCVD	*	BY NEGOTIATION
RCVD	*42C/	DRAFTS AT…
RCVD	*	60 DAYS SIGHT
RCVD	*42A	DRAWEE - NAME & ADDRESS
RCVD	*	ISSUING BANK
RCVD	*43P/	PARTIAL SHIPMENTS
RCVD	*	NOT ALLOWED
RCVD	*43T/	TRANSSHIPMENT
RCVD	*	NOT ALLOWED

RCVD	*44A/	LOADING ON BOARD/DISP/TAKING IN CHARGE AT/F
RCVD	*	SHANGHAI, CHINA
RCVD	*44B/	FOR TRANSPORTATION TO
RCVD	*	HAMBURG, GERMANY

****** RECEIVED MESSAGE ****   3–AUG–2013 08：30   page no. : 5295

Status : MESSAGE DELIVERED

Station : 1   CONTINUATION OF MESSAGE

RCVD	*44C/	LATEST DATE OF SHIPMENT
RCVD	*	130830
RCVD	*	30–AUG–2013
RCVD	*45A/	DESCRIPTION OF GOODS &/OR SERVICES
RCVD	*	1 700 SETS OF DUMBBELL / ART NO. G6610–10KGS
RCVD	*	AT PRICE OF USD 10.67/SET
RCVD	*	TOAL AMOUNT：USD 18 139.00
RCVD	*	CIF HAMBURG, GERMANY（INCOTERMS 2010）
RCVD	*	AS PER S/C NO. KH–SPTSC38
RCVD	*46A/	DOCUMENTS REQUIRED
RCVD	*	+MANUALLY SIGNED COMMERCIAL INVOICE IN TRIPLICATE STATING FOB
RCVD	*	VALUE, INSURANCE PREMIUM AND THIS DOCUMENTARY CREDIT NUMBER.
RCVD	*	+FULL SET OF CLEAN ON BOARD OCEAN BILLS OF LADING WITH 2
RCVD	*	NON–NEGOTIABLE COPIES MADE OUT TO THE ORDER OF BENEFICIARY
RCVD	*	MARKED FREIGHT PREPAID, NOTIFY APPLICANT AND ISSUING BANK AND
RCVD	*	SHOWING THIS DOCUMENTARY CREDIT NUMBER.
RCVD	*	+PACKING LIST IN TRIPLICATE
RCVD	*	+CERTIFICATE OF ORIGIN AUTHENTICATED BY CHAMBER OF COMMERCE

RCVD	*	+BENEFICIARY'S CERTIFICATE CERTIFYING THAT SHIPPING SAMPLE HAVE
RCVD	*	BEEN SENT TO APPLICANT BEFORE SHIPMENT.
RCVD	*	+INSPECTION SHALL BE EFFECTED BEFORE SHIPMENT BY THE BENEFICIARY
RCVD	*	AND RELEVANT REPORTS OR CERTIFICATES SHALL BE ISSUED BY GEORGE
RCVD	*	SMITHS INSPECTION AGENT OR INSPECTOR APPROVED BY THE APPLICANT.
RCVD	*	THE APPLICANT RESERVES THE RIGHT TO REINSPECT THE GOODS AT THE
RCVD	*	DESTINATION PORT.
RCVD	*	+INSURANCE POLICY/CERTIFICATE MADE OUT FOR USD 20 502. 00 AND
RCVD	*	COVERING ALL RISKS AND WAR RISK AS PER C. I. C. OF PICC DATED1/1/1981.
RCVD	*	+ SHIPMENT ADVICE MUST BE SENT TO BENEFICIARY WITHIN 48 HOURS AFTER
RCVD	*	ISSURANCE OF B/L WITH SHIPPING DETAILS AND CONTRACT NUMBER.
RCVD	*	+ALL DOCUMENTS MUST QUOTE THE NUMBER OF THIS LETTER OF CREDIT.
RCVD	*47A/	ADDITIONAL CONDITIONS
RCVD	*	+MAKING SHIPPING MARK AS KD-SPTSC08/SPORTAR/HAMBURG/C/NO. 1-UP
RCVD	*	+MULTIMODAL TRANSPORT DOCUMENTS ACCEPTABLE
RCVD	*	+DRAFTS TO BE PRESENTED FOR NEGOTIATION MUST BE MARKED AS BEING
RCVD	*	DRAWN UNDER THIS CREDIT AND BEAR ITS NUMBER.
RCVD	*	+TO ADVISING BANK: KINDLY COLLECT YOUR ADVISING COMMISSION
RCVD	*	BEFORE RELEASING THE DOCUMENTARY CREDIT TO BENEFICIARY.
RCVD	*	+IF DOCUMENTS PRESENTED ARE FOUND TO BE DISCREPANT, PLEASE
RCVD	*	STATE DISCREPANCIES NOTED.
RCVD	*71R/	CHARGE
RCVD	*	ALL BANK CHARGES OUTSIDE GERMANY
RCVD	*	INCLUDING REIMBURSING BANK
RCVD	*	COM. ARE FOR BENEFICIARY'S
RCVD	*	ACCOUNT
RCVD	*48 /	PERIOD FOR PRESENTATION
RCVD	*	WITHIN 14 DAYS AFTER THE DATE OF
RCVD	*	SHIPMENT BUT WITHIN THE VALIDITY OF
RCVD	*	THE CREDIT
RCVD	*49 /	CONFIRMATION INSTRUCTIONS

RCVD	*	WITHOUT
RCVD	*53A/	REIMBURSING BANK-BIG
		BANK OF NEW YORK
		NEW YORK, NY

****** RECEIVED MESSAGE ****   3-AUG-2013 08：30   page no. : 5296

Status：MESSAGE DELIVERED

Station： 1   CONTINUATION OF MESSAGE

RCVD	*53A/	REIMBURSING BANK – BIG
RCVD	*	IRVTUSEN
RCVD	*	BANK OF NEW YORK
RCVD	*	NEW YORK, NY
RCVD	*76 /	INSTR TO PAYG/ACCPTG/NEGOTG BANK
RCVD	*	+REIMBURSEMENTS CLAIMS UNDER THIS L/C ARE SUBJECT TO U. R. R. 1995
RCVD	*	I. C. C. PUB. NO. 525
RCVD	*	+THE AMOUNT OF EACH DRAWING TO BE ENDORSED ON THE REVERSE
RCVD	*	SIDE OF THIS CREDIT BY THE NEGOTIATION BANK
RCVD	*	+IN CASE DOCUMENTS PRESENTED WITH DISCREPANCY (IES)
RCVD	*	A DISCREPANCY FEE OF USD50. 00 OR EQUIVALENT PLUS OUR TELEX/SWIFT
RCVD	*	EXPENSES (IF APPLICABLE) WILL BE DEDUCTED FROM THE PROCEEDS.
RCVD	*72 /	SENDER TO RECEIVER INFORMATION
RCVD	*	SUBJECT TO UCP2007 REV. PUB 600
RCVD	*	ALL DOC MUST BE SENT IN ONE LOT
RCVD	*	BY ANY COURIER TO ISSUING BANK
RCVD	*	
RCVD	*	
RCVD	*MAC：	Authentication Code
RCVD	*	6588FBA5
RCVD	*CHK：	Check Sum
RCVD	*	4DAF2B97D6DC
RCVD	*	

RCVD　＊SAC：SWIFT Authentication Correct

RCVD　＊COP：P：CBT Primary Copy

User requested copy from OMHQ

（二）进出口商通过银行修改信用证

对上面给出的销售合同和信用证进行审核，发现不符点时，给进口公司写一封函（见表1-7），通知对方修改信用证。

表1-7　　　　　　　　　　　　　信用证修改函

金喆进出口有限公司

JINZHE IMP. & EXP. CO. LTD.

ADD.：ROOM 302，WORLD TRADE CENTER，	TEL：86-21-64331255
277 WU XING ROAD，	FAX：86-21-64331256
SHANGHAI，CHINA	

TO：GLOBAL TRADING UM GMBH

Aug 4，2013

Dear Sir，

　　We are very glad to receive your L/C No. 384010021947，but we are quite sorry to find that it contains some discrepancies with the S/C. Please instruct your bank to amend the L/C as quickly as possible.

　　The L/C is to be amended as follows：

　　1. The credit is amended to be available for 30 days' sight draft.

　　2. Insurance policy in duplicate shall cover the amount "for total invoice value plus 10%".

　　3. Time of shipment and expiry date of the credit has to be extended to Sept. 4th and Sept. 20th in China respectively.

　　4. The name of Beneficiary shall be "JINZHE IMP. AND EXP. CO. LTD.".

　　5. The inspection clause has been amended to read as "Inspection of quantity should be effected before shipment by the beneficiary. Relevant documents or certificates are required to be issued by Shanghai Import and Export Commodity Inspection Bureau or specific inspector accepted by the Beneficiary. Meanwhile, the Applicant reserves the right of reinspection at the destination port".

　　6. This credit is subject to UCP600.

　　Please amend the L/C accordingly.

Yours faithfully，

JINZHE IMP. & EXP. CO. LTD.

Manager

不久，收到银行改证通知书（见表1-8）及信用证修改书（见表1-9）。

表1-8　　　　　　　　　　　　　　　银行改证通知书

中国银行
BANK OF CHINA

修 改 通 知 书

Notification of Amendment

BANK OF CHINA SHANGHAI BRANCH

　　ADDRESS：50 HUQIU ROAD

　　CABLE：CHUNGKUO

　　TELEX：33062 BOCSH E CN

　　SWIFT：BKCHCMBJ300

　　PHONE：021-63232070

　　FAX：021-63232071

2013/08/06

To：致：	WHEN CORRESPONDING	NO. 9711-01
JINZHE IMP. & EXP. CO. LTD. ROOM 302，WORLD TRADE CENTER，277 WU XING ROAD，SHANGHAI, CHINA	PLEASE QUOTE OUR REF. NO.	
Issuing Bank 开证行 DEUTSCHE BANK FILIALE HANNOVER	Transmitted to us through 转递行 REF. NO.	

L/C NO. 信用证号 384010021947	DATE 开证日期 August 2, 2013	Amount 金额 USD 18 139.00	EXPIRY PLACE 有效地 LOCAL
EXPIRY DATE 有效期 2013/09/05	TENOR 期限 30 DAYS	CHARGE 未付费用 RMB 300.00	CHARGE BY 费用承担人 BENE.
RECEIVED VIA 来证方式 SWIFT	AVAILABLE 是否生效 VALID	TEST/SIGN 印押是否相符 YES	CONFIRM 我行是否保兑 NO
AMEND NO. 修改次数 1	AMEND DATE 修改日期 2013/08/06	INCREASE AMT. 增额 USD 0.00	DECREASE AMT. 减额 USD 0.00

DEAR SIRS，敬启者：

WE HAVE PLEASURE IN ADVISING YOU THAT WE HAVE RECEIVED FROM THE A/M BANK A（N）AMENDMENT TO THE CAPTIONED L/C, CONTENTS OF WHICH ARE AS PER ATTACHED SHEET（S）.

兹通知贵公司，我行自上述银行收到修改（书）一份，内容见附件。

THIS AMENDMENT SHOULD BE ATTACHED TO THE CAPTIONED L/C ADVISED BY US, OTHERWISE, THE BENEFICIARY WILL BE RESPONSIBLE FOR ANY CONSEQUENCES ARISING HEREFROM.

本修改需附于有关信用证中，否则，贵公司需对由此而产生的后果承担责任。

REMARKS：备注：

THIS L/C CONSISTS OF TWO SHEET（S），INCLUDING THE COVERING LETTER AND ATTACHMENT（S）.

本信用证连同面函及附件共　2页　纸。

KINDLY TAKE NOTE THAT THE PARTIAL ACCEPTANCE OF THE AMENDMENT IS NOT ALLOWED.

本修改（书）不能部分接受。

THIS AMENDMENT IS ADVISED SUBJECT TO ICC UCP PUBLICATION NO. 600.

本修改之通知系遵循国际商会《跟单信用证统一惯例》第 600 号出版物办理。

YOURS FAITHFULLY

BANK OF CHINA SHANGHAI BRANCH

中国银行上海分行

表 1-9	信用证修改书

```
****** RECEIVED MESSAGE **** 6-AUG-2013 09：30      page no. ：5321
Status：MESSAGE DELIVERED
Station：1                    BEGINNING OF MESSAGE
```

RCVD	* FIN/Session/OSN	: F01	6036	942305
RCVD	* Own Address	: COMMONSHADLN	BANK OF CHINA SHANGHAI BRANCH	
RCVD	*		50 HUQIU RD, SHANGHAI CHINA	
RCVD	*			
RCVD	* Output Message Type	: 700	ISSUE OF A DOCUMENTARY CREDIT	
RCVD	* Input Time	: 1401		
RCVD	* MIR	: 130802DEUTGEBKAXXX5737638647		
RCVD	* Sent by	: AYUDTHBKAXXX	DEUTSCHE BANK	
RCVD	*		FILIALE HANNOVER	
RCVD	* Output Date/Time	: 130806/0945		
RCVD	* Priority	: Normal		
RCVD	*			
RCVD	*20 / SENDER'S REFERENCE			

续表

RCVD	*	384010021947
RCVD	*21 /	RECEIVER'S REFERENCE
RCVD	*	NON REF
RCVD	*52A/	ISSUING BANK
		DEUTSCHE BANK
RCVD	*	FILIALE HANNOVER
RCVD	*31C/	DATE OF ISSUE
RCVD	*	130802
RCVD	*	02-AUG-2013
RCVD	*30 /	DATE OF AMENDMENT
RCVD	*	090806
RCVD	*	06-AUG-2013
RCVD	*26E /	NUMBER OF AMENDMENT
RCVD	*	1
RCVD	*59 /	BENEFICIARY-NAME & ADDRESS
RCVD	*	JINZHE IMP. AND EXP. CO. LTD.
RCVD	*	ROOM 302, WORLD TRADE CENTER,
RCVD	*	277 WU XING ROAD,
RCVD	*	SHANGHAI, CHINA
RCVD	*79 /	NARRATIVE
RCVD	*	1-READ IN FIELD 20 UNDER DATE AND PLACE OF EXPIRY AS 090920 / 20, SEP, 2013.
RCVD	*	2-READ IN FIELD 59 UNDER BENEFICIARY - NAME & ADDRESS AS
RCVD	*	JINZHE IMP. AND EXP. CO. LTD.
RCVD	*	ROOM 302, WORLD TRADE CENTER,
RCVD	*	277 WU XING ROAD,
RCVD	*	SHANGHAI, CHINA
RCVD	*	3-READ IN FIELD 42C UNDER DRAFTS AT⋯ AS 30 DAYS SIGHT
RCVD	*	4-READ IN FIELD 44C UNDER LATEST DATE OF SHIPMENT AS 090904 04 SEP 2013
RCVD	*	5-IN FIELD 46A DOCUMENTS REQUIRED, DELETE:
RCVD	*	+INSPECTION SHALL BE EFFECTED BEFORE SHIPMENT BY THE BENEFICIARY
RCVD	*	AND RELEVANT REPORTS OR CERTIFICATES SHALL BE ISSUED BY GEORGE

RCVD	*	SMITHS INSPECTION AGENT OR INSPECTOR APPROVED BY THE APPLICANT.
RCVD	*	THE APPLICANT RESERVES THE RIGHT TO REINSPECT THE GOODS AT THE
RCVD	*	DESTINATION PORT.
RCVD	*	ADD: +INSPECTION SHOULD BE EFFECTED BEFORE SHIPMENT BY THE
RCVD	*	BENEFICIARY. RELEVANT DOCUMENTS OR CERTIFICATES ARE REQUIRED
RCVD	*	TO BE ISSUED BY CCIC SHANGHAI CO. , LTD. OR SPECIFIC INSPECTOR
RCVD	*	ACCEPTED BY THE BENEFICIARY. MEANWHILE, THE APPLICANT
RCVD	*	RESERVES THE RIGHT OF REINSPECTION AT THE DESTINATION PORT.

****** RECEIVED MESSAGE ****　　　　　6-AUG-2013 09: 30　　　page no. : 5322

Status: MESSAGE DELIVERED

Station: 1　　　　　　　CONTINUATION OF MESSAGE

RCVD	*	6-READ INSURANCE CLAUSE IN FIELD 46A UNDER DOCUMENTS REQUIRED AS
RCVD	*	+INSURANCE POLICY/CERTIFICATE MADE OUT FOR TOTAL INVOICE VALUE
RCVD	*	PLUS 10 PERCENT AND COVERING ALL RISKS AND WAR RISK AS PER C. I. C. OF
RCVD	*	PICC DATED 1/1/1981.
RCVD	*	7-IN FIELD 47A UNDER ADDITIONAL CONDITIONS, ADD: THIS CREDIT IS
RCVD	*	SUBJECT TO ICC PUBLICATION NO. 600.
RCVD	*	
RCVD	*	ALL OTHER TERMS AND CONDITIONS REMAIN UNCHANGED.
RCVD	*	
RCVD	*	
RCVD	*	
RCVD	* MAC:	Authentication Code
RCVD	*	6588FBA5
RCVD	* CHK:	CheckSum
RCVD	*	4DAF2B97D6DC
RCVD	*	
RCVD	* SAC:	SWIFT Authentication Correct
RCVD	* COP:	P: CBT Primary Copy
RCVD	*	

User requested copy from OMHQ

五、实训考核方法

（一）根据合同准确填写开证申请书

（二）准确阅读信用证

（三）准确理解和掌握信用证中的各种条款

（四）准确拟写信用证修改函

模块二　进出口许可证

一、实训目的

（一）学生能掌握国家颁布的进出口许可证的相关条例

（二）学生能根据信用证的要求正确填写进出口许可证

二、理论知识点

（一）出口许可证的申领

根据《出口许可证管理货物目录》和《出口许可证管理货物分级发证目录》的规定，一些特殊物资的出口需办理出口许可证，出口商凭以向海关办理出口报关手续。

出口许可证分为出口配额许可证和出口非配额许可证，对于出口配额许可证须事先按有关规定取得配额证明。申领出口许可证时须提交相关的资料、文件，并根据分级管理的原则，向有关签证机构提出申请。发证机构自收到申请之日起3个工作日内发放出口许可证。发证机构凭加盖经营者公章的申请表取证联和领证人员身份证明材料发放出口许可证。

通过商务部许可证事务局的网站进行网上申请是较为快捷的方式，具体程序参见本模块的第四节"实训单证填制"。

"网络链接"：

（1）《2014年出口许可证管理货物目录》可链接 http：//www. mofcom. gov. cn/article/b/c/201312/20131200446709. shtml

（2）《2014年出口许可证管理货物分级发证目录》可链接 http：//www.

mofcom. gov. cn/article/b/c/201401/20140100448328. shtml

（二）出口许可证的使用

（1）出口许可证的有效期最长不得超过 6 个月，且有效期的截止日期不得超过当年 12 月 31 日。出口许可证应当在有效期内使用，逾期自行失效。

（2）出口许可证一经签发，不得擅自更改证面内容。如需更改，经营者应当在许可证有效期内提出更改申请，并将许可证交回原发证机构，由原发证机构重新换发许可证。

（3）出口许可证管理实行"一证一关"（指许可证只能在一个海关报关）管理。一般情况下，出口许可证为"一批一证"（指许可证在有效期内一次报关使用）。如要实行"非一批一证"（指许可证在有效期内可多次报关使用），应当同时在出口许可证备注栏内打印"非一批一证"字样，但最多不超过 12 次，由海关在许可证背面"海关验放签注栏"内逐批签注核减出口数量。

（4）对出口实行许可证管理的大宗、散装货物溢装数量按照国际贸易惯例办理，即报关出口的大宗、散装货物的溢装数量不得超过出口许可证所列出口数量的 5%。对不实行"一批一证"制的大宗、散装货物，在每批货物出口时，按其实际出口数量进行核扣，最后一批货物出口时，其溢装数量按该许可证实际剩余数量并在规定的溢装上限 5%（原油、成品油在溢装上限 3%）内计算。

（5）国家对部分出口货物实行指定出口报关口岸管理。

（三）出口许可证的缮制

1. 出口商（Exporter）

出口商是指出口合同签订单位，应与出口批准文件一致。出口商代码为《进出口经营者资格证书》、《对外贸易经营者备案登记表》或《外商投资企业批准证书》中的 13 位企业代码。

2. 发货人（Consignor）

发货人是指具体执行合同发货报关的单位。配额以及配额招标商品的发货人应与出口商保持一致。

3. 出口许可证号（Export license No. ）

结构为：××-××-××××××

$\qquad$ （1）-（2）-（3）

（1）为年份。

（2）为发证机构代码。

（3）为顺序号，由发证系统自动生成。

4. 出口许可证有效截止日期（Export license expiry date）

按《货物出口许可证管理办法》确定的有效期，由发证系统自动生成。

5. 贸易方式（Terms of trade）

贸易方式指该项出口货物的贸易性质，包括：一般贸易、进料加工、来料加工、出料加工、外资企业出口、捐赠、赠送等，只能填报一种。

6. 合同号（Contract No.）

合同号是指申请出口许可证时提交出口合同的编号，长度为 17 个英文字符，只能填报一个合同号。

7. 报关口岸（Place of clearance）

报关口岸指出口口岸，只允许填报一个关区。出口许可证实行"一证一关"制。对指定口岸的出口商品，按国家有关规定执行。

8. 进口国（地区）（Country/Region of purchase）

进口国（地区）是指合同目的地。只能填报一个国家（地区）。不能使用地区名，如欧盟等。如对中国保税区出口，进口国（地区）应打印"中国"。

9. 付款方式（Mode of payment）

付款方式包括：信用证、托收、汇付等，只能填报一种。

10. 运输方式（Mode of transport）

运输方式是指货物离境时的运输方式，包括：海上运输、铁路运输、公路运输、航空运输等，只能填报一种。如远洋出口冷冻商品，运输方式不得打印陆运，包括铁路运输、公路运输。

11. 商品名称（Description of goods）、商品编码（Code of goods）

按商务部公布的年度《出口许可证管理货物目录》中的 10 位商品编码填报，商品名称由发证系统自动生成。只能填报一个商品编码并应与出口批准文件一致。

12. 规格、型号（Specification）

只能填报同一商品编码下的 4 种不同规格等级，超过 4 种规格等级的，另行申请许可证。

13. 单位（Unit）

单位是指计量单位。按商务部公布的年度《出口许可证管理货物目录》中的计量单位执行，发证系统自动生成。如合同使用的计量单位与规定的计量单位不一致，应换算成规定的计量单位。无法换算的，可在备注栏注明。

14. 数量（Quantity）

数量是指申请出口商品数量。最大位数为 9 位阿拉伯数字，最小保留小数点后 1 位。如数量过大，可分证办理；如数量过小，可在备注栏内注明。计量单位为"批"的，此栏均为"1"。

15. 单价（币别）（Unit price）

单价（币别）指与第十三项"单位"所使用的计量单位相应的单价和货币种类。计量单位为 1 批的，此栏为总金额。

16、17、18. 总值（Amount）、总值折美元（Amount in USD）、总计（Total）

由发证系统自动计算。

19. 备注（Supplementary details）

用于注明其他需要说明的情况。如不是"一批一证"报关的出口许可证，在此栏注明"非一批一证"。

20. 发证机关签章（Issuing authority's stamp & signature）

发证机构发放出口许可证前在此栏加盖《中华人民共和国出口许可证专用章》。

21. 发证日期（Licence date）

由发证系统自动生成。

出口许可证的具体格式见表2-1。

表2-1　　　　　　　　　　　**出口许可证**

中华人民共和国出口许可证
EXPORT LICENCE OF THE PEOPLES REPUBLIC OF CHINA

1. 出口商 Exporter			3. 出口许可证号 Export license No.		
2. 发货人 Consignor			4. 出口许可证有效截止日期 Export license expiry date		
5. 贸易方式 Terms of trade			8. 进口国 Country/Region of purchase		
6. 合同号 Contract No.			9. 支付方式 Mode of Payment		
7. 报关口岸 Place of clearance			10. 运输方式 Mode of transport		
11. 商品名称 Description of goods			商品编码 Code of goods		
12. 规格、型号 Specification	13. 单位 Unit	14. 数量 Quantity	15. 单价（USD） Unit price	16. 总值（USD） Amount	17. 总值折美元 Amount in USD
18. 总计 Total					
19. 备注 Supplementary details			20. 发证机关签章 Issuing authority's stamp & signature		
			21. 发证日期 Licence date		

中华人民共和国商务部监制（2007）

（三）进口许可证的申领

2014 年实施进口许可证管理的货物有消耗臭氧层物质和重点旧机电产品。消耗臭氧层物质进口许可证由各地商务厅（局）、外经贸委（厅、局）签发，在京中央管理企业的进口许可证由配额许可证事务局签发。重点旧机电产品进口许可证由配额许可证事务局签发。进口经营者应按照规定持相关文件、资料向相应的发证机构申领进口许可证，符合申请规定的，发证机构应在规定的时限内予以发放。

"网络链接"：

（1）《2014 年进口许可证管理货物目录》可链接

http：//www. mofcom. gov. cn/article/b/c/201312/20131200446715. shtml

（2）《2014 年进口许可证管理货物分级发证目录》可链接

http：//www. mofcom. gov. cn/article/b/c/201401/20140100448303. shtml

（四）进口许可证的使用

（1）进口许可证的有效期为 1 年，当年有效。特殊情况需要跨年度使用时，有效期不得超过次年 3 月 31 日，逾期自行失效。

（2）进口许可证一经签发，不得擅自更改证面内容。如需更改，经营者应当在许可证有效期内提出更改申请，并将许可证交回原发证机构，由原发证机构重新换发许可证。

（3）进口许可证管理实行"一证一关"（指许可证只能在一个海关报关）管理。一般情况下，进口许可证为"一批一证"（指许可证在有效期内一次报关使用）。如要实行"非一批一证"（指许可证在有效期内可多次报关使用），应当同时在进口许可证备注栏内打印"非一批一证"字样，但最多不超过 12 次，由海关在许可证背面"海关验放签注栏"内逐批签注核减进口数量。

（4）对进口实行许可证管理的大宗、散装货物溢装数量按照国际贸易惯例办理，即报关进口的大宗、散装货物的溢装数量不得超过进口许可证所列进口数量的 5%。对不实行"一批一证"制的大宗、散装货物，在每批货物进出口时，按其实际进口数量进行核扣，最后一批货物进口时，其溢装数量按该许可证实际剩余数量并在规定的溢装上限 5% 内计算。

（五）进口许可证的缮制

1. 进口商（Importer）

进口商是指进口合同签订单位。进口商代码为《中华人民共和国进出口企业资格证书》、《对外贸易经营者备案登记表》或《外商投资企业批准证书》中的 13 位企业代码。

接受赠送、无偿捐赠、援助进口的货物，该项为"赠送"，编码为"0000000000001"。

2. 收货人（Consignee）

收货人是指实际进口用货单位。

3. 进口许可证号（Import licence No.）

结构为：××-××-××××××

　　　　　（1）-（2）-（3）

（1）为年份。

（2）为发证机构代码。

（3）为顺序号，由发证系统自动生成。

4. 进口许可证有效截止日期（Import licence expiry date）

按《货物进口许可证管理办法》确定的许可证有效期，由发证系统自动生成。

5. 贸易方式（Terms of trade）

贸易方式是指该项进口货物的贸易性质，包括：一般贸易、进料加工、来料加工、外资企业进口、边境贸易、赠送等，只能填报一种。

6. 外汇来源（Terms of foreign exchange）

常见的有：银行购汇、现金、外资等，只能填报一种。

7. 报关口岸（Place of clearance）

报关口岸是指进口口岸，只能填报一个。

进口许可证实行"一证一关"制。对指定口岸的进口商品，按国家有关规定执行。

8. 出口国（地区）（Country/Region of exportation）

出口国（地区）填签约国（地区）名称，只能填报一个。不能使用区域名，如欧盟等。如从中国保税区进口，出口国（地区）应填报"中国"。

9. 原产地国（地区）（Country/Region of origin）

原产地国（地区）指对商品进行实质性加工的国家（地区）。

10. 商品用途（Use of goods）

商品用途包括自用、生产用、内销、维修、样品、加工后返回、加工复出口、加工贸易内销，只能填报一种并应与批准文件一致。

11. 商品名称（Description of goods）、商品编码（Code of goods）

商品编码按商务部公布的年度《进口许可证管理货物目录》中的10位商品编码填报，商品名称由系统自动生成。只能填报一个商品编码并应与进口批准文件一致。

12. 规格、型号（Specification）

只能填报同一商品编码下的4种不同规格型号，超过4种规格型号的，另行申请许可证。

13. 单位（Unit）

单位指计量单位。按商务部公布的年度《进口许可证管理货物目录》中的计量单位执行，由发证系统自动生成。如合同使用的计量单位与规定的计量单位不一致，应换算成规定的计量单位。无法换算的，可在备注栏注明。

14. 数量（Quantity）

数量指申请进口的商品数量，最大位数为9位阿拉伯数字，最小保留小数点后

1 位。如数量过大，可分证办理；如数量过小，可在备注栏内注明。计量单位为"批"的，此栏均为"1"。

15. 单价（币别）（Unit price）

单价（币别）指与第 13 项"单位"所使用的计量单位相应的单价和货币种类。计量单位为 1 批的，此栏为总金额。

16、17、18. 总值（Amount）、总值折美元（Amount in USD）、总计（Total）

由发证系统自动计算。

19. 备注（Supplementary details）

用于注明其他需要说明的情况。如不是"一批一证"报关的进口许可证，在此栏注明"非一批一证"。

20. 发证机关签章（Issuing authority's stamp & signature）

发证机构在发放进口许可证前在此栏加盖"中华人民共和国进口许可证专用章"。

21. 发证日期（Licence date）

由发证系统自动生成。

进口许可证的具体格式见表 2-2。

表 2-2   进口许可证

中华人民共和国进口许可证
IMPORT LICENCE OF THE PEOPLE'S REPUBLIC OF CHINA

1. 进口商： Importer	3. 进口许可证号： Import license No.
2. 收货人： Consignee	4. 进口许可证有效截止日期： Import license expiry date
5. 贸易方式： Terms of trade	8. 出口国（地区）： Country/Region of exportation
6. 外汇来源： Terms of foreign exchange	9. 原产国（地区）： Country/Region of origin
7. 报关口岸： Place of clearance	10. 商品用途： Use of goods
11. 商品名称： Description of goods	商品编码： Code of goods

续表

12. 规格、型号 Specification	13. 单位 Unit	14. 数量 Quantity	15. 单价 Unit price	16. 总值 Amount	17. 总值折美元 Amount in USD
18. 总　计 Total					
19. 备　注： Supplementary details				20. 发证机关签章： Issuing authority's stamp & signature	
				21. 发证日期： License date	

中华人民共和国商务部监制（2007）

三、实训内容与要求

（一）申领进出口许可证的程序

（二）进出口许可证的有效期限

（三）掌握进出口许可证的填写

四、实训单证填制

（一）进出口许可证申领的网上流程

（1）于中华人民共和国商务部配额许可证事务局的官方网站（www.licence.org.cn）下载"许可证电子钥匙申请表"，将填写好的申请表、"对外贸易经营者备案登记表原件与复印件"或"外商投资企业批准证书原件与复印件"及"办理人的身份证原件与复印件"送当地外经贸厅许可证签发机构，接受审批。

（2）安装电子钥匙的驱动程序。在许可证事务局的网站中点击"申领"或"网上企业申领"，填写相关信息，在线填写申报单。

（3）通过审批后，将申报单进行打印并签字盖章，持申报单、合同及相关文件到相关部门领取许可证。

（二）根据信用证的要求正确填写进出口许可证

出口许可证样本参见表2-3。

表2-3　　　　　　　　　　　　**出口许可证**

中华人民共和国出口许可证

EXPORT LICENCE OF THE PEOPLE'S REPUBLIC OF CHINA

1. 出口商： Exporter：大连金喆进出口贸易有限公司	3. 出口许可证号： Export licence No.：2013061269
2. 发货人： Consignor：大连金喆进出口贸易有限公司	4. 出口许可证有效截止日期： Export licence expiry date：2013-10-15
5. 贸易方式： Terms of trade：一般贸易	8. 出口最终目的国（地区）： Country / Region of purchase：美国
6. 合同号： Contract No.：TR-365	9. 付款方式： Mode of payment：L/C
7. 报关口岸： Place of clearance：大连	10. 运输方式： Mode of transport：江海

11. 商品名称：　　　　　　　　　　　　　　商品编码：

Description of goods：全棉布料　　　　　　Code of goods：1841.4624

12. 规格、型号 Specification	13. 单位 Unit	14. 数量 Quantity	15. 单价 Unit price	16. 总值 Amount	17. 总值折美元 Amount in USD
10″×10″	DOZ	12 000	USD 1.2	USD 14 400	USD 14 400
20″×20″	DOZ	8 000	USD 2	USD 16 000	USD 16 000
18. 总　计 Total	DOZ	20 000		USD 30 400	USD 30 400

19. 备　注： Supplementary details 输欧或输美许可证号： 类别号：	20. 发证机关盖章： Issuing authority's stamp 21. 发证日期： Licence date

中华人民共和国商务部监制（2007）

第一联（正本）发货人办理海关手续

五、实训考核方法

（一）掌握进出口许可证的申领办法

（二）正确填写进出口许可证

模块三　集装箱货物托运单

一、实训目的

（一）学生能根据买卖合同和信用证的有关规定完成订舱操作流程

（二）学生熟悉出口托运和订舱的一般程序，能正确填写集装箱货物托运单和订舱单据

二、理论知识点

（一）集装箱班轮订舱的一般程序

集装箱班轮订舱的一般程序如图 3-1 所示。

（1）出口企业即货主在货、证齐备后，填制订舱委托书，委托货代代为订舱，有时还委托其代理报关及货物储运等事项。

（2）货代接受订舱委托后，缮制集装箱货物托运单，随同商业发票、装箱单及其他必要的单证一同向船公司办理订舱。

（3）船公司根据具体情况，如接受订舱，则在托运单的几联单证上编上与提单号码一致的编号，填上船名、航次，并签署，即表示已确认托运人的订舱，同时把配舱回单、S/O 等与托运人有关的单据退给托运人。

（4）托运人持船公司签署的 S/O，填制出口货物报关单、商业发票、装箱单等连同其他有关出口单证向海关办理货物出口报关手续。

（5）海关根据有关规定对出口货物进行查验，如同意出口，则在 S/O 上盖放行章，并将 S/O 退回给托运人。

（6）托运人持海关盖章的由船公司签署的 S/O 要求船长装货。

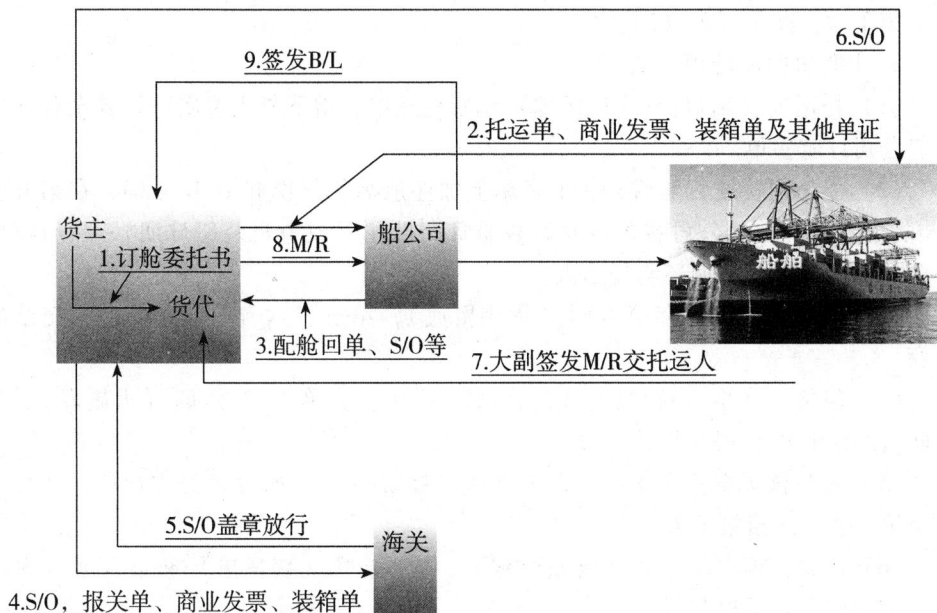

图 3-1 集装箱班轮订舱一般程序图

（7）装货后，由船上的大副签署 M/R（大副收据），交给托运人。

（8）托运人持 M/R 向船公司换取正本已装船提单。

（9）船公司凭 M/R 签发正本提单并交给托运人凭以结汇。

（二）集装箱运输货运单证

货物托运即托运人向承运人订购舱位的过程。托运通常有直接托运和间接托运两种形式，前者由出口商直接向承运人托运，后者由出口商委托货运代理人向承运人托运。在发达的货运市场中，货运代理人有丰富的经验，与各承运人保持着良好的关系，因此，出口商托运货物更多的是委托货运代理人来完成。这样，货物托运环节涉及的单证主要有货物托运委托书（也称订舱委托书）和订舱联单两类，后者由订舱单（也称托运单）、装货单和场站收据等若干联组成，各联的作用不同，但内容基本相同。

1. 集装箱货物装运联单，一般为十联，因此又称十联单

第一联：集装箱货物托运单（货主留底）

第二联：集装箱货物托运单（船代留底）

第三联：运费通知（1）

第四联：运费通知（2）

第五联：装货单（Shipping Order，S/O）——场站收据副本

第六联：场站收据副本——大副联（Mate's Receipt，M/R）

第七联：场站收据（Dock Receipt，D/R）

第八联：货代留底

第九联：配仓回单（1）

第十联：配仓回单（2）

2. 十联单的流转程序如下

（1）托运人（出口商/货运代理）填制托运单，留下货主留底联，其余各联提交船公司订舱签单。

（2）船公司接受订舱后，在十联单上加注船名、航次和 D/R 号码，在第五联（装货单）上加盖船公司签单章并做装船日期批注（或电告装船日期），然后将十联单的第五至第十联返还给托运人。

（3）货运代理可留存第八联（货代留底），第五、六、七、九、十联交给出口商。

（4）报关人（出口商/报关行）将第五联（装货单）、第六联（大副联）、第七联（场站收据）提交报关。

（5）海关核实查验完毕后，在第五联（装货单）上加盖海关放行章，并将第五至第七联退还给报关人。

（6）出口商留存第七联（场站收据），将第五联（装货单）和第六联（大副联）交给船公司凭以装货。

（7）船方装妥货物后，在第六联（大副联）上签字，返还给出口商。

（8）出口商凭船方签署的第六联（大副联）向船公司换取正本提单。

（三）托运委托书及其填写

托运委托书是托运人委托货运代理人向承运人托运货物的委托代理协议。托运人应当在委托书中明确委托事项，提供必要的托运信息，包括提供信用证、商业发票、装箱单等。在信用证结算方式下，委托事项应当以信用证为依据；在其他结算方式下，应当以买卖合同为依据。其主要栏目的具体填写要求如下（参见表3-1）：

（1）发货人。为控制物权和日后提单背书转让方便，应当填写信用证受益人。

（2）收货人。按照信用证中提单制作的要求填写。

（3）被通知人。按信用证中提单制作的要求填写；如信用证无规定，按照买卖合同规定填写；如买卖合同无规定，填写买方名址及联系方式。

（4）第4到第33项，严格按信用证规定填写。

（5）第34项，填写托运人对货运代理人的特别指示。

（四）集装箱货物托运单的缮制

1. 编号（D/R No）

这一栏填写将要签发的集装箱提单号码。

2. 发货人（Shipper）

发货人即托运人，指委托运输人，一般为出口方，填写卖方的名称需与提单一致。

3. 收货人（Consignee）

具体填写方法见海运出口托运单。常采用指示收货人（TO ORDER 或 TO ORDER OF…）的填写方法。不标明具体收货人的名址，以方便单据的转让。

表3-1
出口货物订舱委托书

日期:

（1）发货人	（4）信用证号码	
	（5）开证银行	
	（6）合同号码	（7）成交金额
	（8）装运口岸	（9）目的港
（2）收货人	（10）转船运输	（11）分批装运
	（12）信用证有效期	（13）装船期限
	（14）运费	（15）成交条件
	（16）公司联系人	（17）电话/传真
（3）被通知人	（18）公司开户行	（19）银行账号
	（20）特别要求	

（21）标记、唛码	（22）货号规格	（23）包装件数	（24）毛重	（25）净重	（26）数量	（27）单价	（28）总价
	（29）总件数	（30）总毛重	（31）总净重	（32）总尺码		（33）总金额	

（34）备注

4. 通知人（Notify Party）

填制方法同散装运输托运单。在信用证支付方式下，按来证规定的通知人缮制。如来证不要求在提单上注明通知人的，可提供目的港收货人的名称和地址，并注明仅缮制在副本提单上，以便船公司通知客户提货清关。

5. 集装箱号（Container No.）

6. 封志号（铅封号）、标记与号码（Seal No.，Marks & Nos.）

第五、六栏的内容可以连在一起写。如果托运时已装好箱，即整箱货（FCL），则填集装箱号码及海关查验后作为封箱的铅封关封号，如果为拼箱货（LCL），可先填入货物具体唛头，在场站装箱完毕后，填集装箱号码。但如L/C有规定，则必须严格与信用证规定一致。在集装箱号和铅封号之后，还应加注货物的具体交接方式，如FCL-FCL、CY-CY、LCL-LCL、CFS-CFS、CY-CFS、CFS-CY等。

7. 箱数或件数（No. of Container or Pkgs）

如为托运人装箱的整箱货，可只注集装箱数量，如"3 container"，只要海关已对集装箱封箱，承运人对箱内的内容和数量不负责任。如需注明箱内小件数量，数量前应加"said to container…"；如果是拼箱货，该栏的填制可参照散装运输托运单相同栏目的填制方法，填写货物最大包装件数。

8. 包装种类与货名（Kind of Packages；Description of Goods）

（1）填写包装材料及形式，必须与合同及 L/C 要求一致；（2）货名可只填写统称，如同时出口两种及两种以上货物，需分别填写，不允许只填写其中一种数量较多或金额较大的商品。

9. 毛重（Gross Weight）

填写货物毛重，以千克计。

10. 尺码（Measurement）

此处为货物尺码总数，它不仅包括各种货物之和，还应包括件与件之间堆放时的空隙所占的体积。

11. 集装箱数或件数合计（TOTAL NUMBER OF CONTAINERS OR PACKAGES）

用大写表示集装箱数（整箱托运时）或本托运单项下的商品总件数（拼箱托运时）。

12、13、14. 由场站员或理货员（Terminal Clerk/Tally Clerk）于理货整箱后填写

15. 正本提单份数（No. of Original B（s）／L）

由船方或其代理填写。正本提单份数（No. of Original B（s）/L）按证中规定填写，若证中只规定"Full Set"或"Complete Set"等，未规定具体份数，可掌握 2～3 份，提单份数通常用大写英文数字注明，有的在大写字母之后用括号或斜线隔开，注阿拉伯数字。如："TWO/2"。

16. 签发地点（Place of Issue）

通常为承运人接收货物或装船地址，但有时也不一致，按实际情况填写即可。

17、18. 货物交接方式

货物交接方式一般有 9 种：CY–CY、CY–DOOR、DOOR–CY、DOOR–DOOR、CY–CFS、CFS–CY、CFS–CFS、CFS–DOOR、DOOR–CFS。

19. 货物种类（Type of Goods）

选择确认托运种类，打"√"。冷藏货物需填冷藏温度。危险品必须提供下列内容：危险品的化学成分、国际海运危险品法规号码、包装标志和使用鉴定、港监签证。外包装上注明危险品标志。

20～24 分货物不需转运（a）和需要转运（b）两种情况讲解

20. 前程运输（Pre…Carriage by）

（a）空白。

（b）填第一程船的船名或联合运输过程中在装货港装船前的运输工具。例如：从沈阳用火车将集装箱及货物运到大连新港，再运至目的港，此栏可填"Wagon No. xxxx"。

21. 收货地点（Place of Receipt）

（a）空白或场站。

（b）指前段运输的收货地点，按上例情形，此栏应填沈阳（ShenYang）。

22. 船名、航次（Ocean Vessel Voy. No.）：（a）船名；（b）第二程船名

23. 装货港（Port of Loading）：（a）装货港名称；（b）中转港名称

应按 L/C 规定填写。若证中只笼统规定装货港名称，如："Chinese main port"，制单时应根据实际情况填具体港口名称，并加注"CHINA"；如有重名的，须加注地区名以示区别，如：XINGANG/DALIAN/CHINA 或 XINGANG/TIANJIN/CHINA；若证中同时列明几个启运港，如："XINGANG/ QINHUANGDAO/TANGSHAN"，制单时只填实际装运港的名称。

24. 卸货港（Port of Discharge）：（a）卸货港（目的港）名称；（b）二程卸货港（目的港）名称

25. 交货地点（Place of Delivery）

如为港至港运输，此栏填目的港，如为联合运输，此栏填最终将货物交与收货人的地点（城市）名称。除 FOB 术语外，目的港不能打笼统名称，如信用证规定目的港为"Negoya/Kobe/Yokohama"，此种表示由卖方选港，制单时根据实际只打一个即可，但若来证规定"Option Negoya/Kobe/Yokohama"，则表示由买方选港，制单时应按次序全部照打。

26. 目的地（Final Destination for the Merchant's Reference）

填货物实际到达的目的地，供货主参考。

27～36. 均用中文填写

27、28、29. 分别为发货人或代理人地址、联系人、电话

30. 可否转船

填"N/Y"或"可/否"，注意前后一致。

31. 可否分批

填"N/Y"或"可/否"，如为"Y"，则在备注栏内加以具体说明。

32. 装运期限（Time of Shipment）

装运期限严格按照信用证或合同规定填写，最好用英文书写。如：不迟于2014 年 7 月 8 日，应写成 Not later than July 8, 2014。

装运期可表示为一段时间，例如 Month of Shipment：May, 2014；也可表示为不早于××日，不迟于××日，例如 Shipment not earlier than… and not later than…，latest Shipment be…。

33. 有效期（Expiry Date）

在信用证支付条件下，有效期与运期有着较密切的关系。一般规定信用证至运输单据签发日后 21 天内有效。这一栏填写要参照信用证规定。如果装运期空白不填的话，这一栏也可空白。

34. 制单日期

它必须早于最迟装运期和有效期，可以是开立发票的日期，也可以早于发票日期。

35. 海运费由哪一方支付

如预付费用托收支付，填银行账号。

36. 装箱场站名称

37. 备注：特别说明处

38. 场站签章、日期：在货物入站 CY 或 CFS 后，由场站签收。

集装箱货物托运单格式参见表 3-2。

表 3-2 集装箱货物托运单

Shipper （发货人）		D/R No. （编号）			
Consignee （收货人）					
Notify Party （通知人）		集装箱货物托运单			
Pre-carriage by （前程运输）	Place of Receipt （收货地点）				
Vessel （船名） Voy. No. （航次）	Port of Loading （装货港）				
Port of Discharge （卸货港）	Place of Delivery （交货地点）	Final Destination for the Goods （目的地）			
Container No. （集装箱号）	Seal No. （封志号） Marks & Nos. （标志与号码）	No. of containers or pkgs （箱数或件数）	Kind of Packages/ Description of Goods （包装种类与货名）	Gross Weight 毛重 （千克）	Measurement 尺码(立方米)
TOTAL NUMBER OF CONTAINERS OR PACKAGES （IN WORDS） 集装箱数或件数合计 （大写）					

FREIGHT & CHARGES （运费与附加费）	Revenue Tons （运费吨）	Rate （运费率）	Per （每）	Prepaid （运费预付）	Collect （运费到付）
Ex. Rate （兑换率）	Prepaid at （预付地点）	Payable at （到付地点）		Place of Issue （签发地点）	
	Total Prepaid （预付总额）	No. of Original B（s）/L （正本提单份数）			

Service Type on Receiving CY	Service Type on Delivery CY	
可否转船：	可否分批：	
装期：	有效期：	
金额：		
制单日期：		

三、实训内容与要求

（一）按照本实训指导的货物托运一般程序示意图，写出完整的出口货物托运程序和各程序的具体内容

（二）根据货物托运委托信息表的内容，填写托运委托书

四、实训单证填制

在收到信用证修改通知后，公司即开始安排出口货物的装运事宜，首先要向船公司订舱。订舱文件主要包括商业发票、装箱单、出口货物订舱委托书。

1. 商业发票的填制见表3-3

表3-3　　　　　　　　　　　　　　**商业发票的填制**
COMMERCIAL　INVOICE

(1) SELLER JINZHE IMP. AND EXP. CO. LTD. ROOM 302, WORLD TRADE CENTER, 277 WU XING ROAD, SHANGHAI, CHINA	(3) INVOICE NO. KH-SPTINV01	(4) INVOICE DATE 1-Sep-13
	(5) L/C NO. 384010021947	(6) DATE 3-Aug-13
	(7) ISSUED BY DEUTSCHE BANK	
(2) BUYER GLOBAL TRADING UM GMBH MOOSFELDSTRABE 96 D-746 BALINGEN, W-GERMANY	(8) CONTRACT NO. KH-SPTSC38	(9) DATE 30-Jul-13
	(10) FROM SHANGHAI, CHINA	(11) TO HAMBURG, GERMANY
	(12) SHIPPED BY	(13) PRICE TERM CIF HAMBURG, GERMANY

(14) MARKS	(15) DESCRIPTION OF GOODS	(16) QTY.	(17) UNIT PRICE	(18) AMOUNT
		FOB SHANGHAI VALUE		USD15 989.50
		INSURANCE PREMIUM	USD	199.50
KD-SPTSC08 SPORTAR HAMBURG	DUMBBELL / ART NO. G6610-10KGS	1 700 SETS CIF HAMBURG, GERMANY USD 10.67		USD 18 139.00

C

NO. 1-1700   L/C NO. : 384010021947

TOTAL   USD 18 139.00

（23）ISSUED BY

JINZHE IMP. AND EXP. CO. LTD.

（24）SIGNATURE

×××

3 copies

2. 装箱单的填制见表 3-4

表 3-4   装箱单的填制
PACKING LIST

(1) SELLER JINZHE IMP. AND EXP. CO. LTD. ROOM 302, WORLD TRADE CENTER, 277 WU XING ROAD, SHANGHAI, CHINA	(3) INVOICE NO. KH-SPTINV01	(4) INVOICE DATE 1-Sep-13
	(5) FROM SHANGHAI, CHINA	(6) TO HAMBURG, GERMANY
	(7) TOTAL PACKAGES (IN WORDS) SAY ONE THOUSAND AND SEVEN HUNDRED SETS ONLY	
(2) BUYER GLOBAL TRADING UM GMBH MOOSFELDSTRABE 96 D-746 BALINGEN, W-GERMANY	(8) MARKS & NOS. KD-SPTSC08 SPORTAR HAMBURG C NO. 1-1700	

(9) C/NOS.	(10) NOS. & KINDS OF PKGS.	(11) ITEM	(12) QTY. (pcs.)	(13) G. W. (kg)	(14) N. W. (kg)	(15) MEAS. (m^3)
1-1 700	1 700 CARTONS IN ONE 20 FEET /ART NO. G6610-10KGS CONTAINER	DUMBBELL				
			1 700	17 000	17 000	25.00
	L/C NO. : 384010021947					
TOTAL	1 700 CTNS		1 700	17 000	17 000	25.00

（16）ISSUED BY

JINZHE IMP. & EXP. CO. LTD.

（17）SIGNATURE

×××

3COPIES

3. 出口货物订舱委托书的填制见表 3-5

表 3-5　　　　　　　　　　　　**出口货物订舱委托书的填制**

公司编号　BOX02　　　　　　　　　　　　　　　　　　日期　2013 年 8 月 20 日

(1) 发货人 JINZHE IMP. AND EXP. CO. LTD. ROOM 302, WORLD TRADE CENTER, 277 WU XING ROAD, SHANGHAI, CHINA	(4) 信用证号码：384010021947
	(5) 开证银行：DEUTSCHE BANK
	(6) 合同号码： KH-SPTSC38 ／ (7) 成交金额： USD 18 139.00
	(8) 装运口岸： SHANGHAI, CHINA ／ (9) 目的港： HAMBURG, GERMANY
(2) 收货人 TO ORDER OF SHIPPER	(10) 转船运输：NO ／ (11) 分批装运：NO
	(12) 信用证效期： 2014-9-20 ／ (13) 装船期限： 2013-9-4
	(14) 运费：PREPAID ／ (15) 成交条件： CIF HAMBURG, GERMANY
	(16) 公司联系人 ／ (17) 电话/传真：64331255
(3) 被通知人 GLOBAL TRADING UM GMBH MOOSFELDSTRABE 96 D-746 BALINGEN, W-GERMANY DEUTSCHE BANK FILIALE HANNOVER	(18) 公司开户行： 中国银行 ／ (19) 银行账号： 7938724375
	(20) 特别要求

(21) 标记、唛码	(22) 货号规格	(23) 包装件数	(24) 毛重(kgs)	(25) 净重(kgs)	(26) 数量	(27) 单价(USD)	(28) 总价(USD)
							CIF HAMBURG, GERMANY
KD-SPTSC08 SPORTAR HAMBURG C NO. 1-1700	DUMBBELL /ART NO. G6610-10KGS	1 700 CTNS	17 000	17 000	1 700 SETS	USD 10.67	USD 18 139.00

(29) 总件数	(30) 总毛重	(31) 总净重	(32) 总尺码	(33) 总金额
1 700 CTNS IN ONE 20' CONTAINER	17 000KGS	17 000KGS	25m^3	USD 18 139.00

(34) 备注

五、实训考核方法

（一）掌握货物托运的一般程序

（二）根据有关数据，归纳货物托运委托信息

（三）掌握集装箱货物托运委托书的填写

模块四　发　票

一、实训目的

（一）学生掌握发票的相关内容

（二）学生能根据信用证的要求缮制商业发票

二、理论知识点

（一）商业发票的内容及制作

商业发票（简称"发票"）是出口商向进口商开立的发货价目清单，也是卖方凭以向买方索取所提供的货物或服务的价款的依据。发票是出口商缮制其他出口单据的依据，外贸业务中的各个环节基本上离不开发票，故发票是国际商务单证的核心。

商业发票没有固定的格式，但是其内容必须与信用证或合同的内容严格相符。商业发票包括以下几项内容：

（1）载明"商业发票"（COMMERCIAL INVOICE）或"发票"（INVOICE）字样。

（2）发票编号和签发日期（INVOICE NO. AND DATE）。

（3）合同或订单号码（CONTRACT NO. OR ORDER NO.）。

（4）信用证号（L/C NO.）。

（5）出口商名址（EXPORTER'S NAME AND ADDRESS）。

①出现在发票的最前面。

②出现在发票中间。

（6）收货人名址（CONSIGNEE'S NAME AND ADDRESS）。

收货人名称也称发票抬头，引导发票抬头的词或词组有：

"To"、"To Messrs"、"Sold to"、"Sold to Messrs"、"Messrs"、"For Account and Risk of Messrs"、"For Account of"、"Consigned to"

（7）装运工具及起讫地点（MEANS OF TRANSPORT AND ROUTE）。

①运输工具。

常见的词或词组有：Shipped per/per/by/vessel/ship

②运输路线。

常见的词或词组有：From…To…；From…To…W/T；From…To…Via；From…To…in transit to

（8）唛头及件数（MARKS AND NUMBERS）。

（9）货物描述（DESCRIPTION OF THE GOODS）。

①信用证引导货物内容的词或词组：

A. Description of goods；

B. Covering shipment of；

C. Description of merchandise；

D. Covering the following goods by；

E. Covering Value of；

F. Shipment of goods；

G. Covering.

②《UCP 600》对货物描述的要求。

商业发票中货物描述不得使用统称，必须与信用证中显示的内容相符。

（10）包装种类及件数（NO. & KINDS OF PACKING）。

（11）数量（QUANTITY）。

《UCP 600》第 30 条 a 和 b 对货物数量的规定：

a. "约"（About）或"大约"（Approximately）用于信用证金额或信用证规定的数量或单价时，应解释为允许有关金额或数量或单价有不超过 10% 的增减幅度。

b. 在信用证未以包装单位件数或货物自身件数的方式规定货物数量时，货物数量允许有 5% 的增减幅度，只要总支取金额不超过信用证金额。

（12）单价、价格条件（Price and Price Term）及总金额（Amount）。

①单价包括计价货币、计价单位、单位价格金额和贸易术语四部分，如信用证有具体规定，则应与信用证一致。

②发票金额应与汇票金额相同，且一般不能超过信用证总金额。

③发票币别必须与信用证一致。

④《UCP 600》第 18 条 b 对货物单价、总金额的规定：按照指定行事的被指定银行、保兑行（如有）或开证行可以接受金额超过信用证所允许金额的商业发票，倘若有关银行已兑付或已议付的金额没有超过信用证所允许的金额，则该银行的决定对各有关方均具有约束力。

⑤涉及佣金、折扣时的处理。

A. 实际制单时，来证要求在发票中扣除佣金，则必须扣除。折扣与佣金的处理方法相同，例如：来证要求 "From Each Invoice 8 Percent Commission Must Be Deducted"，且总额为 "USD 20000.00 FOBC8 OSLO"，则填在价格栏中的金额的计算如下：

FOBC8　　　OSLO　　　USD 20 000.00
—C8　　　　　　　　　　　1 600.00
FOB　　　　OSLO　　　USD 18 400.00

B. 有时证内无扣除佣金规定，但金额正好是减佣后的净额，发票应显示减佣后的净额，否则发票金额超证。

C. 有时合同规定佣金，但来证金额内未扣除，而且证内也未提及佣金事宜，则发票不宜显示，等货款收回后另行汇给买方。

⑥运费、保费的处理

A. 有时，来证要求在成交价格为 FOB 时，分别列出运费、保险费，并显示 CIF 的价格，制单时可按照如下格式填写。

B. 有时，来证要求在成交价格为 CIF 时，分别列出运费、保险费，并显示 FOB 的价格，制单时可按照如下格式填写。

例如：TOTAL　FOB VALUE　　　$20000.00
　　　　　　 FREIGHT　　　　 $1200.00
　　　　　　 INSURANCE　　　 $900.00
　　　TOTAL CIF VALUE　　　 $22100.00

（13）声明文句（STATEMENT）。

有时信用证要求在发票内特别加列船名、原产地、进口许可证号码等声明文句。制单时必须列明。声明文句中词语要求内容确切、通顺、简洁。信用证有的条款，不能原文照抄，而要视具体情况重新组织。

（14）出票人签章。

根据《UCP 600》规定，发票可不签字。如果信用证有 "SIGNED COMMERCIAL INVOICE" 字样，则此发票必须签字；若信用证中有 "MANUALLY SIGNED INVOICE" 字样，则必须要有出票人的手签。出票人签字（SIGNATURE OF MAKER）等。

（15）"有错当查" 和 "证实发票"。

为了在发生错误或遗漏时可以更正或更换，有的要求在发票下端注明：E. & O. E.（errors and omissions excepted，有错当查）字样。另外，有些国家的进口商按国家的法令和商业习惯，要求在发票上加注："证明所列内容真实无误"（WE HEREBY CERTIFY THAT THE CONTENTS OF INVOICE HEREIN ARE TRUE & CORRECT.）字样或 "货款已收讫"　（VALUE/PAYMENT RECEIVED UNDER CREDIT NO. ×××ISSUED BY ×××BANK）字样，一般情况下都可以照办。但后一种被称为"证实发票"的，则不能有"E. &. O. E"字样。

商业发票的具体格式见表4-1。

表4-1 　　　　　　　　COMMERCIAL INVOICE

(1) SELLER	(3) INVOICE NO.		(4) INVOICE DATE
	(5) L/C NO.		(6) DATE
	(7) ISSUED BY		
(2) BUYER	(8) CONTRACT NO.		(9) DATE
	(10) FROM		(11) TO
	(12) SHIPPED BY		(13) PRICE TERM

(14) MARKS	(15) DESCRIPTION OF GOODS	(16) QTY.	(17) UNIT PRICE	(18) AMOUNT

(19) ISSUED BY

(20) SIGNATURE　　　　　　　　　　　　　　　　　　3 COPIES

三、实训内容与要求

（一）根据信用证填写商业发票

（二）根据信用证提供的内容审核并修改商业发票

四、实训单证填制

请根据模块一的信用证资料制作商业发票（见表4-2）。

表 4-2   **COMMERCIAL INVOICE**

(1) SELLER JINZHE IMP. AND EXP. CO. LTD. ROOM 302, WORLD TRADE CENTER, 277 WU XING ROAD, SHANGHAI, CHINA	(3) INVOICE NO. KH-SPTINV01	(4) INVOICE DATE 1-Sep-13
	(5) L/C NO. 384010021947	(6) DATE 3-Aug-13
	(7) ISSUED BY DEUTSCHE BANK	
(2) BUYER GLOBAL TRADING UM GMBH MOOSFELDSTRABE 96 D-746 BALINGEN, W-GERMANY	(8) CONTRACT NO. KH-SPTSC38	(9) DATE 30-Jul-13
	(10) FROM SHANGHAI, CHINA	(11) TO HAMBURG, GERMANY
	(12) SHIPPED BY	(13) PRICE TERM CIF HAMBURG, GERMANY

(14) MARKS   (15) DESCRIPTION OF GOODS   (16) QTY.   (17) UNIT PRICE   (18) AMOUNT

                                 FOB SHANGHAI VALUE   USD 15 989.50
                                   INSURANCE PREMIUM   USD   199.50

KD-SPTSC08   DUMBBELL   1 700 SETS
SPORTAR   / ART NO. G6610-10KGS   CIF HAMBURG, GERMANY
HAMBURG   USD 10.67   USD 18 139.00
C
NO. 1-1700   L/C NO. : 384010021947

                             TOTAL   USD 18139.00
(19) ISSUED BY
JINZHE IMP. AND EXP. CO. LTD.

(20) SIGNATURE
×××

                                                   3 COPIES

五、实训考核方法

（一）准确阅读商业发票
（二）根据商业发票的格式准确填写商业发票
（三）根据信用证准确制作商业发票

模块五　商品检验证书

一、实训目的

（一）学生能掌握出口报检的相关程序和相关手续

（二）学生能掌握出口报检所需的单据并且能正确填写商品检验证书等单据

二、理论知识点

（一）出口报检的程序

出口报检的程序包括以下几个方面：

（1）由报检人填写"出口商品检验申请单"。

（2）报检人应提供相关的单据，如双方签订的合同及其附件、信用证、厂检单正本等。

（3）商品检验部门对商品进行检验，签发检验证书或放行单。

"网络链接"：法定检验检疫查询可链接

http：//www. shciq. gov. cn/jsp/ciq＿ hsfdjyjyQy. jsp

（二）出境货物报检单的缮制

出境货物报检单中需由报检人填写的栏目不得留空，若无法填写，以"＊＊＊"代替。

1. 编号

编号由检验检疫机构受理人填写，为 15 位数字。其中，前 6 位为检验检疫机构代码，第 7 位为报检类代码，第 8、9 位为年代码，第 10～15 位为流水号。

2. 报检单位

报检单位是指向检验检疫机构申报检验、检疫、鉴定业务的单位。报检单应加盖报检单位公章。

3. 报检单位登记号

报检单位登记号是指在检验检疫机构登记的号码。

4. 联系人

本栏填写报检人的姓名。

5. 电话

本栏填写报检人的联系电话。

6. 报检日期

报检日期是指检验检疫机构实际受理报检的日期，由检验检疫机构受理人填写。

7. 发货人

发货人是指本批货物贸易合同中的卖方名称或信用证中的受益人名称。如需要出具英文证书的，填写中英文。

8. 收货人

收货人是指本批货物贸易合同中或信用证中的买方名称。如需要出具英文证书的，填写中英文。

9. 货物名称

本栏按贸易合同或发票所列的货物名称填写，根据需要可填写型号、规格或牌号。货物名称不得填写笼统的商品类，如"陶瓷"、"玩具"等。货物名称必须填写具体的类别名称，如"日用陶瓷"、"塑料玩具"等。如填写位置不够，可以附页的形式填报。

10. H. S. 编码

H. S. 编码是指货物对应的海关商品代码，填写 8 位数或 10 位数。

11. 产地

产地是指货物生产/加工的省（自治区、直辖市）以及地区（市）名称。

12. 数/重量

本栏填写报检货物的数/重量，重量一般填写净重。如填写毛重，或以毛重作净重，则需注明。

13. 货物总值

本栏按本批货物贸易合同或发票上所列的总值填写（以美元计）。如同一报检单报检多批货物，需列明每批货物的总值（如报检货物总值与国内、国际市场价格有较大差异，则检验检疫机构保留核价权力）。

14. 包装种类及数量

包装种类及数量是指本批货物运输包装的种类及件数。

15. 运输工具名称、号码

本栏填写货物实际装载的运输工具类别名称（如船、飞机、货柜车、火车等）

及运输工具编号（如船名、飞机航班号、车牌号码、火车车次等）。在报检时未能确定运输工具编号的，可只填写运输工具类别名称。

16．贸易方式

本栏填写一般贸易、来料加工、进料加工和其他等。

17．货物存放地点

货物存放地点是指本批货物存放的地点。填写货物存放的具体地点、仓库等。

18．合同号

合同号是指本批货物贸易合同的编号。

19．信用证号

信用证号是指本批货物的信用证编号。

20．用途

用途是指本批货物的用途，如种用、食用、奶用、观赏或演艺、伴侣、实验、药用、饲用、加工等。

21．发货日期

本栏按本批货物信用证或合同上所列的出境日期填写。

22．输往国家（地区）

输往国家（地区）是指贸易合同中买方（进口方）所在的国家或地区。

23．许可证/审批号

对于实施许可证制度或者审批制度管理的货物，在报检时填写许可证编号或审批单编号。

24．启运地

启运地是指装运本批货物离境的交通工具的启运口岸/地区城市名称。

25．到达口岸

到达口岸是指装运本批货物的交通工具最终抵达目的地停靠的口岸名称。

26．生产单位注册号

生产单位注册号是指生产/加工本批货物的单位在检验检疫机构的注册登记编号。

27．集装箱规格、数量及号码

本栏填写装载本批货物的集装箱规格（如 40 英尺、20 英尺等）以及分别对应的数量和集装箱号码。如集装箱太多，可以附页的形式填报。

28．合同、信用证订立的检验检疫条款或特殊要求

这是指贸易合同或信用证中贸易双方对本批货物特别约定而订立的质量、卫生等条款和报检单位对本批货物检验检疫的特别要求。

29．标记及号码

本栏按出境货物实际运输包装标记填写。如没有标记，填写 N/M。如标记栏填写位置不够，可以附页的形式填报。

30．随附单据

本栏按实际提供的单据，在对应的"□"打"√"。对报检单上未标出的，须

自行填写提供的单据名称。

31. 需要证单名称

本栏按需要检验检疫机构出具的证单，在对应的"□"打"√"，并对应注明所需证单的正副本的数量。对报检单上未标出的，如"通关单"等，须自行填写所需证单的名称和数量。

32. 检验检疫费

本栏由检验检疫机构的计费人员填写。

33. 报检人郑重声明

本栏必须有报检人的亲笔签名。

34. 领取证单

报检人在领取证单时填写领证日期并签名。

中华人民共和国出入境检验检疫出境货物报检单的具体格式见表5-1。

表 5-1　　　　　　　中华人民共和国出入境检验检疫出境货物报检单

报检单位（加盖公章）：						* 编号：_____	
报检单位登记号：		联系人：		电话：		报检日期：　年　月　日	
发货人	（中文）						
	（外文）						
收货人	（中文）						
	（外文）						
货物名称（中/外文）	H.S. 编码	产地	数/重量	货物总值	包装种类及数量		
运输工具名称、号码		贸易方式			货物存放地点		
合同号		信用证号			用途		
发货日期		输往国家（地区）		许可证/审批号			
启运地		到达口岸		生产单位注册号			
集装箱规格、数量及号码							
合同、信用证订立的检验检疫条款或特殊要求		标记及号码		随附单据（划"√"或补填）			
				□合同 □信用证 □发票 □换证凭单 □装箱单 □厂检单	□包装性能结果单 □许可/审批文件 □ □ □ □		

续表

需要证单名称（划"√"或补填）		＊检验检疫费	
□品质证书 ＿正＿副	□植物检疫证书 ＿正＿副	总金额 （人民币元）	
□重量证书 ＿正＿副	□熏蒸/消毒证书 ＿正＿副		
□数量证书 ＿正＿副	□出境货物换证凭单	计费人	
□兽医卫生证书 ＿正＿副	□出境货物通关单		
□健康证书 ＿正＿副	□	收费人	
□卫生证书 ＿正＿副	□		
□动物卫生证书 ＿正＿副	□		
报检人郑重声明： 1. 本人被授权报检。 2. 上列填写内容正确属实，货物无伪造或冒用他人的厂名、标志、认证标志，并承担货物质量责任。 　　　　　　　　　签名：＿＿＿＿＿＿		领取证单	
		日期	
		签名	

注：有"＊"号栏由出入境检验检疫机关填写　　◆国家出入境检验检疫局制

　　表5-2 至表5-6 的内容与表5-1 的内容相似，不再逐一说明。

　　中华人民共和国出入境检验检疫入境货物报检单见表5-2。

　　表5-2　　　　　**中华人民共和国出入境检验检疫入境货物报检单**

报检单位（加盖公章）：　　　　　　　　　　　　　　　　　　　　＊编号：＿＿＿＿＿＿

报检单位登记号：　　　　联系人：　　　　电话：　　　　报检日期：　　年　月　日

收货人	（中文）		企业性质（划"√"）	□合资 □合作 □外资
	（外文）			
发货人	（中文）			
	（外文）			

货物名称（中/外文）	H.S. 编码	产地	数/重量	货物总值	包装种类及数量

运输工具名称、号码				合同号	
贸易方式		贸易国别（地区）		提单/运单号	
到货日期		启运国家（地区）		许可证/审批号	
卸毕日期		启运口岸		入境口岸	
索赔有效期至		经停口岸		目的地	
集装箱规格、数量及号码					
合同订立特殊条款以及其他要求				货物存放地点	
				用途	

续表

随附单据（划"√"或补填）		标记及号码	*外商投资财产（划"√"）	□是 □否
□合同	□到货通知		* 检验检疫费	
□发票	□装箱单		总金额 （人民币元）	
□提/运单	□质保书			
□兽医卫生证书	□理货清单			
□植物检疫证书	□磅码单		计费人	
□动物检疫证书	□验收报告			
□卫生证书	□			
□原产地证书	□		收费人	
□许可/审批文件	□			
报检人郑重声明：			领取单证	
1. 本人被授权报检。			日期	
2. 上列填写内容正确属实。				
签名：＿＿＿＿			签名	

注：有"＊"号栏由出入境检验检疫机关填写　　◆国家出入境检验检疫局制

中华人民共和国出入境检验检疫出境货物换证凭单的具体格式见表5-3。

表5-3　　　　中华人民共和国出入境检验检疫出境货物换证凭单

类别：＿＿＿＿＿＿　　　　　　　　　　　　　　　　　　　　　　编号：＿＿＿＿＿＿＿

发货人		标记及号码	
收货人			
品名			
H.S. 编码			
报检数/重量			
包装种类及数量			
申报总值			
产地		生产单位（注册号）	
生产日期		生产批号	
包装性能检验结果单号		合同/信用证号	
		运输工具名称及编号	
输往国家或地区		集装箱规格及数量	
发货日期		检验依据	

续表

检验检疫结果									
	签字：　　　　　　　　　　　　　　　　　　日期：　　年　　月　　日								
本单有效期									
备注									
分批出境核销栏	日期	出境数/重量	结存数/重量	核销人	日期	出境数/重量	结存数/重量	核销人	

说明：（1）货物出境时，经口岸检验检疫机关查验货证相符且符合检验检疫要求的，予以签发通关单或换发检验检疫证书；（2）本单不作为国内贸易的品质或其他证明；（3）涂改无效。

出入境货物代理报检委托书的具体格式见表5-4。

表5-4　　　　　　　　　　　**出入境货物代理报检委托书**

委托单位		十位编码	
地址		联系电话/经办人	
我单位将于____年____月进口 □ 出口 □ 以下货物			
货物名称		H. S. 编码		件数/重量	
货值		贸易性质		包装性质	
货物起运国		货物产地		合同号或发票号	
企业性质		运单号		信用证号	
经营范围					

随附单据名称、份数及编号：
1. 合同____份；
2. 发票____份；
3. 装箱清单____份；
4. 登记手册____本；编号：____
5. 许可证____份；编号：____

6. 不办、免办证明____份；编号：____
7. 机电证明____份；编号：____
8. 海关免表____份；编号：____
9. 换证凭单或电子转单____份；编号：____
10. _____

我单位郑重声明，保证遵守中华人民共和国出入境检验检疫有关法律、法规的规定和检验检疫机构的各项规章制度。如有违反行为，自愿接受检验检疫机构的处罚并负法律责任。

我单位所委托受托人向出入境检验检疫机构提交的"报检单"和随附各种单据所列内容是真实无讹的。

（以上内容由委托单位填写）			
被委托单位		报检单位注册号	
地址		联系电话	
经办人		报检证号	
（以上内容由被委托单位填写）			
代理报检企业章		委托单位章及其法人代表章	

进口商品检验证书见表5-5。

表 5-5 进口商品检验证书

中华人民共和国上海进出口商品检验局
SHANGHAI IMPORT & EXPORT COMMODITY
INSPECTION BUREAU OF THE PEOPLE'S REPUBLIC
OF CHINA

地址：上海市中山东一路 13 号　　**检 验 证 书**　　　　No. :

Address：13, Zhongshan Road　**INSPECTION CERTIFICATE**　　日期 Date：

　　（E. 1），Shanghai

电话 Tel：8621-32155296

收 货 人：

Consignee：

发 货 人：

Consignor：

品　名：

Commodity：

报验数量/重量：

Quantity/Weight Declared：

运　输：

Transportation：

进口日期：

Date of Arrival：

卸毕日期：

Date of Completion of Discharge：

发 票 号：

Invoice No. :

合 同 号：

Contract No. :

标记及号码：

Mark & No. :

注意：本证书译文如有任何异点，概以中文为主。

（N. B. In case if divergence, the Chinese text shall be regarded as authentic）

兽医检验证书见表 5-6。

表 5-6　　　　　　　　　　**兽医检验证书**

中华人民共和国上海进出口商品检验局
SHANGHAI IMPORT & EXPORT COMMODITY
INSPECTION BUREAU OF THE PEOPLE'S REPUBLIC
OF CHINA

地址：上海市中山东一路 13 号　　**检 验 证 书**　　　　　No. :
Address : 13, Zhongshan Road **INSPECTION CERTIFICATE**　　日期 Date :
　　　（E. 1），Shanghai
电话 Tel：8621-32155296

发 货 人：
Consignor：
收 货 人：
Consignee：
品　　名：　　　　　　　　　　　　标记及号码：
Commodity：　　　　　　　　　　　Mark & No. :
报验数量/重量：
Quantity/Weight Declared：
官方兽医证明如下：
The undersigned Official Veterinarian, certify that：_____

主 任 兽 医
Chief Veterinarian

三、实训内容与要求

（一）熟悉商品检验证书的内容
（二）掌握与商品检验有关的单据的填制

四、实训单证填制

请根据模块一中的信用证资料制作出境货物检验证书，见表 5-7。

表 5-7 　　　　　　　　　　出境货物检验证书

CCIC Shanghai Co. , Limited. 　　　　　　　　　ORIGINAL

No. 361 , Zhao Jia Bang Road , Shanghai

P. C: 200032

Tel: 021-63062406/64189367

Fax: 021-63244587

E-mail: shanghai@ ccic. com

Pre-shipment Inspection Certificate for Quantity

Certificate No. : SH/EXY6170

Date: Sept. 3 , 2013

Applicant: JINZHE IMP. AND EXP. CO. LTD.

　　　　　ROOM 302 , WORLD TRADE CENTER ,

　　　　　277 WU XING ROAD , SHANGHAI, CHINA

Consignor: JINZHE IMP. AND EXP. CO. LTD.

　　　　　ROOM 302 , WORLD TRADE CENTER ,

　　　　　277 WU XING ROAD , SHANGHAI, CHINA

Consignee: GLOBLE TRADING UM GMBH

　　　　　MOOSFELDSTRABE 96 ,

　　　　　D-746 BALINGEN , W-GERMANY

Commodity: DUMBBELL / ART NO. G6610-10KGS

Quantity/WeightDeclared: 1 700 SETS / 17 000 KGS

Invoice No. : KH-SPTINV01

Letter of Credit No. : 384010021947

　　　　　　　　　KD-SPTSC08

Shipping Marks: 　　　SPORTAR

　　　　　　　　　HAMBURG

　　　　　　　　　C

　　　　　　　　　NO. 1-1700

Results of Inspection:

THE SHIPMENT OF DUMBBELL /ART NO. G6610-10 KGS HAS
BEEN INSPECTED BEFORE SHIPMENT AND WAS FOUND TO
BE PACKED IN CARTONS OF 1 SET EACH , 20 CARTONS TO
A PLATE , TOTAL 1700 CARTONS TO ONE 20' CONTAINER.

　　　　　　　　　*　　*　　*　　*

This report is issued without prejudice to the liabilities to the parties concerned.

For and on behalf of

CCIC Shanghai Co. , Limited

Authorized signature (s)

郭哲昕

五、实训考核方法

（一）阅读并准确填制商检证书

（二）熟悉出口报检的程序及所提交的相关单据

模块六　保险单据

一、实训目的

（一）学生了解出口货物保险的投保程序

（二）学生能根据信用证的要求填制投保单和保险单

二、理论知识点

（一）投保业务流程

在 CIF、CIP 条件下，由卖方负责投保，填写投保单。因此，出口方应在办妥运输手续后、货物装船前或货物接受监管前办理投保事宜。

在 FCA、FOB、CFR、CPT 条件下，由买方负责投保，填写投保单。此时出口方应在交货前一定时期内，将预计装运日期通知进口方，以方便进口方及时办理运输手续。进口方办妥运输手续后，应将运输工具和货物等信息通知出口方并催促其按时装运，出口方完成装运后应及时通知进口方，以方便进口方及时办理保险。CFR（或 CPT）合同规定由进口方办理保险，出口方在完成装运后应及时通知进口方有关运输工具和货物等信息，以便进口方及时办理投保事宜。

（二）海洋货物运输险投保单的缮制

由于保险公司出具保险单是以投保单内容为依据的，因此，投保单的制作十分重要。投保单由各保险公司事先印好，其内容与缮制方法如下：

1. 被保险人（Assured's Name）

托收项下的保险单此栏应填出口商名称。CIF 条件下的信用证支付应按信用证要求填制，如信用证规定"To order"，此栏转录，受益人要在保险单背面作空白背书；信用证要求"To order of … 或 in favor of …"，此栏应写成 To order of 加上被保险人名称，并作记名背书；信用证对此无具体规定，受益人应视为被保险人，并作空白背书。

2. 发票号码（Invoice No.）

此栏应与本套单据发票同项内容相一致。

3. 包装数量（Quantity）

此栏填最大包装件数，并与发票、装箱单同项内容一致。散装货填"IN BULK"。如果货物价格以重量计价，除表示件数外，还应注明毛重或净重。

4. 保险货物项目（Description of Goods）

此栏按发票品名填写，如发票品种名称繁多，可填其统称。

5. 保险金额（Amount Insured）

一般按 CIF 发票总值的 110% 填写。信用证项下应按信用证规定计算填入，如无规定，应为发票总额加 1 成的金额。保险金额小数点后的尾数应进位取整，例如 USD2 304.1 应进位取整为 USD2 305。

6. 装载运输工具（Per Conveyance）

海运填写船名，中途转船应在一程船名后加填二程船名，如"By S.S DONG FANG/TOKYO V.108"。空运（By Airplane）填航班名称。

7. 航次、航班或车号（Voy. No.）

海运填航次号，空运填航班号。

8. 开航日期（Slg. Date）

一般填写本批货物运输单据的签发日期，如海运可填"As per B/L"。

9. 起讫地点（From … to …）

在 From 后填装运港（地）名称，在 To 后填目的港（地）名称。需转运时，应在目的港（地）后加注"W/T at …"（转运港/地名称），并与提单或其他运输单据相一致。如海运至目的港，保险承保到内陆城市，应在目的港后注明。例如，"From … To Liverpool and thence to Birmingham"。

10. 赔款偿付地点（Claim Payable at）

本栏包括保险赔款的支付地点和赔付的货币名称，其应按信用证规定缮制。如来证未作规定，或托收项下的，则填目的港（地）名称。

11. 承保险别（Condition）

此栏应按合同或信用证规定的保险险别填写，并注明依据的保险条款名称及其颁布年份。例如，"Covering all Risks and War Risks as Per PICC1/1/1981"。

12. 投保单位签章（Applicant's Signature and Co.'s Name，Add. & Tel. No.）

此栏填进出口商全称、地址和电话，由经办人签名并注明日期。

海运出口货物投保单的具体格式见表6-1。

表 6-1 　　　　　　　　　　海运出口货物投保单

（1）保险人		（2）被保险人	
（3）标记	（4）包装及数量	（5）保险货物项目	（6）保险货物金额

（7）总保险金额：（大写）

（8）运输工具：　　　　（船名）　　　　　　　（航次）

（9）装运港：　　　　　　　　　　　　　（10）目的港：

（11）投保险别：　　　　　　　　　　　（12）货物起运日期：

（13）投保日期：　　　　　　　　　　　（14）投保人签字：

（三）保险单的缮制

保险单是保险公司或其代理人签发的，保证当货物受到保险责任范围内的损失时，由其进行赔偿的书面凭证，是被保险人索赔和保险人进行理赔的依据。在 CIF 和 CIP 合同中，保险单是出口结汇单据之一，由卖方背书后转让。

保险单除包括投保单的上述内容外，还包括以下内容：

（1）总保险金额（TOTAL AMOUNT INSURED），即保险金额的大写数字，以英文表示，末尾应加"ONLY"，以防涂改。

（2）保费（PREMIUM）。一般已由保险公司印就"AS ARRANGED"（按约定）字样。除非信用证另有规定，每笔保费及费率可以不具体表示。

（3）费率（RATE）。一般已由保险公司印就"AS ARRANGED"（按约定）字样。

（4）货损检验及理赔代理人（SURVEYING AND CLAIM SETTLING AGENTS）。一般选择目的港或目的港附近的有关机构为货损检验、理赔代理人，并详细注明代理人的地址。如果保险单上注明保险责任终止在内地而非港口，应填列内地代理人名址。如当地无中国人民保险公司的代理机构，可以注明由当地法定检验机构代为检验。如果信用证自行指定买方选择的代理人，则不应接受。

应该注意的是，根据 UCP600 第二十八条 e 款的规定，保险单日期不得晚于发运日期，除非保险单据表明保险责任不迟于发运日生效。

保险单示例见表 6-2。

表 6-2　　　　　　　　　　　　　　　　　**保险单**

中 国 人 民 保 险 公 司

THE PEOPLE'S INSURANCE COMPANY OF CHINA

总公司设于北京　　　　　　　　　　　　　　一九四九年创立

Head office：BEIJING　　　　　　　　　　　Established in 1949

保险单　　　　　　　　　　　　　　　　　保险单号次

INSURANCE POLICY　　　　　　　　　　　POLICY NO.　　JZ-DRGBD01

中国人民保险公司（以下简称本公司）

THIS POLICY OF INSURANCE WITNESSES THAT THE PEOPLE'S INSURANCE COMPANY OF CHINA (HEREINAFTER CALLED "THE COMPANY")

根　　　　　　据

AT THE REQUEST OF _____

（以下简称被保险人）的要求，由被保险人

(HEREINAFTER CALLED " THE INSURED ") AND IN CONSIDERATION OF THE AGREED PREMIUM

向本公司缴付约定的保险费，

PAID TO THE COMPANY BY THE INSURED, UNDERTAKES TO INSURE THE UNDERMENTIONED

按照本保险单承保险别和背面所载条款与

GOODS IN TRANSPORTATION SUBJECT TO THE CONDITIONS OF THIS POLICY AS PER THE

下列特款承保下述货物运输保险，特立本保险单。

CLAUSES PRINTED OVERLEAF AND OTHER SPECIAL CLAUSES ATTACHED HEREON.

标记 MARKS& NOS.	包 装 及 数 量 QUANTITY	保险货物项目 DESCRIPTION OF GOODS	保 险 金 额 AMOUNT INSURED

总保险金额：

TOTAL AMOUNT INSURED：_____

保费：　　　　　　费率：　　　　　　　装载运输工具：

PREMIUM _____　RATE _____　PER CONVEYANCE S. S. _____

开航日期：　　　　　　　　自　　　　　　　　　至

SLG. ON OR ABT. _____　FROM _____　TO _____

承保险别：

CONDITIONS

所保货物，如遇出险，本公司凭本保险单及其他有关证件给付赔款。

CLAIMS, IF ANY, PAYABLE ON SURRENDER OF THIS POLICY TOGETHER WITH OTHER RELEVANT DOCUMENTS.

所保货物，如发生本保险单项下负责赔偿的损失或事故，

IN THE EVENT OF ACCIDENT WHEREBY LOSS OR DAMAGE MAY RESULT IN A CLAIM UNDER THIS POLICY IMMEDIATE,

应立即通知本公司下述代理人查勘。

NOTICE APPLYING FOR SURVEY MUST BE GIVEN TO THE COMPANY'S AGENT AS MENTIONED HEREUNDER.

　　　　　　　　　　　　　　　　　中国人民保险公司上海分公司

赔款偿付地点　　　　　　　　　　　THE PEOPLE'S INSURANCE CO. OF CHINA

CLAIM PAYABLE AT/IN _____　SHANGHAI BRANCH

日期　　　　　　　　上海

DATE　　　　　　　SHANGHAI　　　郭复北

地址：中国上海中山东一路 23 号

Address：23 Zhongshan Dong Yi Lu, Shanghai, China.　　General Manager

TEL：63234305 63217466-44　Telex：33128 PICCS CN.

Cable：42001 Shanghai

（四）进口投保涉及保险单的形式

对于 FOB（或 FCA）和 CFR（或 CPT）条件下的进口合同，保险由进口方办理。对于进口合同保险，我国一般均采用"预约"方式，具体操作程序为：由我国进口方预先与保险公司签订预约保险合同，其中对预约保险货物的范围、险别和保险费率以及每批货物的最高保险金额、保险费率结算办法做出具体规定；货物进口时，我国进口方在收到国外装船通知后，速将货物名称、数量、保险金额、运输工具名称和种类、航程起讫点、开航日期等信息以书面形式通知保险公司，进口货物一经起运，保险公司则自动按照预约保险合同的规定予以承保。因此，在预约保险方式下，将出口方发来的发运通知或将已填好的预约保险起运通知书通知给保险公司，即视为办妥了保险手续。

以海运为例，发运通知即装船通知（见表6-3）。装船通知没有固定格式，但其内容应按照信用证的规定填制。若信用证没有具体要求，它一般包括如下内容：出口方抬头、装船通知（SHIPPING ADVICE）字样、出口方电话、传真等联络方式、通知对象（TO）、通知方（FROM）、制作和发出日期（DATE）、销售合同号（S/C NO.）、信用证号（L/C NO.）、提单号（B/L NO.）、商品描述（COMMODITY/GOODS）及总金额（TOTAL VALUE）、数量（QUANTITY）、包装（PACKAGES）、毛重（GROSS WEIGHT）、净重（NET WEIGHT）、船名（VESSEL）、装运港（PORT OF LOADING）和目的港（DESTINATION）、预计船舶离港时间（ETD）、预计船舶到达时间（ETA）及制作人/出具人签章等。

表 6-3　　　　　　　　　　　　　装船通知

GOLDEN SEA TRADING CORP.		
ADD. :		
TEL:	FAX:	E-MAIL:
TO:	F. L. SMIDTH & CO. A/S	FROM:　GOLDEN SEA TRADING CORP.
	77, VIGERSLEV ALLE	8TH FLOOR, JIN DU BUILDING,
	DK-2500 VALBY	277 WU XING ROAD,
	COPENHAGEN, DENMARK	SHANGHAI, CHINA
SUBJECT:	SHIPPING ADVICE	DATE:　12-Aug-13
	S/C NO.　JH-FLSSC01	
	L/C NO.　FLS-JHLC01	
	B/L NO.　JH-FLSBL01	
	GOODS　2 ITEMS OF "FOREVER" BRAND BICYCLES	
	TOTALVALUE　USD　82 200.00	
	QUANTITY　1 200 UNITS	
	PACKAGES　CARTON	
	G. W. （KGS.）　39 600.0KGS	
	N. W. （KGS.）　33 600.0KGS	
	MEAS. （m³）　547.2m³	
	VESSEL　YI XIANG　V. 307	
	FROM　SHANGHAI	
	TO　COPENHAGEN	
	ETD　12-Aug-13	
	ETA　3-Sep-13	
	GOLDEN SEA TRADING CORP.	
	×××	

表 6-4 是国际运输预约保险起运通知书。

表 6-4 国际运输预约保险起运通知书

被保险人 编号：

唛头	包装及数量	保险货物项目	价格条件	货价（原币）

合同号：	发票号：	提单号：
运输方式：	运输工具名称：	运费：

开航日期： 年 月 日	运输路线：自 至

投保险别	费率	保险金额	保险费

中国人民保险公司	被保险人签章	备注
年 月 日	年 月 日	

注：本通知书填写一式五份送保险公司。保险公司签章后退回被保险人一份。

（五）保险单的背书行为

以海运为例，海洋货物运输保险单同提单一样可以转让，经保险单上载明的被保险人背书后，即可发生转让的效力，而无须经保险人同意。保险单经被保险人背书转让后，一旦货物出险，善意持有人即享有凭保险单向保险人索取赔偿的合法权利。

1. 空白背书（BLANK ENDORSED），空白背书只注明被保险人（包括出口商名称和经办人的名字）名称。当来证没有规定使用哪一种背书时，也使用空白背书方式。

2. 记名背书，当来证要求"DELIVERY TO（THE ORDER OF）XXX COMPANY（BANK）"或"ENDORSED IN THE NAME OF XXX"，即规定使用记名方式背书。

具体做法是：在保险单背面注明被保险人的名称和经办人的名字后，打上"DELIVERY TO（THE ORDER OF）XXX COMPANY（BANK）"或"ENDORSED IN THE NAME OF XXX"字样。记名背书在出口业务中较少使用。

3. 记名指示背书

当来证保单条款规定为"INSURANCE POLICY OR CERTIFICATE IN NEGOTIABLE FORM ISSUED TO THE ORDER OF XXX"时，具体做法是：只要在保险单背面打上"TO ORDER OF XXX"字样，然后签署被保险人的名称就可以了。

三、实训内容与要求

（一）根据所给的条件填制保险单
（二）根据所给的条件审核并修改保险单
（三）根据信用证和买卖合同审核保险单的可接受性

四、实训单证填制

根据模块一中的信用证内容填写海运出口货物投保单，见表6-5。

表6-5　　　　　　　　　　海运出口货物投保单

（1）保险人	中国人民保险公司	（2）被保险人	JinZhe Imp. And Exp. Co. Ltd.
（3）标记	（4）包装及数量	（5）保险货物项目	（6）保险金额
KD-SPTSC08 SPORTAR HAMBURG C NO. 1-1700	1 700 CTNS 1×20'container	Dumbbell/ART NO. G6610-10KGS	USD 19 952.90

（7）总保险金额：（大写）
UNITED STATES DOLLARS NINETEEN THOUSAND NINE HUNDRED FIFTY TWO AND NINETY CENTS ONLY

（8）运输工具：　（船名）　（航次）　YI XIANG　V.307	（9）装运港：SHANGHAI, CHINA	（10）目的港：HAMBURG, GERMANY

（11）投保险别：OCEAN MARINE CARGO CLAUSES ALL RISKS AND WAR RISK AS PER CIC OF PICC DATED 1/1/1981	（12）货物起运日期：　4-Sep-13

（13）投保日期：30-Aug-13	（14）投保人签字：

五、实训考核方法

（一）保险单填制的准确性

（二）保险单背书行为的规范化

模块七　原产地证书

一、实训目的

（一）学生能掌握原产地证书的种类

（二）学生能正确填写不同的原产地证书

二、理论知识点

（一）原产地证书的概念

原产地证书（CERTIFICATE OF ORIGIN，简称 CO），简称产地证，是证明货物原产于某国（地区）的书面文件。产地证是出口产品进入国际贸易领域的"经济国籍"和"护照"，其作用包括：

（1）产地证是受惠国、地区（出口国、地区）的原产品出口到给惠国、地区（进口国、地区）时享受关税优惠的凭证，是提高出口商品市场竞争力的重要工具；

（2）产地证是进口货物是否适用禁、限措施的凭证；

（3）产地证是进口货物是否适用反倾销税、反补贴税、保障措施关税等贸易政策的凭证；

（4）产地证是海关借以对进口货物进行统计的重要依据；

（5）产地证起到证明商品内在品质、提高商品竞争力的作用。

（二）原产地证书的种类

产地证可分为非优惠性产地证（一般产地证）和优惠性产地证，优惠性产地证包括普惠制原产地证明书和区域性经济集团互惠原产地证书。

在我国，非优惠性产地证可由生产商（厂家）、出口商、贸促会、出入境检验检疫机构出具（若 S/C 或 L/C 中对出具机构未作规定，以上任一机构出具均可）；优惠性产地证（可享受关税优惠之用）一般由出入境检验检疫机构出具。

此外，国际贸易中还有专用产地证。

1. 一般原产地证明书

一般原产地证明书（CO）是证明货物原产于某一特定国家或地区，享受进口国正常关税（最惠国）待遇的证明文件。它的适用范围是：征收关税、贸易统计、保障措施、歧视性数量限制、反倾销和反补贴、原产地标记、政府采购等方面。

2. 普惠制原产地证明书

普惠制原产地证明书（GSP CO FORM A）是具有法律效力的我国出口产品在给惠国享受在最惠国税率基础上进一步减免进口关税的官方凭证。

目前，给予我国普惠制待遇的国家共有 39 个，包括：欧盟 27 国（奥地利、比利时、丹麦、芬兰、法国、德国、希腊、爱尔兰、意大利、卢森堡、荷兰、葡萄牙、西班牙、瑞典、英国、波兰、捷克、匈牙利、斯洛伐克、斯洛文尼亚、拉脱维亚、爱沙尼亚、立陶宛、塞浦路斯、马耳他、保加利亚和罗马尼亚）、瑞士、挪威、列支敦士登、日本、新西兰、澳大利亚、加拿大、俄罗斯、白俄罗斯、乌克兰、哈萨克斯坦和土耳其。美国不给予我国普惠制待遇。

3. 区域性经济集团互惠原产地证书

区域性经济集团互惠原产地证书是具有法律效力的在协定成员国之间就特定产品享受互惠减免关税待遇的官方凭证。随着我国积极参与区域性与双边自由贸易协定，相互给予关税优惠待遇的国家将越来越多。我国进出口企业应加强对区域性与双边自由贸易协定及其互惠原产地证书的认识与应用，在出口贸易中，我国出口商在与对方进行谈判时，我方提供相关的优惠原产地证书，进口商在其报关时可以少缴关税，降低了进口商品的成本，我国出口价格就可以相应高一些。在进口贸易中，要求对方提供相关的优惠原产地证书，我国进口企业同样可以享受我国的优惠关税待遇，从而降低进口商品成本，进而达到利用关税优惠待遇扩大出口、降低进口成本、提高进出口贸易效益的目的。

目前，我国主要有《〈中国–东盟自由贸易区〉优惠原产地证明书》、《〈亚太贸易协定〉原产地证明书》、《〈内地–香港〉CEPA 原产地证明书》、《〈内地–澳门〉CEPA 原产地证明书》、《〈中国与巴基斯坦优惠贸易安排〉优惠原产地证明书》、《〈中国–智利自贸区〉原产地证书》、《〈中国–新西兰自贸区〉原产地证书》、《〈中国–新加坡自贸区〉原产地证书》、《〈中国–秘鲁自贸区〉原产地证书》、《〈中国–哥斯达黎加自贸区〉原产地证书》、《〈中国–冰岛自贸区〉原产地证书》、《〈中国–瑞士自贸区〉原产地证书》等。

（1）《中国–东盟自由贸易区》优惠原产地证明书（FORM E）

2010 年 1 月 1 日中国–东盟自由贸易区正式启动。这是世界上人口最多的自由贸易区，是全球第三大自由贸易区，也是由发展中国家组成的最大自由贸易区。

中国–东盟自由贸易区由中国和东盟 10 国共同组成，拥有 19 亿消费者、近 6

万亿美元国内生产总值和 4.5 万亿美元贸易总额。

自贸区启动后，中国和东盟 6 个老成员国文莱、菲律宾、印度尼西亚、马来西亚、泰国、新加坡之间，超过 90% 的产品实行零关税。中国对东盟平均关税从 9.8% 降到 0.1%，东盟 6 个老成员国对中国的平均关税从 12.8% 降至 0.6%。东盟 4 个新成员国越南、老挝、柬埔寨、缅甸，也将在 2015 年实现 90% 的产品零关税。关税壁垒的逐渐消除，为中国与东盟企业创建了更加便利的发展平台。

（2）《亚太贸易协定》原产地证明书（FORM B）

《亚太贸易协定》的成员国包括中国、韩国、印度、斯里兰卡、孟加拉国和老挝。

（3）《港澳 CEPA》原产地证明书

（4）《中国与巴基斯坦优惠贸易安排》优惠原产地证明书（FORM P）

（5）《中国–智利自贸区》原产地证书（FORM F）

（6）《中国–新西兰自贸区》原产地证书（FORM N）

（7）《中国–新加坡自贸区》原产地证书（FORM X）

（8）《中国–秘鲁自贸区》原产地证书（FORM R）

（9）《中国–哥斯达黎加自贸区》原产地证书（FORM L）

（10）《大陆–台湾自贸区》原产地证书（FORM H）

（11）《中国–冰岛自贸区》原产地证书

（12）《中国–瑞士自贸区》原产地证书

"网络链接"：了解中国"自贸区"可链接 http：//fta. mofcom. gov. cn（"中国自由贸易区服务网"）。

4. 专用产地证

专用产地证是国际组织和国家根据政策和贸易措施的特殊需要，针对某一特殊行业的特定产品规定的原产地证书，主要有输往欧盟蘑菇罐头原产地证明书、烟草真实性证书等。

（三）一般原产地证明书的缮制

1. 产地证书的编号（Certificate No. ）

此栏不得留空，否则证书无效。

2. 出口方（Exporter）

此栏填写出口公司的详细地址、名称和国家（地区）名。若经其他国家或地区，需填写转口商名称时，可在出口商后面加填英文 VIA，然后再填写转口商名称、地址和国家。

3. 收货方（Consignee）

此栏填写最终收货人名称、地址和国家（地区）名。通常是外贸合同中的买方或信用证上规定的提单通知人。如信用证规定所有单证收货人一栏留空，在这种情况下，此栏应加注"TO WHOM IT MAY CONCERN"或"TO ORDER"，但此栏不得留空。若需填写转口商名称时，可在收货人后面加填英文 VIA，然后再填写转口商名称、地址、国家。

4. 运输方式和路线 （Means of transport and route）

此栏填写装运港和目的港、运输方式。若经转运，还应注明转运地。

例 1：从深圳到汉堡走海运，应填为：

FROM SHENZHEN TO HAMBURG BY SEA。

例 2：通过海运，由上海港经香港转运至汉堡港，应填为：

FROM SHANGHAI TO HAMBURG BY VESSEL VIA HONGKONG。

例 3：从深圳到汉堡经香港转运，其中深圳到香港段用卡车运输，香港到汉堡走海运。

FROM SHENZHEN TO HONGKONG BY TRUCK, THENCE TRANSHIPPED TO HAMBURG BY SEA。

5. 目的地国家（地区）（Country/region of destination）

此栏填写目的地国家（地区）。一般应与最终收货人或最终目的港（地）国别相一致，不能填写中间商国家名称。

6. 签证机构用栏（For certifying authority use only）

由签证机构在签发后发证、补发证书或加注其他声明时使用。证书申领单位应将此栏留空。一般情况下，该栏不填。

按照相关规定，产地证必须在装运前申请。一般原产地证明书在装运前 3 天申请，普惠制原产地证明书格式 A 在装运前 7 天申请。如果产地证的申请日期晚于提单的装运日期，那么就要在此栏加盖后发章（“ISSUED RETROPECTIVELY”）。

7. 运输标志（Marks and numbers of packages）

此栏填写唛头。应按信用证、合同及发票上所列唛头填写完整图案、文字标记及包装号码，不可简单填写“按照发票”（AS PER INVOICE NUMBER）或者“按照提单”（AS PEER B/L NUMBER）。货物如无唛头，应填写“无唛头”（“N/M”或“NO MARKS”）字样。此栏不得留空，如唛头多，本栏填写不够，可填写在第 7、8、9 栏内的空白处，如还是不够，可用附页填写。

8. 商品描述、包装数量及种类（Description of goods, number and kind of packages）

商品名称要填写具体名称，不得用概括性表述，例如服装（GARMENT）、食品（FOOD）等。该栏目填写的一般格式是“件数大写”+“（件数的阿拉伯数字）”+“包装种类”+“OF”+“货描”。如，1941 箱自行车，可表述为“ONE THOUSAND NINE HUNDRED AND FORTY ONE (1941) CTNS OF BICYCLES”。

如货物为散装，在商品名称后加注“IN BULK”（散装）字样。

有时信用证要求在所有单据上加注合同号、信用证号等，可加注在此栏内。本栏的末行要打上表示结束的符号（＊＊＊＊＊＊＊＊＊＊＊＊＊＊＊），以防加填内容。

9. 商品编码（H. S. Code）

此栏要求填写 H. S. 6 位数编码，应与报关单一致。若同一证书包含几种商品，则应将相应的税目号全部填写。此栏不得留空。

10. 数量（Quantity or weight）

此栏要求填写出口货物的数量及商品的计量单位。如果只有毛重时，则需填"G. W."。

11. 发票号码及日期（Number and date of invoices）

此栏填写商业发票号码及日期。此栏不得留空，为避免对月份、日期的误解，月份一律用英文表述。例如，2004 年 3 月 15 日应表述为"MARCH. 15，2004"。

12. 出口方声明（Declaration by the exporter）

此栏填写出口人的名称、申报地点及日期，由已在签证机构注册的人员签名并加盖有中英文的印章。

13. 由签证机构签字、盖章（Certification）

此栏填写签证地点、日期。签证机构签证人经审核后在此栏（正本）签名，并加盖签证印章。

China Council for the Promotion of International trade——中国国际贸易促进委员。

China Chamber of International Commerce——中国国际商会。

一般原产地证明书/加工装配证明书申请书的具体格式见表7-1。

表 7-1　　　　　　　　　一般原产地证明书/加工装配证明书申请书

| 申请单位注册号：3502 | 证书号：CCPIT | 全部国产填 P |
| 发票日期： | 发票号： | 含进口成分填 W |

申请人郑重声明：本人被正式授权代表本企业办理和签署本申请书。本申请书及"中华人民共和国出口货物原产地证明书/加工装配证明书"所列内容正确无误，如发现弄虚作假，冒充证书所列货物，擅改证书，本人愿按《中华人民共和国进出口货物原产地条例》的有关规定接受处罚并承担法律责任，现将有关情况申报如下：

商品名称（中英文）		H. S. 编码（不少于 6 位数）	
该批货物实际生产企业			
含进口成分货物主要制造、加工工序			
商品 FOB 总值（以美元计）		最终目的国/地区	
拟出运日期		转口国（地区）	
包装数量或重量			
贸易方式（请选择□打钩）	A. 一般贸易　□　　B. 灵活贸易　□　　C. 其他贸易　□		
证书种类（请选择□打钩）	A. 一般原产地证明书　□　　B. 加工装配证明书　□		
同时申请认证单证名称与份数			

现提交中国出口货物商业发票副本一份，"中华人民共和国出口货物原产地证明书/加工装配证明书"一正三副及其他附件_____份，请予审核签证。

申请单位签章：

申领员签名：

电话或手机：

日　　期：　　年　　月　　日

一般原产地证明书（CERTIFICATE OF ORIGINAL）示例见表7-2。

表7-2　　　　　　　　　　　CERTIFICATE OF ORIGINAL

1. Exporter（full name and address）	Certificate No.
2. Consignee（full name, address, country）	CERTIFICATE OF ORIGIN OF THE PEOPLE'S REPUBLIC OF CHINA
3. Means of transport and route	5. For certifying authority use only
4. Country/region of destination	

6. Marks and numbers of packages	7. Description of goods, number and kind of packages	8. H. S. Code	9. Quantity or weight	10. Number and date of invoices

11. Declaration by the exporter	12. Certification
The undersigned hereby declares that the above details and statements are correct; that all the goods were produced in China and that they comply with the Rules of Origin of the People's Republic of China.	It is hereby certified that the declaration by the exporter is correct.
Place and date, signature and stamp of authorized signatory	Place and date, signature and stamp of certifying authority

China Council for the Promotion of International Trade is China Chamber of International Commerce.

（四）普惠制原产地证明书申请书的缮制

普惠制原产地证明书申请书的内容和缮制方法如下：

（1）"申请单位（盖章）"栏：加盖申请单位公章。

（2）"注册号"栏：填写申请单位在检验检疫机构产地证签证部门注册的注册号。

（3）"证书号"栏：企业应根据检验检疫机构的编号规则，按顺序编号，不得重号或跳号。编号规则为：Gx/申请单位注册号/0001，x代表年份，后4位代表流水号。

（4）"电话"栏：填写申请单位的联系电话。

（5）"日期"栏：填写申报日期。

（6）"生产单位联系人电话"栏：填写该批出口货物的生产企业的全称及联系人的电话。

（7）"商品名称"栏：填写商品名称的中英文，并且与发票证书的商品名称一致。

（8）"H.S.税目号"栏：填写商品H.S.税目号（6位数）。

（9）"包装数量或毛重或其他数量"栏：填写该批出口货物的箱数、毛重或个数等。

（10）"商品FOB总值"栏：根据申报的出口货物的发票上所列的金额以FOB价格填写（以美元计），如出口货物不是以FOB价格成交的，应换算成FOB价格。

（11）"发票号"栏：应填上所附的发票的发票号。

（12）"货物拟出运日期"栏：如实填写货物拟离开起运口岸的日期（年、月、日）。

（13）"最终销售国"栏：即货物即将运抵的最终销售国。

（14）"贸易方式和企业性质"栏：根据实际情况选择，划"√"。

（15）"原产地标准"栏：根据提示及货物实际情况选择1～3项如实填写。

（16）"本批产品系"栏：根据货物运输路线中的起运港、中转港及目的港填写本批产品的运输路线。

（17）"提交单据"栏：申请单位依据所提供的单证划"√"，如提供其他相关单据，一并补填。

（18）"证书种类"栏：在"加急证书"和"普通证书"中选择，划"√"。

（19）"领证人"栏：由已在检验检疫机构产地证签证部门注册备案的申领员签署姓名。

普惠制原产地证明书申请书的具体格式见表7-3。

（五）普惠制原产地证明书的缮制

联合国贸发会议优惠问题特别委员会对原产地证明书格式A的印刷格式，填制方法都有严格明确的规定，对所需纸张的质量、重量、大小尺寸，使用文件作了规定，并要求正本加印绿色检索图案，防止涂改或伪造。因此，填制本证书时必须十分细心。本证书一律不得涂改，不得加盖校正章。本证书一般使用英文填制，也可使用法文。在特殊情况下，第二栏可以使用给惠国的文种。唛头标记不受文种限制，可据实填写。

表7-3　　　　　　　　　　　普惠制原产地证明书申请书

申请单位（盖章）：　　　　　　　　　　　　　　　　证书号：_____

申请人郑重声明：　　　　　　　　　　　　　　　　注册号：_____

本人是被正式授权代表出口单位办理和签署本申请书的。

本申请书及普惠制产地证明书格式A所列内容正确无误，如发现弄虚作假，冒充格式A所列货物，擅改证书，自愿接受签证机关的处罚及负法律责任。现将有关情况申报如下：

生产单位		生产单位联系人电话	
商品名称（中英文）		H.S. 税目号 （以6位数码计）	
商品FOB总值（以美元计）			发票号	
最终销售国		证书种类　"√"	加急证书	普通证书
货物拟出运日期				

贸易方式和企业性质（请在适用处划"√"）

正常贸易 C	来进料加工 L	补偿贸易 B	中外合资 H	中外合作 Z	外商独资 D	零售 Y	展卖 M
包装数量或毛重或其他数量							

原产地标准：

　　本项商品系在中国生产，完全符合该给惠国给惠方案规定，其原产地情况符合以下第_____条：

　　（1）"P"：（完全国产，未使用任何进口原材料）；

　　（2）"W"：其H.S.税目号为_____（含进口成分）；

　　（3）"F"：（对加拿大出口产品，其进口成分不超过产品出厂价值的40%）。

　　本批产品系：1. 直接运输从_____到_____；

　　　　　　　　2. 转口运输从_____中转国（地区）到_____。

申请人说明　　　　　　　　　　　　　　　　　　　领证人（签名）

　　　　　　　　　　　　　　　　　　　　　　　　电话：

　　　　　　　　　　　　　　　　　　　　　　　　日期：　　　年　月　日

现提交中国出口商业发票副本一份、普惠制原产地证明书格式A（FORM A）一正两副，以及其他附件____份，请予审核签证。

注：凡含有进口成分的商品，必须按要求提交"含进口成分受惠商品成本明细单"。

商检局联系记录

1. 证书号码（Reference No. number）

此栏不得留空，否则，证书无效。

2. 出口商名称、地址和国家（Goods consigned from）

此栏填写出口商的详细地址，包括街道名、门牌号码等。中国地名的英文译音应采用汉语拼音。如，中国 杭州 北山路 97 号 邮编：310007（NUMBER 97，BEI SHAN ROAD，HANGZHOU，CHINA. POST CODE NO. 310007）。

3. 收货人名称、地址和国家（Goods consigned to）

根据信用证要求填写给惠国的最终收货人名称（即信用证上规定的提单通知人或特别声明的收货人）。如果信用证未明确最终收货人，可以填写商业发票的抬头人，但不可填写中间商的名称。

欧盟、挪威等国对此栏没有强制性要求。如果商品直接运往上述给惠国，而且进口商要求将此栏留空时，则可以不填。

4. 所知航运方式和航线（Means of transport and route）

此栏一般填写装货、到货地点（如始运港、目的港）及运输方式（如海运、陆运、空运）等内容，对转运商品应加转运港，如 VIA HONGKONG。该栏还要填明预定自中国出口的地点和日期。如，ON/AFTER APRIL 15，2004 FROM SHANGHAI TO NEW YORK VIA SINGAPORE BY SEA。

对输往内陆给惠国的商品，如瑞士、奥地利，由于这些国家没有海岸，因此，如系海运，都须经第三国，再转运至该国，在填写时应注明。如，ON/AFTER MAY 06，2004 BY VESSEL FROM SHANGHAI TO HAMBURG W/T HONGKONG IN TRANSIT TO SWITZERLAND。

5. 供官方使用（For offical use）

此栏在正常情况下留空。在下列特殊情况下，签证当局在此栏加注：

①当货物已出口，签证日期迟于出货日期，签发"后发"证书时，在此栏加盖"ISSUED RETROSPECTIVELY"红色印章。

②当证书遗失、被盗或损毁，签发"复本"证书时，在此栏加盖"DUPLICATE"红色印章，并在此栏注明原证书的编号和签证日期，并声明原证书作废，其文字是 THIS CERTIFICATE IS IN REPLACEMENT OF CERTIFICATE OF ORIGIN NO. …DATED …WHICH IS CANCELLED。

6. 商品顺序号（Item number）

如果同批出口货物包含不同品种，则按不同品种、发票号等分列"1"、"2"、"3"。单项商品，此栏填"1"。

7. 唛头及包装号（Marks and numbers of packages）

如果没有唛头，应填写"NO MARK"（N/M）。如果唛头过多，此栏不够填写，可填写在第 7、8、9、10 栏之截止线以下（附页的纸张要与原证书一般大小），在右上角打上证书号，并由申请单位和签证当局授权签字人分别在附页末页的右下角和左下角手签、盖印。附页手签的笔迹、地点、日期均与证书第 11、12

栏相一致。

8. 包装件数、包装种类及商品的名称（Number and kind of packages, description of goods）

在填写该栏时应注意：

①包装件数必须用英文和阿拉伯数字同时表示。

②商品名称必须具体填写，不能笼统填写"MACHINE"（机器）、"GARMENT"（服装）。

③商品的商标、牌名（BRAND）及货号（ART NO.）一般可以不填。商品名称等项填完后，应在下一行加上表示结束的符号，以防止加填伪造内容。

④国外信用证有时要求填写合同、信用证号码等，可加填在此栏空白处。

9. 原产地标准（Origin criterion）

此栏是国外海关审核的核心项目。对含有进口成分的商品，因情况复杂，国外要求严格，极易弄错而造成退证查询。

①如果本商品完全是出口国自产的，不含任何进口成分，出口到所有给惠国，填写"P"。

②如果出口商品有进口成分，出口到欧盟、挪威、瑞士和日本，填"W"，其后加上出口产品的 H. S. 品目号，如"W"42. 02. 。条件：a. 产品列入了上述给惠国的"加工清单"符合其加工条件；b. 产品未列入"加工清单"，但产品生产过程中使用的进口原材料和零部件要经过充分的加工，产品的 H. S. 品目号不同于所用的原材料或零部 H. S. 品目号。

③含有进口成分的产品，出口到加拿大，填"F"。条件：进口成分的价值未超过产品出厂价的40%。

④含进口成分的产品，出口到波兰，填"W"，其后加上出口产品的 H. S. 品目号。条件：进口成分的价值未超过产品出厂价的50%。

⑤含进口成分的产品，出口到俄罗斯、乌克兰、白俄罗斯、捷克、斯洛伐克5国，填"Y"，其后加上进口成分价值占该产品离岸价格的百分比，如"Y"38%。条件：进口成分的价值未超过产品离岸价格的50%。

⑥输往澳大利亚、新西兰的商品，此栏可以留空。

10. 毛重和其他数量（Gross weight or other quantity）

此栏应按商品的正常计量单位填写，如"只"、"件"、"双"、"台"、"打"等。以重量计算的，则填毛重；只有净重的，填净重亦可，但要标上 N. W. （NET WEIGHT）。

11. 发票的日期和号码（Number and date of invoices）

此栏不得留空。月份一律用英文表示（可用缩写）。此栏的日期必须按照正式商业发票填制。

12. 签证当局的证明（Certificate）

签证单位要填写商检局签证地点、日期。商检局签证人经审核后在此栏（正本）签名，盖签证印章。本栏日期不得早于发票日期（第 10 栏）和申报日期（第 12 栏），而且应早于货物出运日期（第 3 栏）。

13. 出口商声明（Declaration by the exporter）

在生产国横线上填写"中国"（CHINA）。进口国横线上填最终进口国，进口国必须与第 2 栏的国别一致，如转运内陆目的地，应与内陆目的地的国别一致。当货物运往欧盟 27 国范围内，进口国不明确时，进口国可填"E. U. "。

申请单位应授权专人在此栏手签，标上申报地点、日期，并加盖申报单位中英文印章，手签人手迹必须在商检局注册备案。

此栏日期不得早于发票日期（第 10 栏）（最早是同日）。盖章时应避免覆盖进口国名称和手签人姓名。

普惠制原产地证明书（GENERALIZED SYSTEM OF PREFERENCES CERTIFICATE OF ORIGINAL）示例见表 7-4。

表 7-4 GENERALIZED SYSTEM OF PREFERENCES CERTIFICATE OF ORIGINAL

1. Goods consigned from (Exporter's business name, address, country)	Reference No. GENERALIZED SYSTEM OF PREFERENCES CERTIFICATE OF ORIGIN (Combined declaration and certificate)			
2. Goods consigned to (Consignee's name, address, country)	FORM A Issued in THE PEOPLE'S REPUBLIC OF CHINA (country) See notes overleaf			
3. Means of transport and route (as far as known)	4. For official use			
5. Item number	6. Marks and numbers of packages	7. Number and kind of packages; description of goods	8. Origin criterion (See notes overleaf)	9. Gross weight or other quantity	10. Number and date of invoices
11. Certification It is hereby certified, on the basis of control carried out, that the declaration by the exporter is correct.	12. Declaration by the exporter The undersigned hereby declares that the above details and statements are correct; that all the goods were produced in ＿＿＿＿＿＿ (country) and that they comply with the origin requirements specified for those goods in the Generalized System of Preferences for goods exported to ＿＿＿＿ (importing country)			
Place and date, signature and stamp of certifying authority	Place and date, signature of authorized signatory			

（六）普惠制原产地证明书签署的基本程序及方法

1. 注册登记

由申请签发普惠制原产地证明书的企业（公司）事先向当地商检机构办理注册登记手续。登记时须提交下列证件：

A. 经营出口业务的批准文件;

B. 国家工商行政管理部门核发的营业执照;

C. 由申请签证单位法人代表签署的、委托该单位人员办理普惠制原产地证明书申请及手签事宜的委托书一份,及被委托手签人免冠半身一寸近照两张。

2. 签证条件

符合下列条件的出口商品,可以申请签发普惠制原产地证明书:

A. 出口到正式通知对我国实行普惠制待遇的给惠国家;

B. 该商品是给惠国给惠方案中给予我国普惠制待遇的商品;

C. 该商品是"完全原产产品",或虽含有进口成分,但符合原产地规则中的"加工标准"或"百分比标准"等有关规定;

D. 申请单位必须预先在商检机构办理注册登记手续。

3. 申报时必须提供的单据

A. 填制正确、清楚的《普惠制原产地证明书申请书》一份;

B. 缮制正确、清楚,并经申请单位手签人员手签并加盖公章的《普惠制原产地证明书(FORM A)》一套;

C. 正式的出口商业发票副本一份(申请单位使用复印发票需盖章签字,发票不得手写,并注明包装、数量、重量、唛头及运输方式和路线,如无注明,提供装箱单一份);

D. 含有进口成分的商品,必须提交"含进口成分受惠商品成本明细单";

E. 复出口去日本的来料加工产品及其以进养出的商品,还应提交缮制清楚的、经申请单位手签人员手签并加盖公章的"从日本进口原料的证书"一式两份及来料(或进料)发票副本;

F. 必要时,申请单位还应提交信用证、合同、提单及报关单等。

正常情况下,申请单位必须在货物出运前5天申请签证,因某种原因,未能及时申请的,可签发"后发证书"(签往日本的除外)。申请单位应提交以下单据:

A. 解释迟交申请原因的函件;

B. 正常签证所需提供的资料;

C. 提单或运单,以证明货物确已出运。

三、实训内容与要求

(一) 熟悉一般原产地证明书的内容和格式,掌握原产地证书的缮制要领

(二) 审核原产地证书的内容并加以修改

(三) 根据相关数据缮制一般原产地证明书

四、实训单证填制

根据模块一中的信用证内容缮制原产地证书（见表7-5）。

表7-5 原产地证书

1. Exporter JINZHE IMP. AND EXP. CO. LTD. ROOM 302, WORLD TRADE CENTER, 277 WU XING ROAD, SHANGHAI, CHINA	Certificate No. : 456879141653 CERTIFICATE OF ORIGIN OF THE PEOPLE'S REPUBLIC OFCHINA
2. Consignee GLOBAL TRADING UM GMBH MOOSFELDSTRABE 96 D-746 BALINGEN, W-GERMANY	
3. Means of transport and route FROM SHANGHAI, CHINA TO HAMBURG, GERMANY BY SEA	5. For certifying authority use only
4. Country/Region of destination HAMBURG, GERMANY	

6. Marks and numbers	7. Number and kind of packages; description of goods	8. H. S. Code	9. Quantity	10. Number and date of invoices
KD-SPTSC08 SPORTAR HAMBURG C NO. 1-UP CONTAINER NO. YX307HG56087 L/C NO. : 384010021947	1 700 SETS OF DUMBBELL / ART NO. G6610-10KGS ONE20' CONTAINER	9506990000	1700 SETS 17000 KGS	KH-SPTINV01 SEP, 1, 2013

* *

11. Declaration by the exporter The undersigned hereby declares that the above details and statements are correct, that all the goods were produced in China and that they comply with the Rules of Origin of the People's Republic of China. KANGHUA IMP. AND EXP. CO. , LTD. SHANGHAI, SEP. , 3, 2013 张哲	12. Certification It is hereby certified that the declaration by the exporter is correct. 中国国际贸易促进委员会 单据证明专用章 CHINA COUNCIL FOR THE PROMOTION OF INTERNATIONAL TRADE (SHANGHAI) SHANGHAI, SEP. , 3, 2013 王东
Place and date, signature and stamp of authorized signatory	Place and date, signature and stamp of certifying authority

五、实训考核方法

（一）阅读并准确缮制原产地证书

（二）根据信用证或发票要求缮制不同的原产地证书

模块八　进出口报关单

一、实训目的

（一）学生了解出口货物报关的有关法律规定

（二）学生熟练掌握出口报关的程序和出口报关单的填制方法，能够根据相关数据独立完成出口报关单的填制工作

二、理论知识点

（一）出口货物报关的相关法律规定

出口货物报关是指出口货物的发货人或其代理人向海关办理货物出境手续及相关海关事务的过程。根据《中华人民共和国海关法》（简称《海关法》）的规定，出口货物的发货人，除特准的外，应当在货物运抵海关监管区、装运前 24 小时，通过在海关注册的企业、报关员向海关报关。报关流程示意图如图 8-1 所示。

（二）出口货物报关单的概念

出口货物报关单是指出口货物的发货人或其代理人，按照海关规定的格式对出口货物的实际情况作出的书面申明，凭以要求海关对其货物按适用的海关制度办理报关手续的法律文书。

出口货物报关单按介质分类，可分为纸质报关单和电子数据报关单；按海关监管方式分类，可分为进料加工出口货物报关单、来料加工及补偿贸易出口货物报关单和一般贸易及其他贸易出口货物报关单；按用途分类，可分为报关单录入凭单、预录入报关单和报关单证明联。纸质报关单一式五联，分别是海关作业联、企业留存联、海关核销联、出口收汇证明联、出口退税证明联。

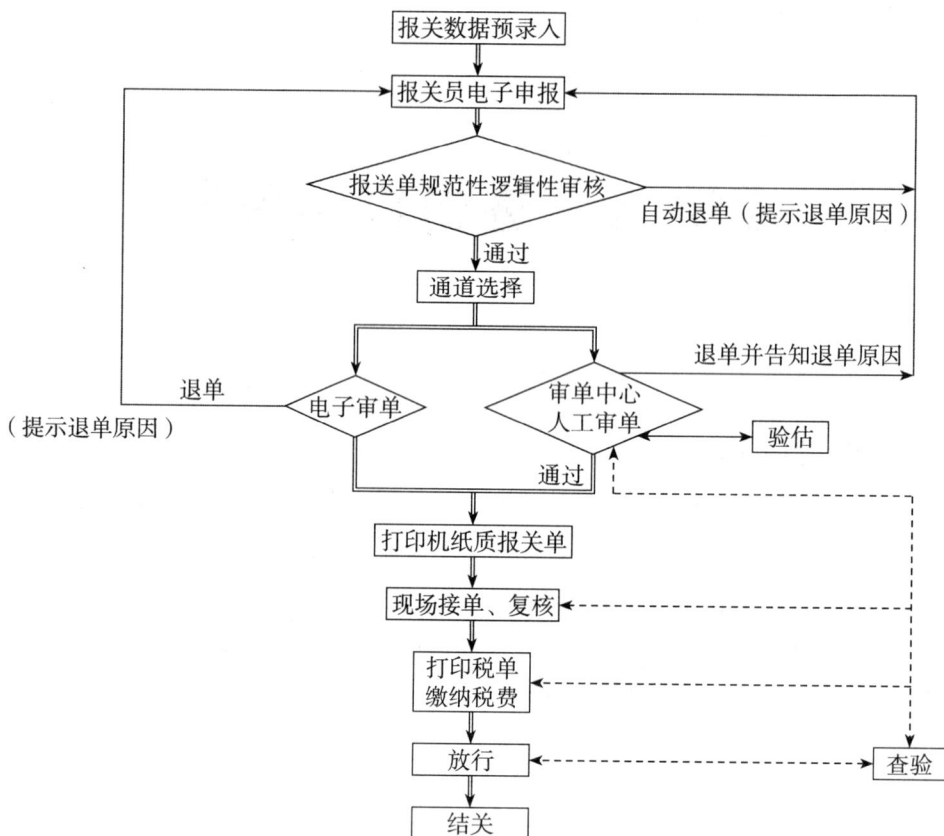

图 8-1   报关流程示意图

（三）报关单填制的一般要求

1. 如实申报

报关人必须按照《海关法》、《中华人民共和国海关进出口货物申报管理规定》和《中华人民共和国海关进出口货物报关单填制规范》的有关规定和要求，向海关如实申报。

2. 两个相符

报关单的填报必须真实，做到"两个相符"：一是"单证相符"，即所填报关单各栏目的内容必须与合同、发票、装箱单、提单以及批文等随附单据相符；二是"单货相符"，即所填报关单各栏目的内容必须与实际进出口货物的情况相符，不得伪报、瞒报、虚报。

3. 准确、齐全、完整、清楚

报关单的填报要准确、齐全、完整、清楚，报关单各栏目内容要逐项详细准确填报，字迹清楚、整洁、端正，不得用铅笔或红色复写纸填写；若有更正，必须在更正项目上加盖校对章。

4. 分单填报

下列情况均应分单填报，即分别填报一份报关单：

（1）不同批文或许可证以及不同合同的货物；

（2）同一批货物中不同贸易方式的货物；

（3）不同备案号的货物；

（4）不同提运单的货物；

（5）不同征免性质的货物；

（6）不同运输方式；

（7）相同运输方式但不同航次或不同运输工具名称的货物；

（8）不同原产地证书的货物；

（9）享受不同税收优惠的货物。

5. 分项填报

在反映进出口商品情况的项目中，下列情况须分项填报：

（1）不同商品编码的商品；

（2）不同商品名称的商品；

（3）不同原产国（地区）/最终目的国（地区）的商品。

一张报关单最多可填报 5 项商品，一份报关单最多可填报 20 项商品。

已向海关申报的进出口货物报关单，如原填报内容与实际进出口货物不一致而又有正当理由的，申报人应向海关递交书面更正申请，经海关核准后，对原填报的内容进行更改或撤销。

（四）出口货物报关单的填制

报关单共有 48 个栏目，其中除"税费征收情况"、"海关审单、批注及放行日期（签章）"栏目由海关负责填写外，其他栏目均由报关员填写。

下面以 H2000 通关系统为例，介绍一般贸易方式下的出口货物报关单各栏目的填制规范。

1. 预录入编号

预录入编号是指预录入单位录入报关单的编号。预录入编号规则由接受申报的海关决定，计算机自动打印。

2. 海关编号

海关编号是指海关接受申报时给予报关单的 18 位数编号，一份报关单对应一个海关编号。出口货物报关单应分别编号，确保同一公历年能按出口唯一地标识本关区的每一份报关单。

3. 出口口岸

此栏填报货物实际离开我国关境的口岸海关的名称及代码。口岸海关名称及代码是指国家正式对外公布并已编入海关"关区代码表"的海关的中文名称及 4 位代码。

4. 备案号

在一般贸易方式下，本栏一般留空。

5. 出口日期

出口日期是指运载所申报出口货物的运输工具办结出境手续的日期。"出口日期"栏目供海关打印报关单证明联用，出口报关单均免于填报。出口日期为 8 位数字，顺序为年（4位）、月（2位）、日（2位）。

6. 申报日期

以电子数据报关单方式申报的，申报日期为海关计算机系统接受申报数据时记录的日期。以纸质报关单方式申报的，申报日期为海关接受纸质报关单并对报关单进行登记处理的日期。

申报日期为8位数字，顺序为年（4位）、月（2位）、日（2位）。本栏在申报时免予填报。

7. 经营单位

经营单位是指对外签订并执行进出口贸易合同的我国境内企业、单位或者个人的名称及海关注册编号。经营单位编码是指经营单位向所在地主管海关办理注册登记手续时，海关为之设置的注册登记编码。经营单位编码为10位数字。本栏填报经营单位的中文名称及编码。

8. 运输方式

本栏应根据货物实际出境的运输方式按海关规定的"运输方式代码表"选择填报相应的运输方式名称或代码。运输方式主要包括水路运输、铁路运输、公路运输、航空运输、邮件运输和其他运输。出境货物按货物运离我国关境最后一个口岸时的运输方式填报。

9. 运输工具名称

本栏填报运输工具和航次号，即"运输工具名称"+"/"+"航次号"。其中水路运输填报船舶英文名称（来我国往港澳小型船舶为监管簿编号）或者"船舶编号"+"/"+"航次号"。

10. 提运单号

本栏填报出口货物提单或运单的编号。

11. 发货单位

发货单位是指出口货物在境内的生产或销售单位，包括自行出口货物的单位、委托进出口企业出口货物的单位等。本栏填报发货单位的中文名称及编码。

12. 贸易方式

本栏根据实际情况，按海关规定的"贸易方式代码表"选择填报相应的贸易方式简称及代码。例如，在"一般贸易"方式下，填写"一般贸易"及代码0110。

13. 征免性质

征免性质是指海关根据《海关法》、《中华人民共和国进出口关税条例》（简称《关税条例》）及国家有关政策对进出口货物实施的征税、减税、免税管理的性质类别。本栏按照海关核发的征免税证明中批注的征免性质填报，或根据进出口货物的实际情况，参照"征免性质代码表"选择填报相应的征免性质简称及代码。例如，在"一般贸易"方式下，填写"一般征税"及代码101。

14. 结汇方式

结汇方式是指出口货物的发货人或其代理人收结外汇的方式。应按照海关规定的"结汇方式代码表"选择填报相应的结汇方式名称或代码。

15. 许可证号

本栏所涉及的填报内容，包括出口许可证、两用物项和技术出口许可证、两用物项和技术出口许可证（定向）、出口许可证（加工贸易）、出口许可证（边境小额贸易）的编号。

"监管证件代码表"中除代码为1、4、x、y的监管证件外，都属于其他"许可证件"，其代码和编号应填在"随附单据"栏，不能填在"许可证号"栏。

16. 运抵国（地区）

运抵国（地区）是指出口货物离开我国关境直接运抵的国家或地区，或者在运输中转国（地区）未发生任何商业性交易的情况下最后运抵的国家或地区。

本栏应按海关规定的"国别（地区）代码表"选择填报相应国别（地区）的中文名称及代码。

对于直接运抵的货物，以货物起始发出的国家或地区为起运国（地区），货物直接运抵的国家或地区为运抵国（地区）。

对于中转货物，起运国（地区）或运抵国（地区）分两种不同情况填报。

（1）对于发生运输中转而未发生任何买卖关系的货物，其运抵国（地区）不变，即以出口货物的最终目的国（地区）为运抵国（地区）填报。

（2）对于发生运输中转并发生了买卖关系的货物，其中转地为运抵国（地区）。

17. 指运港

指运港亦称目的港，是指最终卸货的港口。报关单上的"指运港"栏专指出口货物运往境外的最终目的港。

本栏应根据实际情况按海关规定的"港口航线代码表"选择填报相应的港口中文名称及代码。

对于直接运抵的货物，以货物直接运抵的港口为指运港。对于发生运输中转的货物，仍以最后运抵的港口为指运港。

18. 境内货源地

境内货源地是指出口货物在我国海关境内的生产地或原始发货地（包括供货地点）。

本栏应按"国内地区代码表"选择填报相应的国内地区名称及代码，代码含义与经营单位代码前5位的定义相同。"境内货源地"栏应填报出口货物的生产地或原始发货地。出口货物产地难以确定的，填报最早发运该出口货物的单位所在地。

19. 批准文号

本栏仅用于填报实行出口收汇核销管理的出口收汇核销单上的编号。

20. 成交方式

本栏应根据实际成交价格条款，按海关规定的"成交方式代码表"选择填报相应的成交方式名称或代码。

《2010年国际贸易术语解释通则》（简称《2010通则》）中的11种贸易术语与报关单"成交方式"栏一般对应关系表见表8-1。

表 8-1　　　　　贸易术语与报关单"成交方式"栏一般对应关系表

组　别	E 组	F 组			C 组				D 组		
贸易术语	EXW	FCA	FAS	FOB	CFR	CPT	CIF	CIP	DAT	DAP	DDP
成交方式	FOB				CFR		CIF				

21. 运费

本栏填报出口货物运至我国境内输出地点装载后的运输费用。出口货物成交价格不包含前述运输费用的，本栏免于填报。运保费合并计算的，运保费填报在"运费"栏中。

出口货物报关单中运费与成交方式对应关系表见表 8-2。

表 8-2　　　　　出口货物报关单中运费与成交方式对应关系表

成交方式	运费
CIF	填报
CFR（C&F）	填报
FOB	—

本栏应根据具体情况选择运费单价、运费总价或运费率 3 种方式之一填报，同时注明运费标记，并按海关规定的"货币代码表"选择填报相应的币种代码。

"运费"栏目填报示例见表 8-3。

表 8-3　　　　　　　　"运费"栏目填报示例

标记类别	运费信息	填报格式
1（运费率）	运费率：5%	5/1，或 5
2（运费单价）	运费单价：24 美元/公吨	502/24/2
3（运费总价）	运费总价：7 000 美元	502/7000/3

22. 保费

本栏填报出口货物运至我国境内输出地点装载后的保险费用。出口货物成交价格不包含前述保险费用的，本栏免予填报。运保费合并计算的，运保费填报在"运费"栏中，本栏免予填报。本栏应根据具体情况选择保险费总价或保险费率两种方式之一填报，同时注明保险费标记，并按海关规定的"货币代码表"选择填报相应的币种代码。保险费标记"1"表示保险费率，"3"表示保险费总价。

出口货物报关单中保费与成交方式对应关系表见表 8-4。

表 8-4　　　　　出口货物报关单中保费与成交方式对应关系表

成交方式	保费
CIF	填报
CFR（C&F）	—
FOB	—

23. 杂费

本栏用于填报成交价格以外的，应计入完税价格或应从完税价格中扣除的费用，如手续费、佣金、折扣等费用。应计入完税价格的杂费填报为正值或正率，应从完税价格中扣除的杂费填报为负值或负率。

本栏应根据具体情况选择杂费总价或杂费率两种方式之一填报，同时注明杂费标记，并按海关规定的"货币代码表"选择填报相应的币种代码。杂费标记"1"表示杂费率，"3"表示杂费总价。

24. 合同协议号

本栏填报出口货物合同（包括协议或订单）的编号。

25. 件数

件数是指有外包装的单件出口货物的实际件数，货物可以单独计数的一个包装称为 1 件。

本栏填报有外包装的出口货物的实际件数，散装、裸装货物填报为"1"，一笔交易使用不同种类外包装的，应将各类包装件数相加后填报。有关单据仅列明托盘件数，或者既列明托盘件数，又列明单件包装件数的，本栏填报托盘件数。

26. 包装种类

本栏应根据出口货物的实际外包装种类，按海关规定的"包装种类代码表"选择填报相应的包装种类代码。

27. 毛重

本栏填报出口货物及其包装材料的重量之和，依据合同、发票、提（运）单、装箱单等有关单证所显示的重量确定出口货物的毛重填报。"毛重"计量单位为千克，不足 1 千克的填报为"1"。

28. 净重

本栏填报出口货物的毛重减去外包装材料后的重量，即货物本身的实际重量，计量单位为千克，不足 1 千克的填报为"1"。"净重"依据合同、发票、装箱单等有关单证确定填报。

29. 集装箱号

本栏填报装载出口货物（包括拼箱货物）集装箱的箱体信息，包括集装箱号、集装箱的规格和集装箱的自重。其填报格式为："集装箱号"+"/"+"规格"+"/"+"自重"。所申报货物涉及多个集装箱的，第一个集装箱号填报在"集装箱号"栏中，其余的依次填报在"标记、唛码及备注"栏中。

30. 随附单据

本栏仅填报除出口许可证以外的监管证件代码及编号。其填报格式为："监管证件代码"+"："+"监管证件编号"。

合同、发票、装箱单、出口许可证等随附单证不在"随附单据"栏填报。本栏只填写一个监管证件的信息。所申报货物涉及多个监管证件的，第一个监管证件代码及编号填报在"随附单据"栏中，其余的填报在"标记、唛码及备注"栏中。

"网络链接"：查询海关监管条件可链接

http：//service. customs. gov. cn/default. aspx？ tabid＝9409

31. 生产厂家

生产厂家是指出口货物的境内生产企业的名称。本栏填报其境内生产企业。

32. 标记、唛码及备注

（1）标记、唛码（上部或称左半部）的填报。

1）本栏填报货物标记、唛码中除图形以外的所有文字和数字。

2）无标记、唛码的免于填报。

（2）备注（下部或称右半部）的填报。

本栏用于填报备注内容，包括：

1）所申报货物涉及多个监管证件的，除第一个监管证件（填报在"随附单证"栏）以外的监管证件和代码，应填报在本栏目。其填报格式为："监管证件代码"+"："+"监管证件编号"。

2）所申报货物涉及多个集装箱的，除第一个集装箱号（填报在"集装箱号"栏）以外的集装箱号，应填报在本栏目。其填报格式为："集装箱号"+"/"+"规格"+"/"+"自重"。

33. 项号

本栏填报货物在报关单中的商品排列序号。

34. 商品编号

商品编号是指由出口货物的税则号列及符合海关监管要求的附加编号组成的10位编号。

本栏填报商品编号时应该按照出口商品的实际情况，填报《中华人民共和国海关进出口税则》8位税则号列。有附加编号的，还应填报附加的第9、10位附加编号。

35. 商品名称、规格型号

商品名称即商品品名，是指国际贸易缔约双方同意买卖的商品的名称。商品的规格型号是指反映商品性能、品质和规格的一系列指标，如品牌、等级、成分、含量、纯度、大小、长短、粗细等。

本栏分两行填报：

（1）第一行填报出口货物规范的中文名称，必要时可加注原文。

（2）第二行填报规格型号，包括规格、型号、成分、含量、等级等（一般使用发票、提单或装箱单中的原文）。

36. 数量及单位

数量及单位是指出口商品的实际数量及成交计量单位，以及海关法定计量单位和按照海关法定计量单位换算的数量。

本栏分3行填报：

（1）第一行填报法定第一计量单位及数量。

（2）第二行填报第二法定计量单位及数量。无第二法定计量单位的，本栏为空。

（3）第三行填报成交计量单位及数量。如成交计量单位与海关法定计量单位一致，本栏为空。

37. 最终目的国（地区）

最终目的国（地区）是指已知的出口货物最后交付的国家或地区，即最终实际消费、使用或进一步加工制造的国家或地区。本栏应按海关规定的"国别（地区）代码表"选择填报相应的国家（地区）中文名称及代码。

38. 单价、总价、币制

单价是指出口货物实际成交的商品单位价格的金额部分。总价是指出口货物实际成交的商品总价的金额部分。币制是指进出口货物实际成交价格的计价货币的名称。

单价栏、总价栏只填报单价和总价的数值，无需填报计价单位和计价货币。币制则根据实际成交情况按海关规定的"货币代码表"选择填报相应的货币名称或代码。

39. 征免

征免是指海关依照《海关法》、《关税条例》及其他法律、行政法规，对出口货物进行征税、减税、免税或特案处理的实际操作方式。

本栏根据海关核发的征免税证明或有关政策规定，对报关单所列每项商品依据"征减免税方式代码表"选择填报相应的征减免税方式的名称。例如，在"一般贸易"方式下，填写"照章征税"。

40. 税费征收情况

本栏由海关经办人员填写，主要批注对该份（批）出口货物的税、费征收和减免情况，包括税率、税额的情况。

41. 录入员及录入单位

（1）录入员。由负责将该份报关单内容的数据录入海关计算机系统并打印预录入报关单的实际操作人员签名确认。

（2）录入单位。填报经海关核准，允许其将有关报关单内容输入海关计算机系统的单位。

42. 申报单位

本栏包括申报单位，报关员，申报单位的地址、邮政编码、电话号码等项目。

自理报关的，本栏填报出口企业的名称及海关注册编码；委托代理报关的，本栏填报经海关批准的报关企业名称及海关注册编码。

（1）申报单位。申报单位是指向海关办理进出口货物报关手续的法人。主要有已在海关登记注册的出口发货人、报关企业和临时出口货物的单位。本项填报申报单位的中文名称及编码，并签印。

（2）报关员。报关员是指具体负责该批货物向海关办理报关手续的人员。由该报关员在该栏中签印。

（3）单位地址。填报向海关办理报关手续的单位在境内居住或通信联系的地址。

（4）邮编及电话。填报申报单位所在地区的邮政编码及通讯联系的电话号码。

（5）填制日期。填制日期是指该份报关单的填制日期，由经办的报关员负责填写。电子数据报关单的填制日期由计算机自动打印。

填制日期为8位数字，顺序为年（4位）、月（2位）、日（2位）。

43. 海关审单、批注及放行日期

本栏共分为审单、审价、征税、统计、查验、放行6项，是海关内部作业时签注的总栏目，由上述各项的经办海关人员完成本项任务后将本人姓名或代码手工填制在预录入报关单上。其中"放行"栏一般填写（签注）海关对接受申报的进出口货物完成上述各项任务作出放行决定的日期（包括经办人员的姓名、日期）。

中华人民共和国海关出口货物报关单的具体格式见表8-5。

表8-5　　　　　　　　中华人民共和国海关出口货物报关单

预录入编号：　　　　　　海关编号：

出口口岸		备案号	出口日期	申报日期
经营单位		运输方式	运输工具名称	提运单号
发货单位		贸易方式	征免性质	结汇方式
许可证号	运抵国（地区）		指运港	境内货源地
批准文号	成交方式	运费	保费	杂费
合同协议号	件数	包装种类	毛重（千克）	净重（千克）
集装箱号	随附单据			生产厂家

标记、唛码及备注

项号　商品编号　商品名称、规格型号　数量及单位　最终目的国（地区）　单价　总价　币制　征免

税费征收情况

录入员　　录入单位	兹声明以上申报无讹并承担法律责任	海关审单、批注及放行日期（签章）	
报关员		审单	审价
单位地址	申报单位（签章）	征税	统计
邮编　　电话	填制日期	查验	放行

中华人民共和国海关专用缴款书的具体格式见表8-6。

表 8-6　　　　　　　　　　　中华人民共和国海关专用缴款书

收入系统　　　　　　　　　填发日期：　　年　月　日　　　　　　号码 No.

收款单位	收入机关				缴款单位	名称	
	科目		预算级次			账号	
	收款国库					开户银行	

税号	货物名称	数量	单位	完税价格（￥）	税率（%）	税款金额（￥）

金额人民币（大写）		合计（￥）	

申请单位编号		报关单编号		填制单位	收款国库（银行）
合同（批文）号		运输工具（号）			
缴款期限		提/装货单号		制单人＿＿＿＿＿	
备注				复核人＿＿＿＿＿	

从填发缴款书之日起限 15 日内缴款（期末遇法定节假日顺延），逾期按日征收税款总额 1‰的滞纳金。

　　进出口货物代理报关委托书的具体格式见表 8-7。

表 8-7　　　　　　　　　　进出口货物代理报关委托书

　　　　　　　　　　　　　　　　　　　　　　　　　编号：

委托单位		十位编码	
地　址		联系电话	
经 办 人		身份证号	

　　我单位委托＿＿＿＿＿＿＿＿＿＿公司代理以下进出口货物的报关手续，保证提供的报关资料真实、合法，与实际货物相符，并愿承担由此产生的法律责任：

货物名称		商品编号		件 数	
重　量		价　值		币　制	
贸易性质		货物产地		合同号	
是否退税		船名/航次			
委托单位开户银行			账　号		

随附单证名称、份数及编号：

1. 合同　　　份：　　　　　6. 机电证明　　份、编号：
2. 发票　　　份：　　　　　7. 商检证　　　份：
3. 装箱清单　份：　　　　　8.
4. 登记手册　本、编号：　　9.
5. 许可证　　份、编号：　　10.

（以上内容由委托单位填写）

被委托单位		十位编码	
地　　址		联系电话	
经 办 人		身份证号	

（以上内容由被委托单位填写）

代理（专业）报关企业章及法人代表章	委托单位章及法人代表章

　　　　　　　　　　　　　　　　　　　　　　　　　年　月　日

三、实训内容与要求

（一）根据本模块理论知识点中的出口报关流程示意图，详细写出口货物报关的程序

（二）仔细阅读理论知识点中我国出口货物报关单的填报要领

（三）根据报关单的栏目、填报内容要求，总结归纳有关数据，为报关单的填报做好基础工作

（四）根据所给资料，填制出口报关单并进行出口报关

四、实训单证填制

根据模块一中的信用证内容，填制中华人民共和国海关出口货物报关单（示例见表8-8）。出口商在订妥舱位收到配舱回单后必须向海关办理货物的申报出口手续。报关文件主要包括出口货物报关单、商业发票、装箱单。

表8-8　　　　中华人民共和国海关出口货物报关单（示例）

预录入编号：089635495　　　　　　　海关编号：089635495

出口口岸 吴淞海关		备案号	出口日期 2013.09.04	申报日期 2013.09.01
经营单位 金喆进出口有限公司 3101935046		运输方式 水路运输	运输工具名称 YIXIANG/V.307	提运单号 KH-SPTBL01
发货单位 金喆进出口有限公司		贸易方式 一般贸易 0110	征免性质 一般征税	结汇方式 信用证
许可证号	运抵国（地区） 德国		指运港 汉堡	境内货源地 上海
批准文号	成交方式 CIF	运费 502/1950.00/3	保费 502/1538.37/3	杂费
合同协议号 KH-SPTSC38	件数 1 700	包装种类 纸箱	毛重（千克） 17 000	净重（千克） 17 000
集装箱号 LXLU50687123	随附单据		生产厂家 上海吴淞体育用品厂	

续表

标记、唛码及备注

KD-SPTSC08/SPORTAR/HAMBURG/C/NO.1-UP

SPORTAR

HAMBURG

C

NO.1-UP

项号	商品编号	商品名称、规格型号	数量及单位	最终目的国（地区）	单价	总价	币制	征免
1	9506990000	举重器	1 700 套	德国	10.6700	18 139.00	USD	照章征税
			17 000.00 千克			（304）	美元	

税费征收情况

录入员	录入单位	兹声明以上申报无讹并承担法律责任	海关审单、批注及放行日期（签章）	
报关员	王涛		审单	审价
单位地址　上海吴兴路 277 号		申报单位（签章）金喆进出口有限公司	征税	统计
			查验	放行
邮编　电话　64331255		填制日期　13.09.01	签发官员：孙子武签发日期：2013-09-10	

五、实训考核方法

（一）进出口报关单填制的准确性

（二）熟悉报关流程

（三）提交进出口报关单据的正确性

模块九　海运单据

一、实训目的

（一）掌握出口货物装运出口的程序和海运提单的格式及内容

（二）正确填制海运提单

二、理论知识点

（一）海运提单的概念

海运提单（Bill of Lading，B/L），简称提单。《中华人民共和国海商法》第七十一条规定，提单是指用以证明海上货物运输合同和货物已经由承运人接收或者装船，以及承运人保证据以交付货物的单证。

海运提单的性质及作用包括：

（1）提单是货物收据。证明承运人已经按提单的内容收到货物。

（2）提单是物权凭证。提单合法持有人有权凭提单在目的港向承运人提取货物，也可在货物到达目的港之前，通过转让提单而转移货物所有权，或凭以向银行办理抵押贷款。

（3）提单是承运人与托运人之间所订运输合同的证明。提单条款明确规定了承、托双方之间的权利和义务、责任与豁免，是处理承运人和托运人运输方面争议、纠纷的法律依据。

（4）提单是托运人凭以向银行办理议付、结汇的主要单据之一，并且在运输业务的联系、费用的结算和对外索赔中都具有重要的作用。

（二）提单的内容及缮制

1. 托运人（Shipper）

托运人又称发货人。托运人是指委托运输的人，在贸易中是合同的卖方。一般在填写海运提单 SHIPPER 栏目时，如信用证无特殊规定，都填写卖方的名称。也有的制单人直接把出口公司的章盖在这一栏目中。

2. 收货人（Consignee）

本栏根据信用证要求条款填写，在记名式、不记名式和指示式中选择一个。在信用证结算方式下，"收货人"栏目的常见制作方法主要有 3 种：

（1）记名式，即在"收货人"栏内填写某人或某企业的具体名称。

这种提单只能由提单上所指定的收货人提货，而不得转让给他人。这样的提单在国际贸易中使用不多。信用证中的词句一般为"FULL SET OF B/L CONSIGNED TO ABC COMPANY…"。

（2）不记名式，即在本栏留空或仅填入"TO BEARER"（给持有者）。谁持有这样的提单，谁就可以提货，转让时不必背书，因而风险较大，目前在国际上使用也不多。

（3）指示式。这种提单使用最为普遍。指示式又可分为记名指示式和不记名指示式 2 种。

A. 记名指示式。一般有发货人指示式（TO ORDER OF SHIPPER）、银行指示式（TO ORDER OF XXX BANK）和收货人指示式（TO ORDER OF ABC COMPANY LTD），一般只需要根据信用证的要求，在制单时分别填入。

在信用证项下，"TO ORDER OF XXX BANK"一般大多是指开证行（THE ISSUING BANK）。

信用证上的词句一般为"FULL SET OF B/L MADE OUT TO OUR ORDER"，其中，"OUR"指的就是开证行。

而"TO XXX COMPANY LTD"一般多指开证申请人（THE APPLICANT）。

信用证上的词句一般为"B/L ISSUED TO ORDER OF APPLICANT"，其中，"APPLICANT"指的就是信用证的开证人。

B. 不记名指示式，即在"收货人"一栏填写"TO ORDER"，然后在提单背面由发货人签字盖章进行背书，以示转让物权。

信用证上的词句一般为"FULL SET OF B/L MADE OUT TO ORDER"，凭指示抬头，即"空白抬头"。

如果是托收结算方式，根据合同"收货人"一栏一般填写"TO ORDER"或者"TO ORDER OF SHIPPER"均可，然后由发货人背书。一般不做成代收行指示式抬头，因为 URC522 第十条规定：事先未征得银行的同意，货运不应直接做成银行抬头或银行指示式抬头。

3. 被通知人（Notify party）

在信用证结算方式下，"被通知人"一栏按信用证规定填写。若信用证对此无规定，可将开证申请人作为被通知人。如信用证没有规定，这一栏也可以不填。

如果是托收结算方式，一般可将合同的买方名称填入。

一般来说，被通知人不是提单的当事人，只是收货人的代理人。空白抬头提单注明被通知人，以便承运人在货物到达目的港时，能通知办理报关提货手续。

如果信用证要求两个或两个以上的公司作为被通知人，出口公司应把这两个或两个以上的公司名称及地址完整地填写在这一栏目中。

4. 前段运输（Pre-carriace by）

如果货物需要转运，在这一栏目中填写第一程船的名称；如果货物不需要转运，则此栏空白不填。

5. 收货地点（Place of receipt）

如果货物需要转运，填写收货的港口名称或地点；如果货物不需要转运，则此栏空白不填。

6. 海运船只（Ocean vessel）

此栏填写该批货物的实际装运的船名和航次号；如果货物需要转运，则填写第二程船名及航次号。

7. 装货港（Port of loading）

此栏填写该批货物的实际起运港名称；如果货物需要转运，则填写中转港口的名称。

8. 卸货港（Port of discharge）

此栏填写信用证中的目的港名称。如果货物需要转运，可在目的港（PORT OF DISCHARGE）之后加注"WITH TRANSSHIPMENT AT…"字样。例如，从上海港到汉堡，在香港转运，那么此栏应填写"FROM SHANGHAI TO HAMBURG WITH TRANSSHIPMENT AT HONGKONG"。

如果货运目的港装运到内陆某地，或利用邻国港口过境，则须在目的港后加注"IN TRANSIT TO …"字样。例如"DUBAI IN TRANSIT TO SAUDI ARABIA"（目的港迪拜转运沙特阿拉伯）。

9. 交货地点（Place of delivery 或 Destination）

此栏填写最终目的地名称。如果货物的目的地就是目的港，则此栏空白不填。

10. 集装箱号（Container number）

此栏填写实际的集装箱号码。

11. 标志和号码（Marks and Nos. ）

此栏填写实际的唛头、集装箱号及铅封号等。如无唛头，则填写" NO MARK"。

12. 件数和包装种类（Number and kind of packages）

此栏填写件数和包装种类。

填写此栏时的注意事项包括：

（1）对于提单中的包装货物，则应注意数量和单位。提单下面应加注数量的大写表示，大、小写数量应相一致。

（2）如果是裸装货物，应加注件数，如一辆客车、一台机器等。

（3）如果是散装货物，例如煤、矿石、原油等，此栏可加注"IN BULK"字样；此时数量可以不用大写。

（4）如果是集装箱运输，由托运人装箱的整箱货可加注集装箱数量，如"TWO CONTAINERS ONLY"等。如果海关已对集装箱封箱，承运人对箱内的内容和数量不负责任，提单内应加注"SHIPPER'S LOAD AND COUNT"（SLAC，托运人装货并计数）或"SHIPPER'S LOAD COUNT AND SEAL"（SLCAS，发货人装箱和铅封）字样。如需注明集装箱内小件数量，数量前应加注"SAID TO CONTAIN…"（STC，内容据发货人报称）字样。

（5）如果是托盘装运，此栏应填写托盘数量，同时用括号加注货物的包装件数，如"2 PALLETS（20 CARTONS）"。提单内还应加注"SHIPPER'S LOAD AND COUNT"（SLAC）字样。

（6）如果是两种或多种包装，此栏应填写"FIVE CARTONS、FIVE BALES、SIX CASES"等，件数栏内要逐项列明，同时下面应加注合计数量，如上述包装数量可合计为"16 PACKAGES"，在提单大写件数栏内加注大写合计数量。

（7）如在件数栏内注明"20 CARTONS"，但同时提单又批注有"SHUT OUT 2 CARTONS"或"SHORT LOADED 2 CARTONS"等字样，表示少装2箱，那么发票和其他单据应注明"18 CARTONS"。

（8）提单上不能加注关于包装状况的描述，例如"新袋"（NEW BAG）、旧箱（OLD CARTONS）等词语。

13. 货名（Description of goods）

此栏填写货物名称。货物名称必须与发票、装箱单等单据一致，提单上货物名称的描述可以只写总的名称，而不必如发票上描述得那么细致。

填写此栏时的注意事项包括：

（1）信用证如果没有特别规定，在国际贸易中，商品描述应全部使用英文。

（2）如果来证要求加注中文或法文等，则应遵守信用证的规定，加注中文或法文等。

14. 毛重（Gross weight）

此栏填写总毛重，应与其他单据相一致。如果是裸装货物，没有毛重，只有净重，则在净重千克数前加注"NET WEIGHT"字样。

15. 尺码（Measurement）

此栏填写总尺码（立方米），即货物的体积。

16. 运费条款（Freight clause）

除非信用证有特别要求，一般的海运提单都不填写运费的数额，而只是表明运费是否已付清或什么时候付清。加注字样主要包括：

（1）运费已付（FREIGHT PAID）；

（2）运费预付（FREIGHT PREPAID）；

（3）运费到付（FREIGHT PAYABLE AT DESTINATION）；

（4）运费待付（FREIGHT COLLECT）。

对于含有运费的价格术语（如 CFR、CPT、CIF、CIP），填写（1）或（2）；不含有运费（如 FCA、FOB）的价格术语，则填写（3）或（4）。

如果信用证规定加注运费，一般可加注运费的总金额。如果规定要加注详细的运费，就必须将计算单位、费率等详细列明。

17. 大写总件数（Total packages in words）

此栏的大写总件数与其他单据及提单的小写总件数保持一致。

有时承运人在第 13 ~ 18 栏左侧加注"PARTICULARS FURNISHED BY MERCHANTS"（各项目由货主提供）字样，意思是这些栏目的内容和资料由发货人提供，承运人对此不负责任。

18. 签单地点和日期（Place and date of issue）

海运提单签发的地点和时间，一般为承运人实际装运的地点和时间，货物装运的港口或接受有关方面监管的地方，海运提单必须经装载船只船长签字才能生效。在没有规定非船长签字不可的情况下，船方代理也可以代办。

如果一批货物分几个装运港于同一艘船上运往同一目的港，签发几个不同日期的提单时，则以较迟的日期为装运日期。

19. 正本提单份数（Number of original Bs/L）

此栏填写海运提单正本的签发份数。承运人一般签发两份正本，也可应收货人的要求签发两份以上。签发的份数应用大写数字来表示，如 TWO、THREE、FOUR 等，在栏目内标明。

信用证规定要求出口方提供"全套海运提单"（FULL SET OR COMPOLETE SET OF BILL OF LADING），按国际贸易习惯，一般提供 3 份正本海运提单。这 3 份正本提单同时有效，如果持票人凭其中的一份提取货物，其他两份自动失效。

20. 契约文字

契约文字即提单正面条款，一般包括以下 4 个方面：

（1）已装船条款：SHIPPED ON BOARD THE VESSEL NAMED ABOVE IN APPARENT GOOD ORDER AND CONDITION（UNLESS OTHERWISE

INDICATED) THE GOODS OR PACKAGES SPECIFIED HEREIN AND TO BE DISCHARGED AT THE ABOVE MENTIONED PORT OF DISCHARGE OR AS NEAR HERETO AS THE VESSEL MAY SAFELY GET AND BE ALWAYS AFLOAT (上述外观状况良好之货物或包装（除另有说明者外），已装上述指定船只，并应在上述卸货港或船只所能安全到达并保持浮泊的附近地点卸货）。

（2）内容不知悉条款：THE WEIGHT、MEASURE、MARKS、NUMBERS、QUALITY、CONTENTS AND VALUE, BEING PARTICULARS FURNISHED BY THE SHIPPER, ARE NOT CHECKED BY THE CARRIER ON LOADING （由发货人所提供的重量、尺码、标记、号码、品质、内容及价值各项目，承运人于装船时并未核对）。

（3）承认接受条款：THE SHIPPER, CONSIGNEE AND THE HOLDER OF THIS BILL OF LADING HEREBY EXPRESSLY ACCEPT AND AGREE TO ALL PRINTED, WRITTEN OR STAMPED PROVISIONS, EXCEPTIONS AND CONDITIONS OF THIS BILL OF LADING, INCLUDING THOSE ON THE BACK HEREOF （发货人、收货人及本提单持有人明确表示接受并同意本提单，包括背面所印刷、书写或盖章的一切条款、免责事项和条件）。

（4）签署条款：IN WITNESS WHEREOF, THE CARRIER OR HIS AGENTS HAS SIGNED BILL OF LADING ALL OF THIS TENOR AND DATE, ONE OF WHICH BEING ACCOMPLISHED, THE OTHERS TO STAND VOID。

SHIPPERS ARE REQUESTED TO NOTE PARTICULARLY THE EXCEPTIONS AND CONDITIONS OF THIS BILL OF LADING WITH REFERENCE TO THE VALIDITY OF THE INSURANCE UPON THEIR GOODS （为证明以上各项承运人或其代理人已签署各份内容和日期一样的本提单，其中一份一经完成提货手续，则其余各份均告失效。要求发货人特别注意本提单中关于该批货物保险效力的免责事项和条件）。

21. 代表承运人签字 （Signed for and on behalf of the carrier）

提单签字人应根据签字人的不同情况做出不同批注：

（1）承运人签署的提单。

提单上部：COSCO

提单签字处：COSCO

（签字）

AS CARRIER 或 THE CARRIER

（2）代理人签字的提单。

提单上部：COSCO

提单签字处：ABC SHIPPING COMPANY

（签字）

AS AGENT FOR AND/OR ON BEHALF OF THE CARRIER COSCO 或 AS AGENT FOR AND/OR ON BEHALF OF COSCO AS CARRIER（或 THE CARRIER）

（3）船长签字的提单。

提单上部：COSCO

提单签字处：COSCO（注或不注船名）

（签字）

AS MASTER 或 THE MASTER

（4）代理人签字的提单。

提单上部：COSCO

提单签字处：ABC SHIPPING COMPANY

（签字）

AS AGENT FOR AND/OR ON BEHALF OF THE MASTER XXX OF THE CARRIER COSCO 或 AS AGENT FOR AND/OR ON BEHALF OF XXX AS MASTER （或 THE MASTER）OF COSCO AS CARRIER（或 THE CARRIER）

22. 提单背面的条款

在班轮提单的背面都是印就的条款，是处理承运人与托运人或收货人之间的争议的依据，主要包括：

（1）法律诉讼条款，注明适用有关提单的国际公约；

（2）承运人责任条款；

（3）免责条款；

（4）有关改航、换装、改卸目的港、甲板货物、危险货物、冷藏货物、装货、卸货、交货、共同海损等的条款；

（5）赔偿条款；

（6）运费条款；

（7）留置权条款。

租船提单（Charter party B/L）是承运人根据租船合同签发的提单，通常使用简式提单格式——仅列明船名、装卸港、货物名称、数量及项目。其通常还会加注"Other terms& conditions as per charter party"字样。

该提单并非完整独立的文件，要受租船合同的约束，银行要求提交提单时，通常附租船合同副本，但银行不负责审核合同，仅供各方参考。

海运提单示例见表9-1。

装货单是船公司或其代理人在接受托运人提出的申请后，发给托运人或货运代理人，同时命令船长将单上货物装船的单证。它的主要作用有：①它是承运人确认承运货物的证明；②它是海关对出口货物进行监管的证明；③它是承运人通知码头仓库或装运船舶接货装船的命令。装货单示例见表9-2。

表 9-1　　　　　　　　　　　　　　**海运提单**

托运人 Shipper		B/L　No.
		中 国 对 外 贸 易 运 输 总 公 司
收货人或指示 Consignee or order		北　　京 BEIJING 联　运　提　单 COMBINED TRANSPORT BILL OF LADING
通知地址 Notify address		RECEIVED the foods in apparent good order and condition as specified below unless otherwise stated herein. Thecarrier, in accordance with the provisions contained in this document,
前段运输 Pre-carriage by	收货地点 Place of receipt	(1) undertakes to perform or to procure the performance of the entire transport from the place at which the goods are taken in charge to the place designated for delivery in this
海运船只 Ocean vessel	装货港 Port of loading	document, and (2) assumes liability as prescribed in this document for such transport one of the bills of lading must be surrendered duty indorsed in exchange for the goods or delivery order.

卸货港 Port of discharge	交货地点 Place of delivery	运费支付地 Freight payable at	正本提单份数 Number of original Bs/L

标志和号码 Marks and Nos.	件数和包装种类 Number and kind of packages	货名 Description of goods	毛重（千克） Gross weight （kgs. ）	尺码（立方米） Measurement （m^3）

以 上 细 目 由 托 运 人 提 供
ABOVE PARTICULARS FURNISHED BY SHIPPER

运杂费 Freight and charges	In witness whereof the number of original bills of lading stated above have been signed, one of which being accomplished, the other (s) to be void.
	签单地点和日期 Place and date of issue
	代表承运人签字 Signed for or on behalf of the carrier 　　　　　　　　　　　　　　　　代　　理 　　　　　　　　　　　　　　　　as Agents

海运提单（背面）

1. DEFINITION   Wherever the term "Shipper" occurs hereinafter, It shall be deemed to include also Receiver, Consignee, Holder of this Bill of Lading and Owner of the goods.

2. JURISDICTION   All disputes arising under and or in connection with this Bill of Lading shall be determined by the laws of the People's Republic of China.

3. DEMISE CLAUSE   If the ship is not owned by or chartered by demise to the corporation by whom this Bill of Lading is issued (as may be the case notwithstanding anything that appears to the contrary) this Bill of Lading shall take effect only as a contract of carriage with the Owner or demise charterer as the case may be as principal made through the agency of the said corporation who act as agents only and shall be under no personal liability whatsoever in respect thereof.

4. HAGUE RULES   This Bill of Lading shall have effect in respect of Carrier's liabilities, responsibilities, rights and immunities subject to the Hague Rules contained in the International Convention for the Unification of Certain Rules of Law Relating to Bills of Lading 1924.

5. PACKING AND MARKS   The Shipper shall have the goods properly packed accurately and clearly marked before shipment. The port of destination of the goods should be marked in letters of 5 cm high, in such a way as will remain legible until their delivery.

6. OPTIONAL STOWAGE   (1) The goods may be stowed by the Carrier in containers or similar articles of transport used to consolidate goods. (2) Goods stowed in containers other than flats, pallets, trailers, transportable tanks or similar articles of transport whether by the Carrier or the Shipper, may be carried on or under deck without notice to the Shipper. Such goods whether carried on or under deck shall participate in general average.

7. DECK CARGO. PLANTS AND LIVE ANIMALS   Cargo on deck, plants and live animals are received, handled, carried, kept and discharged at Shipper's or Receiver's risk and the Carrier shall not be liable for loss thereof or damage thereto.

8. FREIGHT   (1) Freight and charges shall be deemed earned on receipt of the goods by the Carrier and shall be paid by the Shipper and non-returnable and non-deductible in any event. Freight payable at destination together with other charges is due on arrival of the goods at the place of destination and shall be paid before delivery of the goods. (2) For the purpose of verifying the freight basis, the Carrier reserves the right to have the goods and the contents of containers, trailers or similar articles of transport inspected in order to ascertain the weight, measurement, value or nature of the goods. In case the particulars of the goods furnished by the Shipper are incorrect, the Shipper shall be liable and bound to pay to the Carrier a sum either five times the difference between the correct freight and the freight charged or to double the correct less the freight charged, whichever sum is the smaller, shall be payable as liquidated damages to the Carrier.

9. LIEN   The Carrier shall have a lien on the goods and any documents relating thereto for all sums payable to the Carrier under this Bill of Lading and for general average contributions to whomsoever due and for the cost of recovering the same, and for that purpose shall have the right to sell the goods by public auction or private treaty without notice to the Shipper. If on sale of the goods, the proceeds fail to cover the amount due and the cost incurred, the Carrier shall be entitled to recover the deficit from the Shipper.

10. TIME BAR, NOTICE OF LOSS   In any event the Carrier shall be discharged from all liabilities

under this Bill of Lading unless suit is brought within one year after the delivery of the goods or the date when the goods should have been delivered. Unless notice of loss of or damage to the goods and the general nature of it be given in writing to the Carrier at the place of delivery before or at the time of the removal of the goods into the custody of the person entitled to delivery thereof under this Bill of Lading, or, if the loss or damage such removal shall be prima facie evidence of the delivery by the Carrier of the goods as described in this Bill of Lading. In the case of any actual or apprehended loss or damage the Carrier and the Shipper shall give all reasonable facilities to each other for inspecting and tallying the goods.

11. THE AMOUNT OF COMPENSATION   (1) When the Carrier is liable for compensation in respect of loss or damage to the goods, such compensation shall be calculated by reference to the invoice value of the goods plus freight and insurance premium if paid. (2) Notwithstanding clause 4 of this Bill of Lading the limitation of liability under the Hague Rules shall be deemed to be RMB. ￥700 per package or unit. (3) Higher compensation may be claimed only when, with the consent of the Carrier, the value for the goods declared by the Shipper which exceeds the limits laid down in this clause has been stated in this Bill of Lading and extra freight has been paid as required. In that case the amount of the declared value shall be substituted for that limit. Any partial loss or damage shall be adjusted pro-rata on the basis of such declared value.

12. LOADING, DISCHARGING AND DELIVERY   The goods shall be supplied and taken delivery of by the owner of the goods as fast as the ship can take and discharge them, without interruption, by day and night. Sundays and Holidays included, notwithstanding any custom of the port to the contrary and the owner of the goods shall be liable for all losses or damages including demurrage and/or equipment detention incurred in default thereof. Discharge may commence without previous notice. If the goods are not taken delivery of by the Receiver in due time from alongside the vessel, or if the Receiver refuses to take delivery of the goods, or in case there are unclaimed goods, the Carrier shall be at liberty to land such goods on shore or any other proper places at the sole risk and expense of the Shipper or Receiver, and the Carrier's responsibility of delivery of goods shall be deemed to have been fulfilled. If the goods are unclaimed during a reasonable time, or whenever the goods will become deteriorated, decayed or worthless, the Carrier may, at his discretion and subject to his lien and without any responsibility attaching to him, sell, abandon or otherwise dispose of such goods solely at the risk and expense of the Shipper.

13. LIGHTERAGE   Any lighterage in or off ports of loading or ports of discharge shall be for the account of the Shipper or Receiver.

14. FORWARDING, SUBSTITUTE OF VESSEL, THROUGH CARGO AND TRANSHIPMENT   If necessary, the Carrier may carry the goods to their port of destination by other persons or by rail or other means of transport proceeding either directly or indirectly to such port, and to carry the goods or part of them beyond their port of destination, and to transship and forward same at Carrier's expense but at Shipper's or Receiver's risk. The responsibility of the Carrier shall be limited to the part of the transport performed by him on the vessel under his management.

15. DANGEROUS GOODS, CONTRABAND   (1) The Shipper undertakes not to tender for transportation any goods which are of a dangerous, inflammable, radioactive, and/or any harmful nature without previously giving written notice of their nature to the Carrier and marking the goods and the

container or other covering on the outside as required by any laws or regulations which may be applicable during the carriage. (2) Whenever the goods are discovered to have been shipped without complying with the subclause (1) above or the goods are found to be contraband or prohibited by any laws or regulations of the port of loading, discharge or call or any place or waters during the carriage, the Carrier shall be entitled to have such goods rendered innocuous, thrown overboard or discharged or otherwise disposed of at the carrier's discretion without compensation and the Shipper shall be liable for and indemnify the Carrier against any kind of loss, damage or liability including loss of freight, and any expenses directly or indirectly arising out of or resulting from such shipment. (3) If any goods shipped complying with the subclause (1) above become a danger to the ship or cargo, they may in like manner be rendered innocuous, thrown overboard or discharged or otherwise disposed of at the Carrier's discretion without compensation except to general average, if any.

16. REFRIGERATED CARGO   (1) The Shipper undertakes not to tender for transportation any goods which require refrigeration without previously giving written notice of their nature and particular temperature range to be maintained. If the above requirements are not complied with, the Carrier shall not be liable for any loss of or damage to the goods howsoever arising. (2) Before loading goods in any insulated space, the Carrier shall, in addition to the Class Certificate, obtain the certificate of the Classification Society's Surveyor or other competent person, stating that such insulated space and refrigerating machinery are in the opinion of the surveyor or other competent person fit and safe for the carriage and preservation of refrigerated goods. The aforesaid certificate shall be conclusive evidence against the Shipper, Receiver and/or any Holder of Bill of Lading. (3) Receivers have to take delivery of refrigerated goods as soon as the ship is ready to deliver, otherwise the Carrier shall land the goods at the wharf at Receiver's or Shipper's risk and expense.

17. TIMBER   Any statement in this Bill of Lading to the effect that timber has been shipped " in apparent good order and condition" does not involve any admission by the Carrier as to the absence of stains, shakes, splits, holes or broken pieces, for which the Carrier accepts no responsibility.

18. BULK CARGO   As the Carrier has no reasonable means of checking the weight of bulk cargo, and reference to such weight in this Bill of Lading shall be deemed to be for reference only, but shall constitute in no way evidence against the Carrier.

19. COTTON   Description of the apparent condition of cotton or cotton products does not relate to the insufficiency of or torn condition of the covering, nor to any damage resulting therefrom, and Carrier shall not be responsible for damage of such nature.

20. OPTIONAL CARGO   The port of discharge for optional cargo must be declared to the vessel's agents at the first of the optional ports not later than 48 hours before the vessel's arrival there. In the absence of such declaration the Carrier may elect to discharge at the first or any optional port and the contract of carriage shall then be considered as having been fulfilled. Any option must be for the total quantity of goods under this Bill of Lading.

21. GOODS TO MORE THAN ONE CONSIGNEE   Where bulk goods or goods without marks or goods with the same marks are shipped to more than one Consignee, the Consignees or Owners of the goods shall jointly bear any expense or loss in dividing the goods or parcels into pro−rata quantities and any deficiency shall fall upon them in such proportion as the Carrier, his servants or agents shall decide.

22. HEAVY LIFTS AND OVER LENGTH CARGO   Any one piece or package of cargo which

exceeding 2 000 kilos or 9 meters must be declared by the Shipper in writing before receipt by the Carrier and/or length Clearly and durably on the outside of the piece or package in letters and figures not less than 2 inches high by the Shipper. In case of the Shipper's failure in his obligations aforesaid, the Shipper shall be liable for loss of or damage to any property or for personal injury arising as a result of the Shipper's said failure and shall indemnify the Carrier against any kind of loss or liability suffered or incurred by the Carrier as a result of such failure.

23. SHIPPER-PACKED CONTAINERS ETC. (1) If a container has not been filled, packed or stowed by the Carrier, the Carrier shall not be liable for any loss of or damage to its contents and the Shipper shall cover any loss or expense incurred by the Carrier, if such loss, damage or expense has been cause by negligent filling, packing or stowing of the container; or the contents being unsuitable for carriage by container; or the unsuitability or defective condition of the container unless the container has been supplied by the Carrier and the unsuitability or defective condition would not have been apparent upon reasonable inspection at or prior to the time when the container was filled, packed or stowed. (2) The provisions of the subclause (1) above also apply with respect to trailers, transportable tanks, flats and pallets which have not been filled, packed or stowed by the Carrier.

24. WAR, QUARANTINE, ICE, STRIKES, CONGESTION, ETC.　Should it appear that war, blockade, pirate, epidemics, quarantine, ice, strikes, congestion and other causes beyond the Carrier's control would prevent the vessel from safely reaching the port of destination and/or discharging the goods thereat, the Carrier is entitled to discharge the goods at the port and the contract of carriage shall be deemed to have been fulfilled. Any extra expenses incurred under the aforesaid circumstances shall be borne by the Shipper or Receiver.

25. GENERAL AVERAGE　General average shall be adjusted in Beijing in accordance with China Council for the promotion of International Trade Provisional Rules for General Average Adjustment Rules 1975.

26. BOTH TO BLAME COLLISION　If the carrying ship comes into collision with another ship as a result of the negligence of the other ship and any act, neglect or default of the master, mariner, pilot or of the servants of the carrier in the navigation or by the management of the carrying ship, the Shipper undertakes to pay the Carrier, or, where the Carrier is not the Owner and in possession of the carrying ship, to pay to the Carrier as trustee for the Owner and/or demise charterer of the carrying ship, a sum sufficient to indemnify the Carrier and/or the Owner and/or demise charterer of the carrying ship against all loss or liability to the other or non-carrying ship or her Owners insofar as such loss or liability represents loss of or damage to his goods or any claim whatsoever of the Shipper, paid or payable by the other or non-carrying ship or her Owners to the Shipper and set-off, recouped or recovered by the other or non-carrying ship or her Owners as part of their claim against the carrying ship or her Owner or demise charterer or the Carrier. The foregoing provisions shall also apply where the Owners, operators, or those in charge of any ship or ships or objects, other than, or in addition to, the colliding ships or objects, are at fault in respect to a collision, contact, stranding or other accident.

27. U. S. A. CLAUSE　With respect to the goods carried to or from the United Sates of America, notwithstanding any other term hereof the Bill of Lading shall have the effect subject to the provisions of the Carriage of Goods by Sea Act of the United Sates of America, 1936. Neither the Carrier nor the vessel shall, in any event, be or become liable for any loss of or damage to such goods in an amount exceeding

Dollars 500 per package lawful money of the United States of America, or in case of goods not shipped in packages, per customary freight unit unless the nature and value of such goods has been declared by the Shippers before shipment and inserted in the Bill of Lading.

表 9-2　　　　　　　　　　　　　　　装货单

中 国 外 轮 代 理 公 司
CHINA　OCEAN　SHIPPING　AGENCY
装 货 单
SHIPPING　ORDER

货

托运人

Shipper _____

编号　　　　　　　　　船名
No. _____S/S _____

目的港
For _____

兹已将下列完好状况之货物装船，特签署此收货单。

Receive on board the undermentioned goods in apparent good order and condition and sign the accompanying receipt for the same.

标记及号码 Marks & Nos.	件数 Quantity	货名 Description of Goods	重量（千克） Weight Kilos	
			净重 Net Weight	毛重 Gross Weight

共计件数（大写）

Total Number of Package in Writing

日期　　　　　　　　　时间
Date _____Time _____

装入何舱

Stowed _____

实收

Received _____

理货员签名　　　　　　　经办员
Tallied by _____Approved by _____

收货单是货物装船后，承运船舶的大副签发给托运人表示已收到货物并已装船的货物收据。它的主要作用有：①它是划分船、货双方责任的重要依据；②它是据以换取已装船提单的单证。收货单示例见表9-3。

表9-3   收货单

中 国 外 轮 代 理 公 司

CHINA   OCEAN   SHIPPING   AGENCY

收 货 单

MATE'S   RECEIPT

货

托运人

Shipper _____

编号		船名
No. _____	S/S _____	

目的港

For _____

兹已将下列完好状况之货物装船，特签署此收货单。

Receive on board the undermentioned goods in apparent good order and condition and sign the accompanying receipt for the same.

标记及号码 Marks & Nos.	件数 Quantity	货名 Description of Goods	重量（千克） Weight Kilos	
			净重 Net Weight	毛重 Gross Weight

共计件数（大写）

Total Number of Package in Writing_____

日期		时间	
Date _____		Time _____	

装入何舱

Stowed _____

实收

Received _____

理货员签名		大副	
Tallied by _____		Chief Officer _____	

（三）UCP600 对提单的规定

托运委托书是货运代理人填制托运单的重要依据，而托运单又是承运人签发提单的重要依据。托运委托书、托运单、承运人签发的提单都必须符合 UCP600 第二十条和第二十七条的有关规定。

1. 关于提单内容

根据 UCP600 第二十条第一款的规定，提单无论其称谓如何，其表面上应包括以下内容：

（1）显示承运人名称并由下列人员签署：承运人或承运人的具名代理或代表，或船长或船长的具名代理或代表。承运人、船长或代理的任何签字必须分别表明承运人、船长或代理的身份。代理的签字必须显示其作为承运人或船长的代理或代表签署提单。

（2）通过下述方式表明货物已在信用证规定的装运港装载于具名船只上：预先印就的措辞，或注明货物已装船日期的装船批注。提单的出具日期将被视为装运日期，除非提单包含注明装运日期的装船批注，在此情况下，装船批注中显示的日期将被视为装运日期。如果提单上有"预期船"字样或类似有关限定船只的词语时，装上具名船只必须由注明装运日期以及实际装运船只名称的装船批注来证实。

（3）注明货物将从信用证中规定的装货港运至卸货港。

（4）表明正本提单的签发份数。

（5）提单应当含有承运条件或参阅承运条件的出处（简式或背面空白的提单），但银行对此类承运条件内容不予审核。

（6）未注明运输单据受租船合约约束。

2. 关于转运的定义

根据 UCP600 第二十条第二款的规定，转运是指在信用证规定的装货港到卸货港之间的海运过程中，将货物由一艘船卸下再装上另一艘船的运输。

3. 关于转运的规定

根据 UCP600 第二十条第三款的规定，只要同一提单包括运输全程，则提单就可以注明货物将被转运或可被转运。银行可以接受注明将要发生或可能发生转运的提单。即使信用证禁止转运，只要提单上证实有关货物已由集装箱、拖车或子母船运输，银行仍可接受注明将要发生或可能发生转运的提单。对于提单中包含的声明承运人保留转运权利的条款，银行将不予理会。

4. 关于清洁提单

根据 UCP600 第二十七条的规定，银行只接受清洁运输单据。清洁运输单据指未载有明确宣称货物或包装有缺陷的条款或批注的运输单据。"清洁"一词并不需要在运输单据上出现，即使信用证要求运输单据为"清洁已装船"的。

5. 关于第三方提单

根据 UCP600 第十四条（k）款的规定，除非信用证另有规定，银行将接受以信用证受益人以外的一方作为发货人的运输单据。

三、实训内容与要求

（一）根据所给的条件填制海运提单
（二）根据所给的信用证内容审核并修改海运提单

四、实训单证填制

根据模块一的信用证内容填制海运提单（见表9-4）。

表9-4　　　　　　　　　　　海运提单

Shipper JINZHE IMP. AND EXP. CO. LTD. ROOM 302，WORLD TRADE CENTER， 277 WU XING ROAD， SHANGHAI, CHINA			BILL OF LADING B/L No.：KH-SPTBL01	
Consignee TO THE ORDER OF SHIPPER				
Notify party GLOBAL TRADING UM GMBH MOOSFELDSTRABE 96 D-746 BALINGEN，W-GERMANY DEUTSCHE BANK FILIALE HANNOVER			中国远洋运输公司 CHINA OCEAN SHIPPING COMPANY	
* Pre-carriage by	* Place of receipt SHANGHAI, CHINA CY			
Ocean vessel, Voy. No. YI XIANG, V. 307	Port of loading SHANGHAI, CHINA			
Port of discharge	* Final destination HAMBURG，GERMANY	Freight payable at	Number original Bs/L 3/3	
Marks and numbers	Number and kind of packages/description	Gross weight	Measurement（m³）	

续表

KD-SPTSC08 SPORTAR HAMBURG C NO. 1-UP	1 700 SETS OF DUMBBELL/ ART NO. G6610-10KGS	17 000 KGS	25 CBM
	L/C NO.：384010021947		
	SHIPPER'S LOAD COUNT AND SEAL FREIGHT PREPAID		
CONTAINER NO. YX307HG56087/ SEAL 0085795624			

ORIGINAL

TOTAL PACKAGES（IN WORDS）	SAY ONE THOUSAND AND SEVEN HUNDRED SETS ONLY
Freight and charges	PREPAID

Place and date of Issue

4 SEP. 2013 SHANGHAI

Signed for the carrier

COSCO SHANGHAI BRANCH

王子琪

* Applicable only when document used as a Through Bill of Loading

五、实训考核方法

（一）海运提单填制的准确性

（二）海运提单背书行为的规范性

模块十 汇 票

一、实训目的

（一）学生能掌握汇票的相关内容及格式
（二）学生能正确填写汇票

二、理论知识点

（一）我国《票据法》对汇票（Draft，Bill of Exchange）的定义是：汇票是出票人签发的，委托付款人在见票时或者在指定日期无条件支付确定的金额给收款人或者持票人的票据。汇票有三个基本当事人，即出票人、受票人（付款人）和受款人（收款人）。

（二）汇票的种类
1. 按出票人，可分为银行汇票和商业汇票；
2. 按汇票的付款时间，可分为即期汇票和远期汇票；
3. 远期汇票按承兑人，可分为银行承兑汇票和商业承兑汇票；
4. 按汇票是否跟随单据，可分为光票和跟单汇票。

（三）汇票的内容
《票据法》第二十二条规定，汇票必须记载下列事项：表明"汇票"的字样；无条件支付的委托；确定的金额；付款人名称；收款人名称；出票日期；出票人签章。汇票上未记载前款规定事项之一的，汇票无效。

（四）汇票的缮制

1. 信用证项下汇票的填写

信用证结算方式下的汇票缮制，不仅要严格符合信用证的要求，还要符合汇票的规范制法。

（1）出票依据（DRAWN UNDER）

出票依据是表明汇票起源于交易是允许的。一般内容有三项：开证行名称、信用证号码和开证日期。出票依据是说明开证行在一定的期限内对汇票的金额履行保证付款责任的法律根据，是信用证项下汇票不可缺少的重要内容之一。

（2）利息（INTEREST）

此栏由结汇银行填写，用以清算企业与银行间利息费用。

（3）号码（NUMBER）

一般填写商业发票的号码。

（4）小写金额（AMOUNT IN FIGURES）

一般填写确切的金额数目。除非信用证另有规定，汇票金额所使用的货币应与信用证和发票所使用的货币一致。在通常情况下，汇票金额为发票金额的100%，但不得超过信用证规定的最高金额。如果信用证金额有"大约"等字样，则有10%的增减幅度。

（5）付款期限（TENOR）

汇票期限的填写应按照信用证的规定。即期的汇票要打上"AT SIGHT"。在汇票"AT"与"SIGHT"之间的空白处用虚线连接，表示见票即付。

如远期汇票，应在"AT"后打上信用证规定的期限。

信用证中有关汇票期限的条款有以下几种：

①以交单期限为起算日期。如"This L/C is available with us by payment at 60 days after receipt of full set of documents at our counters"。

此条款规定付款日期为对方柜台收到单据后的60天，因此在填写汇票时只须写："At 60 days after receipt of full set of documents at your counters"。

注意，信用证中的"OUR COUNTERS"（我们的柜台），系指开证行柜台，而在实际制单中，应改为"YOUR"（你们的）的柜台，指单据到达对方柜台起算60天。

②有的汇票是以装船日期为起算日期的。如"We hereby issue our irrevocable documentary letter of credit No. 194956 available at 30 days after B/L date by drafts"。

那么在制单时就要填写"30 days after B/L date"。制单时，从提单日期起算30天。

③也有少数汇票的起算日期是以发票日期起算的。如"Drafts at 60 days from invoice date"。因此，在制单时应在此栏目里填写"At 60 days from invoice date"。从发票开出日期起算60天。

（6）受款人（PAYEE）

受款人又称收款人（PAYEE），一般是汇票的抬头人，是出票人指定的接受票款的当事人。有的是以出口商或以其所指定的第三者为受款人。在国际票据市场上，汇票的抬头人通常有三种写法：

①记名式抬头（DEMONST RATIVE ORDER），即在受款人栏目中填写："付给×××人的指定人"（PAY TO THE ORDER OF ×××），这种类型的抬头是最普遍使用的一种。

②限制性抬头（RESTRICTIVE ORDER），即在受款人栏目中填写"仅付给×××人"（PAY TO ××× ONLY）或"限付给×××人，不许转让"（PAY TO ××× ONLY, NOT TRANSFERABLE）。

③持票人抬头（PAYABLE TO BEARER），即在受款人栏目中填写"付给持票人"（PAY TO BEARER）。

在国际结算业务中，汇票的受款人一般都是以银行指示为抬头的。常见的信用证对汇票的受款人一般有三种做法：

①来证规定由中国银行指定，或其他议付行，或来证对汇票受款人未作明确规定。通常汇票的受款人应打上："PAY TO THE ORDER OF BANK OF CHINA"（由中国银行指定）。

②当来证规定由开证行指定时，在汇票的这一栏目应打上："PAY TO THE ORDER OF ××× BANK"（开证行的名称）。

③当来证规定由偿付行指定时，在汇票的这一栏目应打上："PAY TO THE ORDER OF ××× BANK"（偿付行名称）。

（7）大写金额（AMOUNT IN WORDS）

用大写英语文字表示，并在文字金额后面加上"ONLY"，以防止涂改。如"SAY UNITED STATES DOLLARS FIVE THOUSAND SIX HUNDRED ONLY"。信用证使用的货币、上面所使用的小写金额应与大写金额相一致。

《票据法》第八条规定，票据金额以中文大写和数码同时记载，二者必须一致，二者不一致的，票据无效。

（8）付款人及付款地点

汇票的付款人（PAYEE）即汇票的受票人（DRAWEE），也称致票人。在汇票中表示为"此致×××"。凡是要求开立汇票的信用证，证内一般都指定了付款人。如果信用证没有指定付款人，按照惯例，一般做成开证行为付款人。填制汇票的一般做法是：

①当信用证规定须开立汇票而要求明确规定有付款人时，应理解为开证行就是付款人，从而打上开证行的名称、地址；

②当信用证的条款为"DRAFTS DRAWN ON APPLICANT"时，应填写该信用证的开证人名称及地址；

③当信用证要求为"DRAWN ON US"时，应理解"US"为开证行名称及地址。

还有，付款人旁边的地点就是付款地点。它既是汇票金额的支付地，也是要求付款地，或拒绝证书做出地。

（9）出票人签字（SIGNATURE OF DRAWER）

出票人（DRAWER）即签发汇票的人，在进出口业务中，通常是出口商（即信用证的受益人）。

汇票的出票人栏目，一般打上出口商的全称，并由出口商经理签署或盖章。

汇票的出票人一般是信用证指定的受益人，按来证照打。汇票的出票人也应当同其他单据的签署人名称相符。

汇票必须注明出票地点，因为如果在一个国家出票，在另一个国家付款时，假如发生争议，要确定以哪个国家的法律为依据，来判断汇票所具备的必要项目是否齐全，从而使之有效。对此，各国采用出票地法律或行为地法律的原则，即以出票行为的当地法律，认为汇票已具备必要项目而生效时，付款地点也同样认为有效。

2. 在填制汇票时应注意的项目

（1）汇票金额不得超过信用证金额，如来证金额有"大约"（ABOUT）字样，则可允许有 10% 的增减幅度。

（2）汇票收款人栏一般填写议付行。

（3）汇票付款人必须按信用证的规定详细填制，如无规定，则以开证行为付款人。

3. 托收项下汇票的填写

托收结算方式下汇票的填制，有九个项目需要填写：

（1）托收汇票须在出票条款栏内或其他位置加注"FOR COLLECTION"。

（2）汇票号码（NUMBER），一般填写发票号码。

（3）小写金额（AMOUNT IN FIGURES），即托收总金额，也就是发票金额；先打币制，紧接着是以阿拉伯数字表示的金额，小数点后保留两位，第三位小数四舍五入，应端正地打在虚线内，不得涂改。

（4）出票地点和日期（PLACE AND DATE OF ISSUE），一般由银行代填。

（5）支付方式和付款期限（TENOR AND MODE OF PAYMENT），支付方式一般为 D/P 或者 D/A，填写在 AT 的前面，付款期限应填写在 AT 与 SIGHT 的中间。如远期见票后 60 天，则填"AT 60 DAYS SIGHT"；如为"即期"，则为"AT * * * * SIGHT"。

（6）"收款人栏目"一般填写托收银行。

（7）大写金额（AMOUNT IN WORDS），先打货币名称，再用英文大写表明托收金额，大小写应相一致。句尾加打一个"ONLY"。

（8）付款人（DRAWEE），即汇票右下角的"TO"栏，根据合同规定填写买方（进口商名称和地址）。

（9）出票人签字（SIGNATURE OF THE DRAWER），在汇票右下角打出或盖上出口方公司名称并由负责人签字或盖章。

（五）汇票的份数

在没有特殊规定时，汇票一般是一式两份，在醒目的位置上印着"1"、"2"

字样，表示第一联和第二联，两联在法律上无区别，其中一联生效则另一联自动作废。

汇票的具体格式见表 10-1。

表 10-1   BILL OF EXCHANGE

```
No. _____

For _____          _____

( amount in figure )                          ( place and date of issue )

At _____ sight of this FIRST   Bill of Exchange ( SECOND being unpaid )

pay to _____ or order the sum of

_____
                        ( amount in words )

Value received for _____ of _____
                    ( quantity )         ( name of commodity )

Drawn under _____

L/C No. _____ dated _____


To：                                            For and on behalf of


                                            _____

                                                    ( Signature )
```

三、实训内容与要求

（一）阅读信用证和商业发票，归纳汇票填制信息

（二）学习 ISBP681 和我国票据法关于商业汇票填制与签发的有关规定

（三）根据所给的条件开出汇票，对汇票进行背书转让并进行普通承兑

（四）计算汇票的到期日

四、实训单证填制

根据模块一中的信用证要求，填写汇票（见表10-2）。

表10-2　　　　　　　　　　　　汇票的填制

BILL OF EXCHANGE

No.　KH-SPTINV01

For　USD18 139.00　　　　SHANGHAI　　　　DATE　　SEP. 8，2013

At　30 DAYS AFTER　　　sight of this FIRST Bill of Exchange（SECOND of the same tenor

and date unpaid）Pay to　　BANK OF CHINA　　　　　　or order the sum of

SAY US DOLLAR EIGHTEEN THOUSAND ONE HUNDRED AND THIRTY NINE ONLY

Drawn under　　　DEUTSCHE BANK

L/C No.　　384010021947　　Dated　　　　　AUG. 3，2013

To

　　DEUTSCHE BANK

　　FILIALE HANNOVER

五、实训考核方法

（一）根据汇票的格式准确填写汇票

（二）根据信用证的要求填制汇票

模块十一　　出口退税单据

一、实训目的

（一）明确出口退税的作用、流程及出口退税额的计算

（二）熟悉出口退税单据

二、理论知识点

（一）出口退税的作用

出口退税是指已报关离境的商品，由税务机关将其出口前在生产和流通各环节中已缴纳的国内流转税（包括增值税和消费税）税款退还给出口企业，使出口产品以无税成本进入国际市场，加强其市场竞争力，扩大产品出口。出口退税的作用是增强本国产品在国际市场上的竞争力。

（二）出口退税的基本流程

1. 出口单位办理出口退税登记。

2. 货物出口报关，取得出口货物报关单出口退税专用联。

3. 出口收汇，取得银行结汇水单。

4. 进入外贸企业出口退税申报系统申报退税。

5. 出口单位提交出口退税单据申报退税。

6. 退税主管部门审批。

7. 退税款划入企业账户。

（三）出口退税应提交的单据

1. 购进出口货物的增值税专用发票（第二联：抵扣联）。

2. 出口商品统一发票（第四联：税务机关存根联）。

3. 出口货物报关单（出口退税专用联）。

4. 银行结汇水单。

5. 外贸企业出口退税汇总申报表。

6. 外贸企业出口退税进货明细申报表。

7. 外贸企业出口退税出口明细申报表。

（四）外贸企业出口退税额的计算。

1. 外贸企业一般贸易出口货物退还增值税的计算

外贸企业出口货物退还增值税应依据购进货物的增值税专用发票所注明的进项金额和出口货物对应的退税率计算。

（1）外贸企业以及实行外贸企业财务制度的工贸企业收购货物出口，其出口销售环节的增值税免征；其收购货物的成本部分，因外贸企业在支付收购货款的同时也支付了生产经营该类商品的企业已纳的增值税税款，因此，在货物出口后按收购成本与退税率计算退税退还给外贸企业，征、退税之差计入企业成本。

外贸企业出口货物增值税的计算应依据购进出口货物增值税专用发票上所注明的进项金额和退税率计算。

应退税额＝外贸收购不含增值税购进金额×退税率

【例11-1】某进出口公司 2014 年 3 月出口美国平纹布 2 000 米，进货增值税专用发票列明单价 20 元/平方米，计税金额 40 000 元，退税率 13%，其应退税额为：

2 000×20×13% ＝5 200（元）

（2）外贸企业收购小规模纳税人出口货物增值税的退税规定

①凡从小规模纳税人购进持普通发票特准退税的抽纱、工艺品等 12 类出口货物，同样实行销售出口货物的收入免税，并退还出口货物进项税额的办法。由于小规模纳税人使用的是普通发票，其销售额和应纳税额没有单独计价，小规模纳税人应纳的增值税也是价外计征的，这样，必须将合并定价的销售额先换算成不含税价格，然后据以计算出口货物退税。

对出口企业购进小规模纳税人特准的 12 类货物出口，提供的普通发票应符合《中华人民共和国发票管理办法》的有关规定，否则不予办理退税。

②凡从小规模纳税人购进税务机关代开的增值税专用发票的出口货物，按规定的方法计算退税。

（3）外贸企业委托生产企业加工出口货物的退税规定

外贸企业委托生产企业加工收回后报关出口的货物，按购进国内原辅材料的增值税专用发票上注明的进项金额，依原辅材料的退税率计算原辅材料应退税额。支付的加工费，凭受托方开具货物的退税率，计算加工费的应退税额。

【例11-2】某进出口公司 2014 年 6 月购进牛仔布委托加工成服装出口，取得牛仔布增值税专用发票一张，注明计税金额 10 000 元（退税率 13%），取得服装加工费计税金额 2 000 元（退税率 17%），该企业的应退税额：

10 000×13% +2 000×17% = 1 640（元）

2. 外贸企业进料加工复出口货物退还增值税的计算

进料加工是指有进出口经营权的企业，为了加工出口货物而从国外进口原料、材料、辅料、元器件、配套件、零部件和包装材料（以下统称进口料件），加工货物收回后复出口的一种贸易方式。进料加工贸易按进口料件的国内加工方式不同，可分为作价加工和委托加工两种。

作价加工复出口货物的退税计算公式：

出口退税额＝出口货物的应退税额－销售进口料件的应抵扣税额

$$销售进口料件的应抵扣税额 = 销售进口料件金额 × 复出口货物退税率 - 海关已对进口料件实征的增值税税额$$

式中，"销售进口料件金额"是指外贸企业销售进口料件的增值税专用发票上注明的金额；"复出口货物退税率"是指进口料件加工的复出口货物退税率；"海关已对进口料件实征的增值税税额"是指海关完税凭证上注明的增值税税额。

【例 11-3】某进出口公司 2014 年 3 月发生以下业务：

3 月 1 日，以进料加工贸易方式进口一批玉米，到岸价格 126 万美元，海关按 85% 的免税比例征收进口增值税 20 万元。

3 月 5 日，该公司以作价加工的方式销售玉米给某厂加工柠橡酸出口。开具销售玉米的增值税专用发票，销售金额 1 100 万元，税额 143 万元。

3 月 20 日，收回该批玉米加工的柠橡酸，工厂开具增值税专用发票，销售金额 1 500 万元。

3 月 25 日，该公司将加工收回的柠橡酸全部报关出口（外汇牌价 1 美元等于 8 元人民币，玉米增值税征税率 13%，柠橡酸出口退税率 13%）。

计算上述业务应退税额。

销售进口料件的应抵扣税额＝1 100 × 13% -20 = 123（万元）

应退税额＝1 500 ×13% -123 = 72（万元）

三、实训内容与要求

（一）掌握出口退税的申报

（二）了解出口退税的相关内容

四、实训单证填制

(一) 出口退税申报和办理退税流程

外贸企业出口退税申报系统是"出口退税计算机网络管理系统"的出口退税系统之一,外贸企业申报退税必须使用该系统进行申报,申报前有关的出口报关单必须已通过"电子口岸执法系统"出口退税子系统进行报送。

1. 退税申报数据录入:包括基础数据采集中的进货明细申报数据录入和出口明细申报数据录入。

2. 数据加工处理:按顺序逐项检查。

3. 生成预申报数据:保存 E 盘。

4. 预审反馈处理:确认正式申报数据。

5. 退税正式申报。

6. 打印申报表,包括外贸企业出口退税出口明细申报表、外贸企业出口退税进货明细申报表和外贸企业出口退税汇总申报表。

7. 外贸企业在出口退税申报系统操作完毕,把退税资料整理齐全并提交退税部门申请出口退税。

8. 经退税部门审批同意后,将退税款汇入出口单位在银行开立的账户。

(二) 出口退税实例具体运作

1. 计算申报退税额

业务背景:3 月 26 日,广东美味贸易有限公司以 FOB 条件出口沙茶酱一批,金额为港币 78 450 元,折合成人民币为 60 068.38 元。4 月 26 日,已办理出口收汇核销手续,于 5 月 7 日向退税部门办理退税申报。

计算步骤:

(1) 确定适用的退税办法

广东美味贸易有限公司 (一般纳税人) 适用"先征后退"的退税办法。

(2) 确定计算基础

以购进的广东省增值税专用发票 (见表 11–1) 的收购金额 (不含增值税) 为计算基础。

(3) 确定适用的退税率

出口沙茶酱的退税率为 15%。

(4) 计算退税额

应退税额 = 出口收购金额 (不含增值税) × 退税率

$$= 60\,068.38 \times 15\%$$

$$= 90\,10.26\ (元)$$

2. 广东美味贸易有限公司会计人员通过外贸企业出口退税申报系统申报后，生成并打印以下申报表：

（1）外贸企业出口退税汇总申报表（见表 11-2）

表 11-1

4400091140

广东省增值税专用发票（第二联：抵扣联）

No.00854699

开票日期：2013 年 03 月 24 日

购货单位	名　称：广东美味贸易有限公司 纳税人识别号： 地址、电话： 开户行及账号：中国建行汕头分行 8030559455 1243 5678				密 码 区		
货物或应税劳务名称	规格型号	单位	数量	单价	金额	税率	税额
沙茶酱	200g×60 瓶	件	30	167.52136752	5 025.64	17%	854.36
沙茶酱	20kg×1 罐	件	280	196.59119658	55 042.74	17%	9 357.26
合计					¥60 068.38		¥10 211.62
价税合计（大写）	⊗柒万零贰佰捌拾圆整				（小写）¥70 280.00		
销货单位	名　称： 纳税人识别号： 地址、电话： 开户行及账号：				备 注		

收款人：　　　　复核：　　　　开票人：　　　　销货单位：

表 11-2

外贸企业出口货物退税汇总申报表

（适用于增值税一般纳税人）

申报年月：2010 年 4 月　申报批次：01

申报日期：2010 年 5 月 7 日

海关代码：

金额单位：元至角分，美元

第二联：抵扣联　购货方扣税凭证

纳税人识别号（章）：　（章）★	出口企业申报		审单情况	主管退税机关审核	机审情况
纳税人名称：	出口企业申报	1 份			
出口退税出口明细申报表	1 份			本次机审通过退税增值税税额	元
出口发票	1 张	张			
出口报关单	1 张，出口额 10 065.00 美元			其中：上期结转疑点退增值税	元
代理出口货物证明	张				
收汇核销单	1 张，收汇额 10 065.00 美元			上期申报数据退增值税	元
远期收汇证明	张，收汇凭证			本次机审通过退消费税税额	元
出口退税进项明细申报表	1 份			其中：上期结转疑点退消费税	元
增值税专用发票	1 张，专用发票 1 张			上期申报数据退消费税	元
普通发票	张，其中非税控专用发票 张				
其他凭证	张，专用税票 张			本次机审通过退数据增值税税额	元
总进货金额	张，总进货金额 60 068.38 元			结余疑点数据退增值税额	元
本月申报退税额	元			结余疑点数据退消费税额	元
其中：增值税	10 211.62 元，消费税 元				
消费税	10 211.62 元，消费税 元				
进料应抵扣税额	9 010.26 元，消费税 元				
其中：增值税	9 010.26 元，消费税 元				
	元		审单情况	授权人申明	
	申请开具单证			（如果你已委托出口货物退税代理人，请填写下列资料）	
代理出口货物证明	份，记录			为代理出口货物退税申报事宜，现授权为本纳税人的代理申	
代理进口货物证明	份，记录			报人，任何与本申报表有关的来文件都可寄予此人。	
进料加工贸易证明	份，记录				
来料加工免税证明	份，记录			授权人签字　　　（盖章）	
出口货物转内销证明	份，记录			年　月　日	
补办报关单证明	份，记录				
补办收汇单证明	份，记录				
补办代理出口证明	份，记录				
内销抵扣专用发票	张，其中非税控专用发票 张				
	申报人申明			审核人	受理税务机关（签章）

此表各栏目填表内容是真实、合法的，与实际出口货物情况相符，此次申报的出口业务不属于"四自三不是"等违背正常出口经营程序的的出口业务。否则，本企业愿承担由此产生的相关责任

财务负责人：　　　　　　　　　　（公章）

企业负责人：　　　年　月　日

受理人　审单人：　　　签批人　审核人　　受理税务机关（签章）

受理日期：　年　月　日　　　年　月　日　　　年　月　日

（2）外贸企业出口退税进货明细申报表（见表 11-3）

表 11-3

外贸企业出口退税进货明细申报表

企业代码：
企业名称：
纳税人识别号：

所属期：2010 年 04 月　申报批次 01

金额单位：元至角分，美元元至角分，美元

序号	关联号	税种	进货凭证号	开票日期	商品代码	商品名称	计量单位	数量	计税金额	征税率（%）	征税税额	退税率（%）	应退税额	专用税票号	备注
01	1234560l	/	44000911400085469 9	2010.03.24	2010039800 0	其他食品	千克	5 960	60 068.38	17	10 211.62	15	9 010.26		

企业填表人：　　　　财务负责人：　　　　企业负责人：　　　　制表日期：2010 年 5 月 7 日

第 1 页

表 11-4

外贸企业出口退税出口明细申报表

所属期：2010 年 04 月　申报批次 01

金额单位：元至角分、美元

企业代码：
企业名称（章）：
纳税人识别号：

序号	关联号	出口发票号	报关单号	出口日期	核销单号	商品代码	商品名称	计量单位	美元离岸价	出口数量	出口进货金额	退税率（%）	应退增值税税额	应退消费税税额	代理证明号	进料加工手册号	备注
01	12345601	44652174	12345678	2010.03.26	98765432 1	2010039 8000	其他食品	千克	10 065	5 960	60 068.38	15	9 010.26				

企业填表人：　　　　财务负责人：　　　　企业负责人：

制表日期：2010 年 5 月 7 日

第 1 页

3. 整理退税资料并提交退税部门申请退税

在上述有关申报表打印完毕后，广东美味贸易有限公司退税员及时将退税资料按以下顺序整理齐全，并提交退税部门办理退税申请：

（1）外贸企业出口货物退税汇总申报表（见表11-2）。

（2）外贸企业出口退税进货明细申报表（见表11-3）。

（3）外贸企业出口退税出口明细申报表（见表11-4）。

（4）广东省增值税专用发票（第二联：抵扣联）（见表11-1）。

（5）广东省出口商品统一发票（第四联：税务机关存根联）（见表11-5）。

（6）中国银行出具的"收账通知"和"出口收汇通知"（见表11-6和11-7）。

（7）中华人民共和国海关出口货物报关单（见表11-8）。

表11-5

广东省出口商品统一发票

Guangdong Province Export Goods Unify Invoice

发票代码：144000925170

发票号码：44652174

购货单位：香港食品公司

Purchase：

地址：香港九龙　　　　　电话：　　　　　开票日期：2013 年 3 月 26 日

Add：　　　　　　　　　Tel：　　　　　Issue date：Year　Month　Date

合同号码： Contract No.	101001	贸易方式 Trade Method	一般贸易	收汇方式 Foreign Exchange Collection Form	电汇
开户银行账号 Bank Where Account Opened & A/C Number	中国银行汕头分行 80355945512435678	发运港 Port of Departure	汕头	转运港 Port of Transshipment	
信用证号 L/C No.		运输工具 Means of Transportation	海运	目的港 Port of Destination	香港

订单号码 P. O. NO.	品名规格 Description and Specification of Goods	单位 Unit	数量 Quantity	销售单价 Unit Price	销售总额 Total Sales Amount
				FOB 汕头 HKD	HKD
TC10F056	沙茶酱　20 千克×1 罐 沙茶酱　200 克×60 瓶	箱 箱	280 30	255.00 235.00	71 400.00 7 050.00
合计金额 大写（币种） Total Amount （Currency）	港币 柒万捌仟肆佰伍拾圆零角零分		小写） Total Amount		HKD78 450.00
备注 Notes					

销货单位：广东美味贸易有限公司

地址：　　　　　　　　　　　　　　Address of Seller：

电话：　　　　　　　　　　　　　　Tel：

传真：　　　　　　　　　　　　　　Fax：

第四联：税务机关存根联

表 11-6　　　　　　　　　　**中国银行出具的收账通知**

中国银行

BANK OF CHINA

收账通知

2010.4.22　　日期：04/22/13

转讫时间：10：16：25

08(04)

客户名称：广东美味贸易有限公司

客户账户：803055945512435678

汇入金额：　　　　　　　　　　　　　　　　入账净额

　　　　HK 78 450. 00　　　　　　　　　　　HK 78 450. 00

业务编号：IR41A00297310　　　　　　　　　汇款方式：T/T

汇入编号：10007022（D）275　　　　　　　汇入日期：04/01/13

汇款行名：LCHBHKHH　　　　　　　　　　　大额流水号：

付款人名：41-265-10-100131-6　　　　　　付款人国别：HKG

申报号码：4405000001 01 100422 P012

国外银行扣费：

我行扣费：CNY

核销号码：987654321

汇款附言：3/101010

经办：　　　　　　　　　　　　复核：

表 11-7　　　　　　　　　　**中国银行出具的出口收汇通知**

中国银行

BANK OF CHINA

中国银行出口收汇通知

日期：04/22/13

时间：10：16：26

2010.4.22

转讫

08(04)

客户名称：广东美味贸易有限公司

收汇账号：803055945512435678

对付账号：803055945512345678

入账金额：HK 78 450. 00

业务编号：90022626　　　　　　　　　（流水号：IR41A00297310）

付款人名：S. E. N　CO. CTD

付款国别：HKG

申报号码：4405000001 01

核销号码：987654321

附　　言：3/101010

经办：　　　　　　　　　　　　复核：

表 11-8   **中华人民共和国海关出口货物报关单**

预录入编号：   海关编号：

出口口岸 皇岗海关　5301	备案号		出口日期 2013.03.27	申报日期 2013.03.26
经营单位 广东美味贸易有限公司 44051XXXXX	运输方式 公路运输	运输工具名称 5000580479275／	提运单号 粤 ZHN87 港	
发货单位 广东美味贸易有限公司 44051XXXXX	贸易方式 一般贸易 0110	征免性质 一般征税 101	结汇方式 电汇	
许可证号	运抵国（地区） 香港 110	指运港 香港 1039	境内货源地 汕头特区 44051	
批准文号 987654321	成交方式 3	运费	保费	杂费
合同协议号 101001	件数 310	包装种类 2	毛重（千克） 6 626	净重（千克） 5 960
集装箱号 0	随附单据 B：4405002100111104000		生产厂家	

标记唛码及备注

项号	商品编号	商品名称、规格型号	数量及单位	最终目的国（地区）	单价	总价	币制	征免
1	21039090	沙茶酱 20 公斤×1 罐	5 600.000 千克 280 箱	香港 110	235	71 400	港币 110	照章（1）
2	21039090	沙茶酱 200 克×60 瓶	3 600.000 千克 30 箱	香港 110	235	7 050	港币 110	照章（1）

税费征收情况

录入人　录入单位	兹声明以上申报无讹并承担法律责任	海关审单批注及放行日期（签章） 审单　　　　　审价
报关员 单位地址 邮编　　　电话	申报单位（签章） 填制日期	征税　　　　　统计 查验　　　　　放行

验讫章
（17）

五、实训考核方法

（一）掌握出口退税的程序
（二）正确填写出口退税单据

模块十二　其他单据

一、实训目的

（一）掌握进出口合同中涉及的其他单据，包括装箱单、重量单、尺码单、受益人证明和装船通知

（二）了解装箱单、重量单、尺码单、受益人证明和装船通知的使用背景

二、理论知识点

（一）包装单据

包装单据（Packing Documents）指一切记载或描述商品包装情况的单据，是商业发票的附属单据，也是一项重要的运输单据。在进口地海关验货、公证行检验和进口商核对货物时，都以包装单据为依据。出口方根据不同商品按信用证条款提供适当的包装单据，以既能符合信用证的规定，为银行所接受，又能满足客户的要求为原则。对于不同特征的货物，进口商可能对某一个或某几个方面比较关注，因此希望对方重点提供某一方面的单据，包括不同名称的各式单据，它们的制作方法和主要内容基本一致。比较常见和习惯使用的包装单据包括表示包装情况的装箱单、表示重量情况的重量单和表示商品体积的尺码单。

1. 装箱单（Packing List）

装箱单是发票的补充单据，它列明了信用证或合同中买卖双方约定的有关包装事宜的细节，以便国外买方在货物到达目的港时供海关检查和核对货物。装箱单的有关内容可以加列在商业发票上，但如信用证有明确的要求，就必须严格按照信用证的约定制作。

2. 重量单（Weight Note）

重量单，又称磅码单，是用以说明货物重量的清单。重量单也是发票的补充单据，可作为买方计算总价、重量和运费的依据，同时也是买方安排运输和存仓的参考。在货物到岸后买方开出的重量单，通常是用于缺量索赔的。

3. 尺码单（Measurement List）

尺码单是用以说明货物尺码细节的清单。其作用在于便于买方安排运输、装卸和仓储，同时它也是计算运费的重要依据。尺码单偏重于说明每件货物的尺码和总尺码，即在装箱单内容的基础上再重点说明不同规格项目的尺码和总尺码。如果不是统一尺码，应逐件列明。

4. 装箱单、重量单和尺码单的特点

装箱单、重量单和尺码单均具有以下特点：

（1）为了与发票保持一致，装箱单、重量单和尺码单的号码和日期两栏与发票完全相同。

（2）装箱单、重量单和尺码单一般不显示收货人、价格、装运情况，对货物描述一般都使用统称概述。

（3）装箱单着重表现货物的包装情况，从最小包装到最大包装所使用的材料和包装方式都应列明，其对重量和尺码内容，一般只体现累计总额；重量单在装箱单的基础上，详细列明货物的毛重、净重、皮重；尺码单则侧重于说明每件货物的尺码和总尺码。

（4）装箱单、重量单和尺码单的制作都要以信用证、合同备货单、出货单为凭据。如信用证中有特别要求，则应严格遵守。

5. 信用证中有关包装单据的条款举例

（1）Separate packing list in full details required. 装箱单必须作详细的缮制。

（2）Packing list showing gross and net weights expressed in kilos of each type of goods required. 装箱单以千克计算，表明货物的毛重和净重。

（3）Signed packing list, one original and one copy. 签字装箱单，一正一副。

（4）Detailed weight and measurement list showing the detail of colors, sizes and quantities in each carton and also net weight and gross weight. 重量和尺码明细单，详注每箱的颜色、尺寸和数量以及净重和毛重。

（5）Detailed packing list in quadruplicate show gross weight, net weight, measurement, color and quantity breakdown for each package, if any applicable. 详细装箱单一式四份，如适用，请标明毛重、净重、尺码、颜色和每包的破损数量。

（二）装船通知（Shipping Advice）

1. 装船通知的概述

装船通知（Shipping Advice or Shipment Advice）是出口商在货物装船后给进口方或其指定人的通知。它一般在货物装运后 1~2 天内发出，其目的是方便进口方办理保险或准备提货、租仓。如果因出口方未及时发送装船通知而使进口方不能及时办理保险或接货，出口方就应负责赔偿进口方由此而导致的一切合理损失。装船通知的作用具体如下：

（1）在 CFR 条件下，提醒买方及时向保险公司办理货物运输保险手续。

（2）在 FOB、CIF 条件下，提醒买方做好进口报关提取货物和付款的准备工作。

基于上述原因，买方通常在合同或信用证中规定，在议付时必须提供该装船通知的副本，与其他单据一起向银行议付。

2. 信用证中有关装船通知的条款举例

（1）Beneficiary's certified copy of cable/telex dispatched to applicant within 48 hours after shipment advising L/C No. , name of vessel /flight number, date, quantity, weight and value of the shipment. 受益人保证电报或电传副本将在装船后 48 小时内发送给申请人，该装船通知包括该批货物的信用证编号、船名或航次、日期、数量、重量和价值。

（2）Shipping advice showing the name of the carrying vessel, date of shipment, marks, amount and the number of this documentary credit must be sent by registered airmail to the applicant. The relative postal registration receipt and a copy of the shipping advice must be attached to the documents. 载有承运船船名、装运日期、唛头、总额和信用证编号的装船通知必须用挂号航空邮件的形式发送给申请人。相关的邮政挂号收据和装运通知副本必须随附在该文件中。

（3）Shipment advice must be sent by telex to the applicant with details of shipment including value, name of vessel and date of shipment quoting their policy No. . Copy of this telex should be presented with documents upon negotiation. 装船通知以电传方式将货物装运情况及预约保单号码通知保险公司，并在议付时提交电传副本。

（4）Insurance covered by openers. All shipments under this credit must be advised by beneficiary immediately after shipment direct to the applicant and to the openers referring to cover note No. giving full details of shipments. A copy of this advice is to accompany each set of documents. 开证人负责投保。本信用证项下的所有货物装船后，应由受益人直接通知申请人及开证人，通知书上应注明预约保单的号码，并说明装船的详情。这份通知书副本必须随附在整套单据上进行议付。

（三）受益人证明

1. 定义

受益人证明（Beneficiary's Certificate/Statement）也称出口商证明（Exporter's Certificate），是一种由受益人自己出具的证明，证明自己履行了信用证规定的任务或证明自己按信用证的要求办事，如证明所交货物的品质、证明运输包装的处理、证明按要求寄单等。

2. 种类

（1）寄单证明（Beneficiary's Certificate for Dispatch of Documents）

寄单证明是受益人证明中最常见的一种。通常是受益人根据规定，在货物装运前后一定时期内，邮寄/传真/快递给规定的收受人全套或部分副本单据，并将证明随其他单据交银行议付。

如 CERTIFICATE FROM THE BENEFICIARY STATING THAT ONE COPY OF THE DOCUMENTS CALLED FOR UNDER THE L/C HAS BEEN DISPATCHED BY COURIER SERVICE DIRECT TO THE APPLICANT WITHIN 3 DAYS AFTER SHIPMENT.

（2）寄样证明（Beneficiary's Certificate for Dispatch of Shipment Sample）

例如：CERTIFICATE TO SHOW THAT THE REQUIRED SHIPMENT SAMPLES HAVE BEEN SENT BY DHL TO THE APPLICANT ON JULY 10, 2005.

（3）电抄本（Telex/Cable/Fax Copy）

电抄本是根据信用证规定，在货物运出前后的一定期限内，由发货人按信用证规定的内容，用传真通知信用证规定的收电人，并以传真或另缮制发电证明书，作为已发电的证明，交银行作为议付的单证。

（4）履约证明

履约证明是证实某件事实、货物符合成交合约或来自某产地的证明文件。例如交货品质证明，是由发货人按信用证的规定，证明所交货物的品质符合合同的规定，可直接作为银行议付的单证。有时信用证中规定要求信用证受益人提供的工厂品质证明书也属于这类证明。

（5）包装和标签证明

【例12-1】某信用证要求：A CERTIFICATE FROM THE BENEFICIARY TO THE EFFECT THAT ONE SET OF INVOICE AND PACKING LIST HAS BEEN PLACED ON THE INNER SIDE OF THE DOOR OF EACH CONTAINER IN CASE OF FCL CARGO OR ATTACHED TO THE GOODS OR PACKAGES AT AN OBVIOUS PLACE IN CASE OF LCL CARGO.

受益人应证明已把一套发票和箱单贴在集装箱箱门内侧（整箱货）或拼箱货的显眼的地方。

【例12-2】BENEFICIARY CERTIFICATE IN TRIPLICATE STATING THE SHIPMENT DOES NOT INCLUDE NON- MANUFACTURED WOOD DUNNAGE, PALLETS, CRATING OR OTHER PACKAGING MATERIALS; THE SHIPMENT IS COMPLETELY FREE OF WOOD BARK, VISIBLE PESTS AND SIGNS OF LIVING PESTS.

要求三份单据，证明货物未再加工、非木制包装、无树皮、无肉眼可见虫害、无活虫。

（6）其他

如 BENEFICIARY'S CERTIFICATE STATING ORIGINAL B/L OF ONE SET CARRIED BY THE CAPTAIN OF THE VESSEL.

一套正本提单已交由船长携带。

CERTIFICATE TO SHOW GOODS ARE NOT OF ISRAELI ORIGIN AND DO NOT CONTAIN ANY ISRAELI MATERIAL.

货物须保证非以色列产并且不含以色列的材料。

3. 信用证中有关受益人证明书条款举例

(1) COPY OF LETTER FROM BENEFICIARY TO OUR APPLICANT EVIDENCING A NON NEGOTIABLE BILL OF LADING TOGETHER WITH COPY OF OTHER DOCUMENTS WERE SENT DIRECTLY TO THEM AFTER ONE DAY FROM SHIPMENT DATE.

一张受益人发给开证人的证明信，证明一份非议付提单和其他单据一起已经在装船后一天直接寄给开证人了。

(2) A STATEMENT FROM THE BENEFICARY EVIDENCING THAT：PACKING EFFECTED IN 25KGS/CTN BOX.

一份受益人声明书，证明货物包装在每只 25 公斤的箱内。

(3) A CERTIFICATE FROM BENEFICIARY STATING THAT THE FOLLOWING DOCUMENTS HAVE BEEN SENT TO THE APPLICANT BY SPEED POST AFTER SHIPMENT EFFECTED：①1/3 ORIGINAL BILL OF LADING；②CERTIFICATE OF QUALITY ISSUED BY CCIB/ CCIC IN DUPLICATE.

受益人证明一份，证明以下单据已经在装船后，快递邮寄给开证人了：①1/3 的正本提单；②一式二份由 CCIB/CCIC 出具的质量证明书。

(4) BENEFICARY'S DECLARATION CERTIFYING THAT THE ORIGINAL OF EXPORT LICENCE HAS BEEN SENT TO THE APPLICANT BY EXPRESS COURIER BEFORE SHIPMENT EFFECTED.

受益人证明书，证明正本出口许可证已在装船前快递邮寄给开证人。

(四) 包装单据的缮制

1. 装箱单的缮制

重量单（除重量栏外）和尺码单（除尺码栏外）的制作要点与装箱单基本一致，在此以装箱单为例（见表 12-1）做一说明。

表 12-1　　　　　　　　　　装箱单样本

(1) SELLER	(3) INVOICE NO.	(4) INVOICE DATE
	(5) FROM	(6) TO
	(7) TOTAL PACKAGES (IN WORDS)	

续表

(2) BUYER				(8) MARKS & NOS.			
(9) C/NOS.	(10) NOS. & KINDS OF PKGS.	(11) ITEM	(12) QTY. (pcs.)	(13) G. W. (kg)	(14) N. W. (kg)	(15) MEAS (m³)	
TOTAL							

(16) ISSUED BY

(17) SIGNATURE

装箱单无统一格式，各出口企业的装箱单大致相同。其主要内容和缮制方法如下，请参照装箱单样本中的序号：

（1）卖方（SELLER）：填写出口企业的名称、地址，应与发票同项内容一致。

（2）买方（BUYER）：填写进口企业的名称、地址，应与发票同项内容一致。

（3）发票编号（INVOICE NO.）：填写出口发票号码或填写"as per invoice"。

（4）发票日期（INVOICE DATE）：填写出口发票日期。

（5）发自（FROM）：填写出单企业全称。

（6）发向（TO）：填写受单企业全称。

（7）总箱数（TOTAL PACKAGES）：填写所有包装件数的总和。

（8）唛头（MARKS & NOS）：与发票一致，有时注实际唛头，有时也可以只注"as per invoice NO. …"。

（9）合同号（C/NOS.）：填写此批货物的合同号。

（10）箱号和包装种类（NOS. & KINDS OF PKGS.）：箱号又称包装件号码。在单位包装货量或品种不固定的情况下，需注明每个包装件内的包装情况，因此包装件应编号。包装种类应注明包装的类型和方式。例如，Carton No. 1－5 are packed in new gunny bags；Carton No. 6－10 are packed in cartons.

（11）品名（ITEM）：品名必须和信用证的描述相符。

（12）数量（QTY.）：注明箱内每件货物的包装件数。例如，"bag 10"，

"drum 20"、"bale 30"。

（13）毛重（G. W.）：注明每个包装件的毛重。信用证或合同中未要求，也可以不注明，但如信用证要求"detailed packing list"，则此处应逐项说明。

（14）净重（N. W.）：注明每个包装件的净重。此包装件内不同规格、品种、花色的货物要分别列出，并在最后的合计栏（total）处累计其总量。信用证或合同中未要求，也可以不注明，但如信用证要求"detailed packing list"，则此处应逐项说明。

（15）外箱尺寸（MEAS）：注明每件包装的体积，并标明总尺码。

（16）出单人（ISSUED BY）：填写出单企业的全称，应与发票内容一致。

（17）签章（SIGNATURE）：出单人签章应与商业发票相符，如果信用证规定中性包装，此栏可以不填。

2. 重量单的缮制

重量单无固定格式，由出口商自行拟制。其主要栏目内容有：①重量单名称；②编号及日期；③商品名称；④唛头；⑤毛重；⑥净重；⑦皮重；⑧总件数。

重量单应注明每个包装件、每个货物类别的毛重、净重、皮重及总重，其中"@"表示单件货物的重量，"/"表示货物的总重量（由"单件货物的重量×件数"可得）。在单位包装货量或品种不固定的情况下，应分列说明。

3. 尺码单的缮制

尺码单无固定格式，由出口商自行拟制。其主要栏目内容包括单据名称、编号、日期、货物名称、货物数量、尺码及签字等。尺码单上一般要求列明每件货物的尺码和总尺码，并提供货物包装件的体积。货物的包装件可以按照信用证的要求，用"长×宽×高"来表示，也可用立方米来表示。尺码单应对货物的单位包装箱尺寸作重点说明，尺码用公制表示。

4. 包装单据缮制中的注意事项

（1）装箱单上的总件数和重量单上的总重量应与发票和提单上的总件数或总重量相一致。

（2）包装单据所列的情况应与货物的包装内容完全相符，例如，"The good are to be packed in cartons, 200 boxes per carton, 4 dozens per box"。

（3）如信用证要求将两种单据分别开列，应提供两套单据。信用证只要求出具其中一种时，应将其他单据的名称删去。单据的名称也必须和信用证的要求相符，如信用证规定为"weight memo"，则单据名称不能用"weight list"。

（4）如果来证要求用"中性包装单"（neutral packing list），则包装单名称打"packing list"，但包装单内不打卖方和开证行的名称，也不要加盖任何签章，由第三人填制。这是因为进口商在转让单据时，不愿将原始出口商暴露给其买主。

（5）制作重量单和尺码单的主要依据都是商业发票。重量单除重量栏外、尺码单除尺码栏外，其余栏目的制作要点与装箱单基本一致。如采用托盘装运，还应分别注明托盘本身的重量和尺码。

（五）装船通知的缮制

装船通知的缮制方法如下：

（1）出口企业名称：装船通知应标明出口企业，一般出口方的名称都已事先印好。

（2）单据名称：对于装船通知的名称，叫法比较多，如 SHIPPING ADVICE，SHIPPING STATEMENT, SHIPMENT DETAILS 等等。当以信用证为支付方式时，名称应符合信用证的要求。

（3）抬头（TO…）：可以是买方，或者是买方指定的人或保险公司。若抬头为买方指定的保险公司，则应同时注明预约保单（COVER NOTE）号码，也可以用统称，如"TO WHOM IT MAY CONCERN"（开启者）。若信用证有要求，应按规定填写。

（4）制单日期：填写制作装船通知的日期，一般在货物装船后 3 天内。若信用证有要求，应按规定填写。

（5）参考号码：包括发票号（INV. NO.）、提单号（B/L NO.）、信用证编号（L/C NO.）及船名（VESSEL NAME），若发送装船通知的目的是让买方即时投保，一般还有预约保单号码（OPEN POLICY NO./COVER NOTE NO.），各项内容要与提单一致。

（6）有关装运情况：包括装运港（PORT OF LOADING）、目的港（PORT OF DISCHARGE）、装运期（SHIPPING DATE），都按合同或信用证的规定填写，一般与提单一致。预计开船日期和到达日期（ETD、ETA）按船期表所列的日期填写。

（7）商品描述部分：包括品名（COMMODITY）、唛头（MARKS）、数量（QUANTITY）、发票总值（VALUE），可以按商业发票的内容填写。

（8）签名（SIGNATURE）：填写出口企业的名称及签章。

（六）受益人证明的缮制

1. 受益人证明的主要内容

（1）出口公司的名称和地址。

（2）单据名称。

（3）抬头：填进口公司的名称或采用笼统称呼，如"TO WHOM IT MAY CONCERN"。

（4）制单日期：应与证明的内容相符。如提单日期是 4 月 28 日，而需要证明的事项应该在提单日期之后的 2 天内作出，则制单日期既不能早于 4 月 28 日，也不能晚于 4 月 30 日。但如果证明的内容是关于包装或货物品质等方面的，则制单日期只要在发票日期之后、议付日期之前即可。

（5）参考编号：一般应注明信用证编号、发票编号和合同编号。

（6）证明内容：根据信用证的要求缮制，但有时应对所用时态作相应变化，另见"注意事项"中的第（2）条。

（7）签署：作为证明，应有出口方签章。

2. 受益人证明的注意事项

（1）单据名称应恰当。单据名称因所证明事项的不同而略异，可能是寄单证明、寄样证明（船样、样卡和码样等）、取样证明，货物产地、品质、唛头、包装和标签情况等的证明，电抄形式的装运通知，产品生产过程证明，商品业已检验证明，以及环保、人权方面的证明（非童工、非狱工制造）等。

（2）证明的内容应严格与合同或信用证的规定相符，但有时也应做必要的修改。如信用证规定"BENEFICIARY'S CERTIFICATE EVIDENCING THAT TWO COPIES OF NON-NEGOTIABLE B/L WILL BE DESPATCHED TO APPLICANT WITHIN TWO DAYS AFTER SHIPMENT"，在具体制作单据时应将要求中的"WILL BE DESPATCHED"改为"HAVE BEEN DESPATCHED"；又如，对于"BENEFICIARY'S CERTIFICATE STATING THAT CERTIFICATE OF MANUFACTURING PROCESS AND OF INGREDIENTS ISSUED BY ABC CO. SHOULD BE SENT TO SUMITOMO CORP."的要求，"SHOULD BE SENT"最好改为"HAD/HAS BEEN SENT"。

（3）证明文件通常以"THIS IS TO CERTIFY"（或 DECLARE，STATE，EVIDENCE 等）或"WE HEREBY CERTIFY"等开始。

（4）因属于证明性质，按有关规定，证明人（受益人）必须签字。

（5）单据一般都应在规定的时间内做出。

三、实训内容与要求

（一）掌握装箱单、重量单、尺码单、受益人证明和装船通知的相关内容

（二）根据信用证的内容填写装箱单、重量单、尺码单、受益人证明和装船通知

四、实训单证填制

根据模块一中的信用证要求，填写装运通知书（见表12-2）和受益人证明（见表12-3）。

表 12-2   **装运通知书**

金 喆 进 出 口 有 限 公 司

JINZHE IMP. AND EXP. CO. LTD.

Tel：86-21-64331255   Fax：86-21-64331256

ADD. ：ROOM 302, WORLD TRADE CENTER, 277 WU XING ROAD, SHANGHAI, CHINA

TO：GLOBAL TRADING UM GMBH   DATE：5-Sep-13

　　MOOSFELDSTRABE 96 D746 BALINGEN, W, GERMANY

FROM：JINZHE IMP. AND EXP. CO. LTD

SHIPPING ADVICE

S/C NO. ：	KH-SPTSC38
L/C NO. ：	384010021947
B/L NO. ：	KH-SPTBL01
GOODS：	DUMBBELL / ART NO. ：G6610-10KGS
VALUE （USD）：	18 139. 0
QUANTITY：	1700 ETS
PACKAGES：	one 20' container
G. W. （KGS. ）：	17 000
N. W. （KGS. ）：	17 000
MEAS. （m³）：	25. 000
VESSEL：	YI XIANG V. 307
FROM：	SHANGHAI, CHINA
TO：	HAMBURG, GERMANY
ETD：	4-Sep-13
ETA：	29-Sep-13

BEST REGARDS

表 12-3   **受益人证明**

金 喆 进 出 口 有 限 公 司

JINZHE IMP. AND EXP. CO. LTD.

DATE：5-Sep-13

ADD. ：	ROOM 302, WORLD TRADE CENTER, 277 WU XING ROAD, SHANGHAI, CHINA	TEL：	86-21-64331255
		FAX：	86-21-64331256
		E-MAIL：	BOX01@ SIFT. SIFT. EDU
TO：	GLOBAL TRADING UM GMBH MOOSFELDSTRABE 96 D746 BALINGEN, W, GERMANY		

S/C NO. :　　　　　　　　　　　KH-SPTSC38
L/C NO. :　　　　　　　　　　　384010021947
INVOICE NO. :　　　　　　　　　KH-SPTINV01
B/L NO. :　　　　　　　　　　　KH-SPTBL01
GOODS：　　　　　　　　　　　DUMBBELL / ART NO.：G6610-10KGS

VALUE：　　　　　　　　　　　USD 18 139. 00
QUANTITY：　　　　　　　　　1 700 SETS

KANGHUA IMP. AND EXP. CO., LTD. 王 昌

WE CERTIFY THAT SHIPPING SAMPLE HAS BEEN SENT TO APPLICANT BEFORE SHIPMENT.

五、实训考核方法

（一）正确使用装箱单、重量单、尺码单、受益人证明和装船通知
（二）正确填写装箱单、重量单、尺码单、受益人证明和装船通知

模块十三　制单操作

一、实训目的

（一）了解出口单据的种类，掌握出口制单结汇的方法及原则

（二）保证单据内容不互相矛盾，符合买卖合同或信用证的规定

（三）正确填写相关的出口单据

二、理论知识点

（一）制单要求

1. 正确

正确是一切单证制作的前提，要做到四个"一致"：

（1）证、同一致：信用证的基本条款应该与合同内容保持一致；

（2）单、证一致：保证及时收汇；

（3）单、单一致：保证及时收汇；

（4）单、货一致：单据必须真实反映货物，如所装货物不符合合同条款要求，买方在收货检验后仍然有权根据合同向卖方索赔和追偿损失。

2. 完整

完整指信用证规定的各项单据必须齐全，不可缺少；单据的种类、每种单据的份数和单据本身的必要项目都必须完整。

3. 及时

及时指按信用证规定的交单期到银行交单结汇，即处理单证要在一定时间内完成。

4. 简洁

单证的内容应力求简洁，避免不必要的烦琐。其具体要求是单证格式的规范化，内容排列的行次整齐、字迹清晰、纸面洁净、格式美观等。

5. 严谨

严谨是对单证工作的总体要求，包括：

（1）单证中的各种条款必须订得严密；

（2）单证必须经过严格的审核；

（3）单证的处理必须合理谨慎。

（二）制单原则

在信用证项下，制单时必须贯彻单证相符、单单相符的原则。在无信用证的情况下，单证相符则指各种单据应与买卖合同相符。制单不仅要以审单标准为基础，而且要提出更高的要求，主要包括：

（1）单、证一致；

（2）单、单一致；

（3）单、货一致；

（4）单、同一致。

（三）制单环节

1. 核对

核对指核对货和证、货和合同是否一致。这是正确制单、审单的前提和保障。

2. 核算

核算指对各种单据中涉及的数据的核对，如货物的尺码、毛（净）重、单价、总值等。发票与各单据的内容应一致，数据计算应正确，描述商品品名、金额、毛重、皮重、净重的措辞必须一致。

3. 配齐

配齐指按信用证或合同的要求，把本批出口货物所需要的各种单据按需要的份数准备妥当。

4. 制单

制单一般可以先从发票和装箱单开始，因为发票是一切单证的中心，要做到逐条逐句，对照制单；纵横交叉制单，仔细严格；单据齐全，数字正确。纵的制单，以信用证为中心，达到"单证相符"；横的制单，以发票为中心，达到"单单相符"。

5. 审单

审单的内容包括：（1）单据的种类及份数是否符合要求；（2）各种单据的内容是否完整，签章是否有遗漏，背书是否正确；（3）各种单据的相同和相应栏目的内容是否一致；（4）单据的名称和内容是否与信用证规定相符；（5）各种单据的签发日期是否符合要求；（6）各种单据的签发人名称和签字是否符合信用证的要求。

（四）交单

单证交付是指受益人在规定的时间内向议付行送交信用证项下的全套单证。一般来说，外贸公司可将单据送交银行预审、改单，直至正式交单，但注意，最后交单期不得晚于以下三个日期：

（1）信用证的有效期；

（2）信用证规定的交单日期；

（3）运输单据出单后的第 21 天。

（五）出口结汇单据时间顺序的排列

1. 发票日期（8 日）

发票的签发日期最早，因为货物装运日期必须符合信用证的规定，但只有知道货物的详细情况，才能安排运输，我们完全可以在货物发运前缮制发票，而且，货物在报关出口时，商检、海关等都需要发票做原始审验凭证。所以，在信用证规定的提交给银行的单据的制作中，我们可以坚持这一原则，即发票签发日期最早。

装箱单、重量单、尺码单等单据的缮制目的是说明发票所载货物的详细重量或货物包装的体积状况，它们是对发票内容的补充。签发这类单据时要注意有关内容与发票内容一致，签署人与发票人为同一人，特别是出具日期与发票日期应相同或略迟于发票日期，但绝不能早于发票日期。

2. 商检证书日期（15 日）

商检证书日期不能晚于提单日期。

3. 保险单日期（16 日）

保险单日期稍早于货物装运日期，强调"稍早"，主要是为了使制单工作更合理化、顺序化。如果保险单的出单日期太超前，很多不确定的内容可能会导致误认、漏认、多认，保险单毕竟需要与运输单据互相对照吻合，因此，保险单据的签发日期要早于运输单据的签发日期。

4. 提单签发日期（17 日）

签发提单的日期应晚于信用证的开证日期，但应早于提交单据的日期。提单的签发日期要早于信用证中规定的最迟装运期。一般来说，信用证都会规定提交单据的期限，如无该项规定，提单也必须在装运日期后的 21 天内提交给银行；否则，银行会拒绝受理。

5. 信用证最迟装运日期（19 日）

6. 信用证有效期（29 日）

信用证中的所有业务必须在信用证的有效期内进行。

7. 汇票有效期（29 日）

汇票出具日期最晚。需要汇票时，我们应把握汇票出票日期最晚的原则。也就是说，受益人要在做好了信用证要求的其他单据后再缮制汇票，除非信用证另有规定。缮制汇票是出口制单的最后一个环节。汇票的出票日期就是议付日期，其不得超过信用证的有效期和最迟交单期。实际做法是，受益人交来汇票不打日期，待银行审单相符时，由银行审单员盖上当日的日期戳，作为出票日期/议付日期。

三、实训内容与要求

（一）指出出口制单的方法及原则

（二）阅读信用证并根据信用证的要求缮制全套单据

四、实训单证填制

请根据以下跟单信用证通知书（见表13-1）和信用证（见表13-2）的相关内容填写相关单据，包括汇票（见表13-3）、提单（见表13-4）、商业发票（见表13-5）、保险单（见表13-6）、装箱单（见表13-7）和原产地证明书（见表13-8）。

表13-1　　　　　　　　　　　　　　　跟单信用证通知书

ADDRESS：50 HUQIU ROAD CABLE：CHUNG KUO TELEX：3062 BOCSH E CN SWIFT：BKCHCMBJ30	中国银行 BANK OF CHINA 跟单信用证通知书 Notification of Documentary Credit　　DATE：2013/04/20
To（致）：JINZHE TRADING CO.，LTD. NO.1267 ZHONGSHAN ROAD，DALIAN，CHINA	WHEN CORRESPONDING PLEASE QUOTE OUR REF. NO.：
ISSUING BANK Chemical Bank New York 55 Wall Street，Room 1702，New York，U.S.A.	Transmitting through（转递行）
L/C NO.（信用证号） DRG-JZLC01 DATED（开证日期） APRIL 14TH 2013	Amount（金额） USD 188 256.00

续表

Dear sirs（敬启者）,

We have pleasure in advising you that we have received from the a/m bank a（n）letter of credit,
兹通知贵公司，我行收自上述银行开来的信用证一份，

（　）pre-advising of	预先通知	（　）mail confirmation of	邮寄证实书
（　）telex issuing	电传开立	（　）ineffective	未生效
（x）original	正本	（　）duplicate	副本

contents of which are as per attached sheet（s）. This advice and the attached sheet（s）must accompany the relative documents when presented for negotiation.
现随附通知。贵公司交单时，请将本通知书及相关单据一并提示。

（x）Please note that this advice does not constitute our confirmation of the above L/C nor does it convey any engagement or obligation on our part.
本通知书不构成我行对此信用证之保兑及其他任何责任。

（　）Please note that we have added our confirmation to the above L/C, negotiation is restricted to ourselves only.
上述信用证已由我行加具保兑，并限向我行交单。

This L/C consists of two sheet（s）, including the covering letter and attachment（s）.
本信用证连同面函及附件共 2 张。

If you find any terms and conditions in the L/C which you are unable to comply with and or any error（s）, it is suggested that you contact applicant directly for necessary amendment（s）of as to avoid any difficulties which may arise when documents are presented. 如本信用证中有无法办到的条款及/或错误，请径与开证申请人联系，进行必要的修改，以排除交单时可能发生的问题。	FOR BANK OF CHINA, Dalian Branch 中国银行 大连分行 信用证通知章 Yours faithfully

---

表 13-2　　　　　　　　　　　　　　信用证

34127 B BOCSH CN

6229

1705 03/25 04803089 TCH0063

0325004658

ZCZC

FROM：CHEMICAL BANK NEW YORK

OUR REF：NY980520004658001T01

TO: BANK OF CHINA, DALIAN BRANCH

　　50 HUQIU ROAD, DALIAN

　　THE PEOPLE'S REP. OF CHINA

FOR USD 188 256. 00 ON DATE 14/04/2013

PLEASE ADVICE BENEFICIARY OF THE FOLLOWING IRREVOCABLE LETTER OF CREDIT ISSUED BY US IN THEIR FAVOR SUBJECT TO UCP 600:

DOCUMENTARY CREDIT NUMBER: DRG-JZLC01

DATE AND PLACE OF EXPIRY: June 10th 2013, IN U. S. A.

APPLICANT: DRAGON TOY CO. , LTD. 1180 CHURCH ROAD, NEW YORK, PA 19446 U. S. A.

BENEFICIARY: JINZHE CO. , LTD. NO. 1267 EAST NANJING ROAD, DALIAN, CHINA

AMOUNT: USD 188 256. 00

SAY UNITED STATES DOLLARS ONE HUNDRED AND EIGHTY EIGHT THOUSAND TWO HUNDRED AND FIFTY SIX ONLY.

AVAILABLE WITH: ANY BANK

BY: NEGOTIATION OF BENEFICIARY'S DRAFT（S）AT 30 DAYS' SIGHT DRAWN ON CHEMICAL BANK, NEW YORK, ACCOMPANIED BY THE DOCUMENTS INDICATED HEREIN.

COVERING SHIPMENT OF:

COMMODITY ART. NO. QUANTITY

TELECONTROL RACING CAR

18812　　2 000 PIECES

18814　　2 000 PIECES

18817　　2 000 PIECES

18818　　2 000 PIECES

SHIPPING TERMS: CIF NEW YORK

SHIPPING MARK: JZ-DRGSC01/DRAGON TOY/NEW YORK/NO. 1-UP

DOCUMENTS REQUIRED:

– 3 COPIES OF COMMERCIAL INVOICE SHOWING VALUE IN U. S. DOLLARS AND INDICATING L/C NO. AND CONTRACT NO.

– 2 COPIES OF PACKING LIST SHOWING GROSS/NET WEIGHT AND MEASUREMENT OF EACH CARTON.

CERTIFICATE OF ORIGIN IN TRIPLICATE ISSUED BY CHINA CHAMBER OF INTERNATIONAL COMMERCE.

– 2 COPIES OF INSURANCE POLICY OR CERTIFICATE ENDORSED IN BLANK FOR THE INVOICE VALUE OF THE GOODS PLUS 110% COVERING ALL RISKS AND WAR RISK AS PER AND SUBJECT TO OCEAN MARINE CARGO CLAUSES OF THE PEOPLE'S INSURANCE COMPANY OF CHINA DATED 1/1/1981.

– 3/3 SET AND ONE COPY OF CLEAN ON BOARD OCEAN BILLS OF LADING MADE OUT TO ORDER AND BLANK ENDORSED MARKED FREIGHT PREPAID AND NOTIFY APPLICANT.

PARTIAL SHIPMENTS: PERMITTED

TRANSSHIPMENTS: PERMITTED

SHIPMENT FROM: DALIAN, CHINA   TO: NEW YORK

NOT LATER THAN: MAY 31, 2013

DOCUMENTS MUST BE PRESENTED WITHIN 15 DAYS AFTER SHIPMENT, BUT WITHIN VALIDITY OF THE LETTER OF CREDIT

INSTRUCTIONS TO THE PAYING/ACCEPTING /NEGOTIATING BANK

NEGOTIATING BANK IS TO FORWARD ALL DOCUMENTS IN ONE AIRMAIL TO CHEMICAL BANK NEW YORK, 55 WALL STREET, ROOM 1702, NEW YORK, NEW YORK 10041 U. S. A.

ATTN: LETTER OF CREDIT DEPARTMENT

END OF MESSAGE

NN/

62814 CBC VW

(WRU)

34127 8B BOCSH CN

NNNN

表 13-3	汇 票

BILL OF EXCHANGE

JZ_DRGINV01

USD   188 256. 00   DALIAN   27−May−13

(amount in figure)   (place and date of issue)

At ＊ ＊ ＊ ＊ ＊ ＊ ＊ ＊ ＊ ＊ ＊ ＊ ＊ ＊ sight of this FIRST Bill of Exchange (SECOND of exchange being unpaid)

pay to BANK OF CHINA, DALIAN BRANCH   or order the sum of

SAY UNITED STATES DOLLARS ONE HUNDRED AND EIGHTY EIGHT THOUSAND AND TWO HUNDRED AND FIFTY SIX ONLY.

(amount in words)

Value received for   600 SETS   of   TELECONTROL RACING CAR

                    (quantity)   (name of commodity)

Drawn under   CHEMICAL BANK NEW YORK

    L/C No. DRG−JZLC01   dated 14−Apr−13

To: CHEMICAL BANK NEW YORK   For and on behalf of

55 WALL STREET, ROOM 1702,   JINZHE TRADING CO. , LTD.

NEW YORK, NEW YORK 10041

                                ×××

                                (Signature)

表 13-4

提 单
BILL OF LADING

(1) SHIPPER: JINZHE TRADING CO., LTD. Address: NO. 1267 ZHONGSHAN ROAD, DALIAN, CHINA	(10) B/L NO.: JZ-DRGBL01

(2) CONSIGNEE: TO ORDER	COSCO 中国远洋运输（集团）总公司 CHINA OCEAN SHIPPING (GROUP) CO.

(3) NOTIFY PARTY: DRAGON TOY CO., LTD. 1180 CHURCH ROAD, NEW YORK, PA 19446 U. S. A.	ORIGINAL Combined Transport BILL OF LADING

(4) PLACE OF RECEIPT: DALIAN CY	(5) OCEAN VESSEL: CHENG FEN	
(6) VOYAGE NO.: V. 208	(7) PORT OF LOADING: DALIAN	
(8) PORT OF DISCHARGE: NEW YORK	(9) PLACE OF DELIVERY: NEW YORK CY	

(11) MARKS:	(12) NOS. & KINDS OF PKGS.:	(13) DESCRIPTION OF GOODS:	(14) G. W. (kg)	(15) MEAS (m³)
JZ-DRGSC01 DRAGON TOY NEW YORK NO. 1-600	 600 CARTONS	TELECONTROL RACING CAR	9 200	99. 533
		FREIGHT PREPAID L/C NO. DRG-JZLC01		

(16) TOTAL NUMBER OF CONTAINERS OR PACKAGES (IN WORDS):
SAY SIX HUNDRED CARTONS ONLY

FREIGHT & CHARGES	REVENUE TONS	RATE	PER	PREPAID	COLLECT
PREPAID AT	PAYABLE AT		(17) PLACE AND DATE OF ISSUE: DALIAN　20-May-13		

续表

TOTAL PREPAID	(18) NUMBER OF ORIGINAL B (S) L: THREE

LADEN ON BOARD THE VESSEL   (21) SIGNED FOR THE CARRIER:

(19) DATE: (20) BY: COSCO DALIAN SHIPPING CO. , LTD.

20-May-09   郭复北

                 COSCO DALIAN SHIPPING CO. , LTD.

                 AS AGENT FOR THE CARRIER CHINA   郭复北

ENDORSEMENT: JINZHE TRADING CO. , LTD.

　　　×××   20-May-13   3 COPIES

表 13-5   商业发票

COMMERCIAL INVOICE

(1) SELLER JINZHE TRADING CO. , LTD.	(3) INVOICE NO. JZ-DRGINV01	(4) INVOICE DATE 9-May-09
Address: NO. 1267 ZHONGSHAN ROAD, DALIAN, CHINA	(5) L/C NO. DRG-JZLC01	(6) DATE 14-Apr-09
	(7) ISSUED BY CHEMICAL BANK NEW YORK	
(2) BUYER DRAGON TOY CO. , LTD.	(8) CONTRACT NO. JZ-DRGSC01	(9) DATE 1-Apr-09
Address: 1180 CHURCH ROAD, NEW YORK, PA 19446 U. S. A.	(10) FROM DALIAN	(11) TO NEW YORK
	(12) SHIPPED BY CHENG FEN V. 208	(13) PRICE TERM CIF NEW YORK

(14) MARKS	(15) DESCRIPTION OF GOODS	(16) QTY.	(17) UNIT PRICE	(18) AMOUNT
JZ-DRGSC01 DRAGON TOY NEW YORK NO. 1-600	TELECONTROL RACING CAR ART. NO. 18812	 2 400 PCS	CIF NEW YORK USD 19. 88	 USD 47 712. 00
	18814	2 000 PCS	USD 20. 66	USD 41 320. 00
	18817	2 000 PCS	USD 21. 94	USD 43 880. 00
	18819	2 400 PCS	USD 23. 06	USD 55 344. 00
			TOTAL:	USD 188 256. 00

续表

Packing：AS PER SALES CONTRACT NO. JZ-DRGSC01 DATED APRIL 1ST, 2009；AS PER L/C NO. DRG-JZLC01 DATED APRIL 14, 2013.

ART NO.18812 AND 18819 PACKED IN 400 CARTONS OF 12 PIECES EACH AND THEN TO TWO 20′FCL CONTAINERS.

ART NO.18814 AND 18817 PACKED IN 200 CARTONS OF 20 PIECES EACH AND THEN TO TWO 20′FCL CONTAINERS.

TOTAL GROSS WEIGHT 9 200KGS

TOTAL NET WEIGHT 7 200KGS

(19) TOTAL VALUE：SAY US DOLLARS ONE HUNDRED AND EIGHTY-EIGHT THOUSAND TWO HUNDRED AND FIFTY-SIX ONLY.

(20) ISSUED BY

JINZHE TRADING CO. , LTD.

(21) SIGNATURE

×××

3 COPIES

表 13-6　　　　　　　　　　保险单

中 国 人 民 保 险 公 司

THE PEOPLE'S INSURANCE COMPANY OF CHINA

总公司设于北京　　　　一九四九年创立

Head office：BEIJING　　　Established in 1949

保 险 单　　　　　　　　　保险单号次

INSURANCE POLICY　　　　POLICY NO. : JZ-DRGBD01

中国人民保险公司（以下简称本公司）

THIS POLICY OF INSURANCE WITNESSES THAT THE PEOPLE'S INSURANCE COMPANY OF CHINA (HEREINAFTER CALLED "THE COMPANY")

根据　　金喆贸易有限公司

AT THE REQUEST OF　JINZHE TRADING CO. , LTD.

（以下简称被保险人）的要求，由被保险人

(HERE IN AFTER CALLED "THE INSURED") AND IN CONSIDERATION OF THE AGREED PREMIUM

向本公司缴付约定的保险费，

BEING PAID TO THE COMPANY BY THE INSURED, UNDERTAKES TO INSURE THE UNDERMENTIONED

按照本保险单承保险别和背面所载条款与

GOODS IN TRANSPORTATION SUBJECT TO THE CONDITIONS OF THIS POLICY AS PER THE

下列条款承保下述货物运输保险，特立本保险单。

CLAUSES PRINTED OVERLEAF AND OTHER SPECIAL CLAUSES ATTACHED HEREON.

标记 MARKS & NOS.	数量 QUANTITY	保险货物项目 DESCRIPTION OF GOODS	保险金额 AMOUNT INSURED
JZ-DRGSC01 DRAGON TOY NEW YORK NO. 1-600	8 800 PIECES	TELECONTROL RACING CAR	USD 207 082. 00

总保险金额：

TOTAL AMOUNT INSURED: SAY US DOLLARS TWO HUNDRED AND SEVEN THOUSAND EIGHTY TWO ONLY.

保费 PREMIUM	费率 RATE AS ARRANGED	装载运输工具 PER CONVEYANCE S. S. CHENG FEN V. 208

开航日期
SLG. ON OR ABT. AS PER BILL OF LADING 　　自 FROM　DALIAN 　　至 TO NEW YORK

承保险别：

CONDITIONS　　COVERING ALL RISKS AND WAR RISK AS PER AND SUBJECT TO OCEAN MARINE

CARGO CLAUSES OF PICC DATED 1/1/1981

所保货物，如遇出险，本公司凭本保险单及其他有关证件给付赔款。

CLAIMS, IF ANY, PAYABLE ON SURRENDER OF THIS POLICY TOGETHER WITH OTHER RELEVANT DOCUMENTS.

所保货物，如发生本保险单项下负责赔偿的损失或事故，

IN THE EVENT OF ACCIDENT WHEREBY LOSS OR DAMAGE MAY RESULT IN A CLAIM UNDER THIS POLICY IMMEDIATE

应立即通知本公司下述代理人查勘：

NOTICE APPLYING FOR SURVEY MUST BE GIVEN TO THE COMPANY'S AGENT AS MENTIONED HEREUNDER：

所保货物，如遇出险，本公司凭本保险单及其他有关证件给付赔款。

GODWIN INSURANCE COMPANY

P. O. BOX 17764

NEW YORK, U. S. A.

FAX：215-393-8576

续表

赔款偿付地点
CLAIM PAYABLE AT/IN   NEW YORK IN USD   中国人民保险公司大连分公司
日 期   大连   THE PEOPLE'S INSURANCE CO. OF CHINA
DATE   18-May-09   DALIAN   DALIAN BRANCH
地址：中国大连中山东一路23号
TEL：83234305 83217466 - 44 Telex：33128   孙博
PICCS CN.
Address：23 Zhongshan Dong Yi Lu Dalian, China.   General Manager
Cable：42008 Dalian

ENDORSEMENT：JINZHE TRADING CO. , LTD.

×××   18-May-09   2 COPIES

表 13-7	装箱单

PACKING LIST

(1) SELLER JINZHE TRADING CO. , LTD.	(3) INVOICE NO. JZ-DRGINV01	(4) INVOICE DATE 2013-5-9
Address： NO. 1267 ZHONGSHAN ROAD, DALIAN, CHINA	(5) FROM DALIAN	(6) TO NEW YORK
	(7) TOTAL PACKAGES (IN WORDS) SAY SIX HUNDRED CARTONS ONLY	
(2) BUYER DRAGON TOY CO. , LTD.	(8) MARKS & NOS. JZ-DRGSC01	
Address： 1180 CHURCH ROAD, NEW YORK, PA 19446 U. S. A.	DRAGON TOY NEW YORK NO. 1-600	

(9) C/NOS. (10) NOS. &KINDS (11) ITEM (12) QTY. (PCS.) (13) G. W. (kg)
(14) N. W. (kg) (15) MEAS (m^3) OF PKGS.

		TELECONTROL RACING CAR			
1-200	200 CTNS	18812	2 400	2 400	1 800	24. 8832
201-300	100 CTNS	18814	2 000	2 200	1 800	24. 8832
301-400	100 CTNS	18817	2 000	2 200	1 800	24. 8832
401-600	200 CTNS	18819	2 400	2 400	1 800	24. 8832
TOTAL	600 CTNS		8 800	9 200	7 200	99. 533

续表

SHIPPING MARKS	WEIGHT AND MEAS. PER EXPORT CARTON：			
JZ-DRGSC01	ART. NO.	G. W. (KGS.)	N. W. (KGS.)	MEAS. (m^3)
DRAGON TOY	18812	12	9	0.124
NEW YORK	18814	22	18	0.249
NO. 1-600	18817	22	18	0.249
	18819	12	9	0.124

（16）ISSUED BY

JINZHE TRADING CO., LTD.

（17）SIGNATURE

××××

2 COPIES

表 13-8　　　　　　　　　　原产地证明书

1. Exporter (full name and address) JINZHE TRADING CO., LTD. NO. 1267 ZHONGSHAN ROAD, DALIAN, CHINA	Certificate No. JZ-DRGORG01
2. Consignee (full name, address, country) DRAGON TOY CO., LTD. 1180 CHURCH ROAD, NEW YORK, PA 19446 U. S. A.	CERTIFICATE OF ORIGIN OF THE PEOPLE'S REPUBLIC OF CHINA
3. Means of transport and route FROM DALIAN TO NEW YORK BY SEA	5. For certifying authority use only
4. Destination port NEW YORK U. S. A.	

6. Marks and numbers of packages	7. Description of goods： number and kind of packages	8. H. S. Code	9. Quantity or weight	10. Number and date of invoices
JZ-DRGSC01 DRAGON TOY NEW YORK NO. 1-600	600 CARONTS (SAY SIX HUNDRED CARTONS ONLY) TELECONTROL RACING CAR	9503. 8000 9	200KGS	JZ-DRGINV01 09-May-09

＊ ＊

11. Declaration by the exporter	12. Certification
The undersigned hereby declares that the above details and statements are correct, that all the goods were produced in China and that they comply with the Rules of Origin of the People's Republic of China. JINZHE TRADING CO. , LTD. DALIAN <div align="right">日期：MAY 14, 2009</div>	It is hereby certified that the declaration by the exporter is correct. 郭哲昕 DALIAN <div align="right">日期：MAY 16, 2009</div>
Place and date/signature and stamp of certifying authority	Place and date/signature and stamp of certifying authority

China Council for the Promotion of International Trade is China Chamber of International Commerce.

2 COPIES

五、实训考核方法

（一）信用证阅读的准确性

（二）各种出口单据制作的完整性及准确性

模块十四　信用证结算方式下的审单

一、实训目的

在前期各实训操作的基础上，根据信用证、UCP600 和 ISBP681 的规定，对准备提交单据的种类、格式、内容、出具日期、签署等做出全面审核，如果发现不符点或遗漏，及时提出修改、补充意见，保证所有单证相互之间不矛盾，符合信用证的规定。

二、理论知识点

（一）UCP600 关于审核单据的标准

UCP600 第十四条对信用证项下的单据的银行审核标准做出了较为详细的规定，这些规定为受益人自己审核信用证中要求的单据提供了依据。

1. 银行只负责审核单据表面是否相符。

2. 不因任何原因缩减的 5 个审单日。各审单银行应自收到提示单据的翌日起（算），在最多不超过 5 个银行工作日的时间内确定提示是否相符。该期限不因单据提示日适逢信用证有效期或最迟提示期或在其之后而被缩减或受到其他影响。这就要求受益人应提早交单，以免银行提出不符点时，信用证已经过期。

3. 交单期限。装运单据必须由受益人或其代表按照相关条款在不迟于装运日后的 21 个公历日内提交，但无论如何不得迟于信用证的到期日。

4. 单证相符。单据中内容的描述不必与信用证、信用证对该项单据的描述以及国际标准银行实务完全一致，但不得与该项单据中的内容、其他规定的单据或信用证相冲突。

5. 货物描述。除商业发票外，其他单据中的货物、服务或行为描述若需规定，可使用统称，但不得与信用证规定的描述相矛盾。

6. 其他单据的制作。如果信用证要求提示运输单据、保险单据和商业发票以外的单据，但未规定该单据由何人出具或单据的内容，只要所提交单据的内容看来满足其功能需要且其他方面与第十四条（d）款相符，银行将对提示的单据予以接受。

7. 多余的单证。提示信用证中未要求提交的单据，银行将不予置理。如果收到此类单据，可以退还给提示人。

8. 单证日期。单据的出单日期可以早于信用证开立日期，但不得迟于信用证规定的提示日期。

9. 单据的地址及联系方式。当受益人和申请人的地址显示在任何规定的单据上时，不必与信用证或其他规定的单据中显示的地址相同，但必须与信用证中述及的各自地址处于同一国家内。用于联系的资料（电传、电话、电子邮箱及类似方式）如作为受益人和申请人地址的组成部分，将被不予置理。然而，当申请人的地址及联系信息作为按照第十九条、第二十条、第二十一条、第二十二条、第二十三条、第二十四条或第二十五条出具的运输单据中收货人或通知方详址的组成部分时，则必须按照信用证规定予以显示。

10. 托运人、发货人。显示在任何单据上的货物的托运人或发货人不必是信用证的受益人。

（二）单据审核的依据

信用证下各单据审核的依据是：

1. 有效的信用证和随附的修改书（如果有的话）；

2. 信用证适用的 UCP；

3. ISBP681。

（三）单据审核的基本原则

单据的审核是对已经缮制的单据对照前述的三个依据或合同（非信用证付款方式下）进行及时的检查、核对，如发现问题，及时更正，以达到安全收汇的目的。信用证项下单据的审核原则是：

1. 及时性。其要求货物出口装运后，及时填制并审核有关单据，从而保证能及时发现和更正单据上的可能差错，以有效避免因审核不及时造成的各项工作的被动。

2. 全面性。其要求一方面，要根据前述三个审核依据对所有的提交单据的种类、形式、内容、份数、日期、签署做全面的审核，不放过任何一个不符点；另一方面，要加强与各有关部门的联系，使发现的问题能得到及时、妥善的处理。

3. 正确性。其要求做到单单相符、单证相符。单单相符是指根据 UCP600 及 ISBP681 的规定，按照非镜像原则，保证各单据之间的相关内容不存在矛盾之处。非镜像原则是指只要不相互矛盾，即使文字上有所不同，也不应视为单单不符。单证相符是要求按照非镜像原则，保证各单据的种类、形式、内容、份数、日期、签署等与信用证、UCP、ISBP 及商业习惯都一致。

此外，也要审核所有单据是否做到了单货相符、单约相符。单货相符是指单证上的货物记载与实际装运货物一致；单约相符是指提交的单据在种类、份数、内容上保持一致。单货相符、单约相符不是信用证的审核原则，恰恰相反，银行只审核单据表面而不管货物实际情况如何。然而，从履行买卖合同义务的角度考虑，单据上的货物记载与实际出运的货物不一致、提交的单据与合同的规定不一致很可能构成卖方违约。我们要求单货相符、单约相符的目的，就是要在信用证单据的审核过程中，同时审核买卖合同的履行情况，做到诚实守约。

（四）单据审核的方法

单证审核的方法概括起来为纵横交错法，即先进行以信用证为依据的各项单据的审核，保证单证相符，然后进行以商业发票为中心的其他单据的审核，保证单单相符。

1. 综合审核的要点

（1）单证及份数是否齐全；

（2）文件类型是否符合要求；

（3）单证是否按规定进行了认证；

（4）单证之间的货物描述、数量、金额、重量、体积、运输标志等是否一致；

（5）单证日期是否符合要求。

2. 汇票审核的要点

（1）付款人名称、地址是否正确；

（2）金额的大、小写是否一致；

（3）付款期限是否符合信用证的规定；

（4）汇票金额是否超出信用证金额；

（5）出票人、受款人、付款人是否符合信用证的规定；

（6）币制名称是否与信用证和发票上的一致；

（7）出票条款是否全面、正确；

（8）是否按需要进行了背书；

（9）是否由出票人作了签署；

（10）汇票份数是否作了说明。

3. 商业发票审核的要点

（1）抬头人是否符合信用证的规定；

（2）签发人是否为受益人；

（3）货物描述是否完全符合信用证的要求；

（4）货物数量是否符合信用证的规定；

（5）单价和价格条件是否符合信用证的规定；

（6）提交的正副本份数是否符合信用证的要求；

（7）是否载有信用证要求表明和证明的内容；

（8）金额有否超出信用证的金额。

4. 保险单据的审核要点

（1）是否为保险公司或其代理出具；

（2）投保加成是否符合信用证的规定；

（3）保险险别是否符合信用证的规定；

（4）保险单据的类型是否与信用证的要求一致；

（5）保险单据的正副本份数是否齐全；

（6）保险单据上的币别是否与信用证上的币别一致；

（7）包装件数、唛头等是否与发票和其他单据上的一致；

（8）运输工具、起运地及目的地是否与信用证和其他单据一致；

（9）如转运，保险期限是否包括了全程运输；

（10）保险单的签发日期是否早于或等于运输单据的签发日期；

（11）以受益人为投保人的保险单据是否已经由投保人背书。

5. 运输单据的审核要点

（1）单证类型是否符合信用证的规定；

（2）起运地、转运地、目的地是否符合信用证的规定；

（3）装运日期/出单日期是否符合信用证的规定；

（4）收货人和被通知人是否符合信用证的规定；

（5）商品名称是否与信用证和发票上的相矛盾；

（6）运费预付或运费到付是否已正确标明；

（7）正副本份数是否符合信用证的要求；

（8）运输单据上是否有不良批注；

（9）包装件数是否与其他单据一致；

（10）唛头是否与其他单据一致；

（11）全套正本单证是否都由承运人或其代理人正确地盖章及签字；

（12）是否已正确背书。

6. 其他单据

装箱单、重量单、产地证书、商检证书等是否单单相符和单证相符。

（1）信用证分析单（见表 14-1）

表 14-1　　　　　　　　　　　　　　信用证分析单

开证行		开证日期		信用证编号		
申请人		受益人		合同号码		
通知行		保兑行		议付行		
信用证金额		增减幅度		有效期		到期地点	
汇票付款人		汇票付款期限			汇票金额	

续表

装运港			目的港								
装运期限			可否转船				可否分批装运				
运输标志			交单日								
货物描述											

单据名称	提单	发票	装箱单	重量单	保险单	产地证	FORM A	寄单证明	寄单邮据	寄样证明	寄样邮据	检验证明
单据份数												

运输单据	抬头					险种				
				保险						
	通知					加成率		赔款地点		
	运费支付									
特别事项										

（2）出口货物信息明细表（参见表 14-2）

表 14-2 　　　　　　　　　　　**出口货物信息明细表**

货号	单价	数量	总值	单位	包装	件毛重	件净重	总毛重	总净重	件尺码	总尺码	其他

（3）已填制单据信息表（见表 14-3）

表 14-3 　　　　　　　　　　　**已填制单据信息表**

	汇票	发票	装箱单	提单	保险单	产地证	其他单证 1	其他单证 2
编号								
内容								
签发日								
份数								

（4）信用证审单记录表（参见表 14-4）

表 14-4 **信用证审单记录表**

	不符点	改正意见
汇票	1. 2. 3. ⋮	1. 2. 3. ⋮
发票	1. 2. 3. ⋮	1. 2. 3. ⋮
提单 ⋮	1. 2. 3. ⋮	1. 2. 3. ⋮

三、实训内容与要求

（一）编制信用证分析单，根据试验数据中的信用证及信用证修改书填制该表

（二）编制出口货物信息明细表，并根据出口合同和提单填制该表

（三）编制已填制单据信息表，并根据已填制的单据填制该表

（四）编制信用证审单记录表

（五）根据上述信息，进行各单证的纵横审核，结果记录在信用证审单记录表中，同时就各项不符点提出修改意见

四、实训单证填制

（一）基础资料

1. 不可撤销信用证（见表 14-5）

表 14-5   不可撤销信用证

DBS BANK   ORIGINAL

SHANGHAI BRANCH

SHANGHAI BRANCH Suite 2301, J F News Tower, 300 Han Kou Road, Shanghai 200001 People's Republic of China Tel: 86-21-5618838 Telex: 30436 DBSSH CN Fax: 86-21-5618711	IRREVOCABLE NUMBER DOCUMENTARY CREDIT 0016100293496 PLACE AND DATE OF ISSUE: Shanghai, April 10th, 2013 DATE AND PLACE OF EXPIRY Aug. 15th, 2013, Malaysia

APPLICANT
LIDA TRADING COMPANY LIMITED
ADD: NO.1267 EAST NANJING ROAD
     SHANGHAI, CHINA
     FAX: 021-64042588
	BENEFICIARY
	NANKAI WORSTED SPINNING SDN., BHD.
	ADD: LOT 20051, GONG BADAK
	     INDUSTRIAL ESTATE 21300
	     KUALA LUMPUR, MALAYSIA

ADVISING BANK: BANK OF COMMERCE MALAYSIA BERHAD KUALA LUMPUR BRANCH 15 LEBUH PANTAI 10300 KUALA LUMPUR MALAYSIA	AMOUNT: * * * USD * * * * * * * *418, 925.52 * * * * * SAY US DOLLARS FOUR HUNDRED EIGHTEEN THOUSAND NINE HUNDRED AND TWENTY FIVE AND POINT FIFTY-TWO * CREDIT AVAILABLE WITH: BANK OF COMMERCE MALAYSIA BERHAD

PARTIAL SHIPMENTS: ALLOWED
TRANSSHIPMENT: ALLOWED
SHIPPED FROM: KELANG,
SHIPPED TO: MALAYSIA
LATEST SHIPMENT: SHANGHAI,
                       CHINA
                       July 31st, 2013
	* BY: NEGOTIATION
	AGAINST PRESENTATION OF THE DOCUMENTS
	DETAILED HEREIN AND OF YOUR
	DRAFTS IN DUPLICATE AT SIGHT
	DRAWN ON: DBS BANK, SHANGHAI BRANCH
	* BEARING OUR DOCUMENTARY CREDIT NO.

DOCUMENTS REQUIRED:

01 FULL SET OF CLEAN ON BOARD BILLS OF LADING MADE OUT TO ORDER, ENDORSED IN BLANK MARKED "FREIGHT PAYABLE AT DESTINATION" AND NOTIFY APPLICANT.

02 PACKING LIST IN 3 ORIGINAL/S AND 3 COPY/IES, INDICATING CONTRACT NUMBER, SHIPPING MARKS, TOTAL PACKAGES, GROSS AND NET WEIGHT OF EACH PACKAGE AND PACKAGE NUMBER FOR EACH SPECIFICATION OR ITEM.

03 YOUR SIGNED COMMERCIAL INVOICE IN 3 ORIGINAL/S AND 3 COPY/IES, INDICATING CONTRACT NUMBER, SHIPPING MARKS, NAME OF CARRYING VESSEL, NUMBER OF THE L/C AND SHIPMENT NUMBER IN CASE OF PARTIAL SHIPMENT.

04CERTIFICATE OF INSPECTION IN TRIPLICATE ISSUED BY MALAYSIA TEXTILE INSPECTION BUREAU.

05 CERTIFICATE OF ORIGIN ISSUED BY GOVERNMENT AUTHORITY.

MERCHANDISE DESCRIPTION:

100% Wool Hosiery Yarn Art. No. 2/48nm, raw white in hank 19440kgs@ US $ 11. 20 Art. No. 2/32 nm, raw white in hank 13536kgs@ US $ 10. 32

Art. No. 1/40nm, raw white in cone 6120kgs@ US $ 10. 05. as per Contract No. YN－NK942 dated April 1st, 2013

The goods are dispatched in three equal monthly lots during May/June/July, documents of which should be the same.

SPECIAL INSTRUCTIONS:

1) ALL BANK CHARGES OUTSIDE CHINA INCLUDING REIMBURSEMENT COMMISSIONS ARE FOR BENEFICIARY'S ACCOUNT.

2) USD35. 00 WILL BE CHARGED FOR EACH SET OF DISCREPANT DOCUMENTS PRESENTED. THIS DISCREPANCY FEE WILL ALWAYS BE FOR ACCOUNT OF THE BENEFICIARY.

3) B/L MUST INDICATE NAME, ADDRESS AND TEL. NO. OF SHIPPING COMPANY AGENT IN SHANGHAI.

4) ONE SET OF NON－NEGOTIABLE DOCUMENTS MUST BE FAXED TO APPLICANT WITHIN 24 HOURS AFTER SHIPMENT. A CERTIFICATE TO THIS EFFECT IS REQUIRED.

INSTRUCTIONS TO NEGOTIATING/PAYING BANK:

1. UPON RECEIPT OF DOCUMENTS CONFORMING TO THE TERMS OF THIS CREDIT, WE WILL REMIT PROCEEDS AS PER YOUR INSTRUCTIONS.

2. DOCUMENTS MUST BE DISPATCHED DIRECTLY TO US AT DBS SHANGHAI BRANCH, Suite 2301, JF News Tower, 300 Han Kou Road, Shanghai 200001, China ATTN. TRADE SERVICES (IMPORT LC) IN TWO CONSECUTIVE REGISTERED AIRMAILS.

WE HEREBY ISSUE THIS DOCUMENTARY CREDIT IN YOUR FAVOUR. WE AGREE WITH DRAWERS, ENDORSERS, AND BONA FIDE HOLDERS OF DRAFTS DRAWN UNDER AND IN COMPLIANCE WITH THE TERMS AND CONDITIONS OF THIS CREDIT THAT THE SAME WOULD BE DULY HONORED IF NEGOTIATED/PAID WITHIN THE VALIDITY DATE OF THIS CREDIT. THE NEGOTIATING/PAYING BANK MUST ENDORSE THE AMOUNT NEGOTIATED/ PAID ON THE REVERSE OF THIS CREDIT.

THIS CREDIT IS SUBJECT TO THE UNIFORM CUSTOMS AND PRACTICES FOR DOCUMENTARY CREDITS ICC PUBLICATION NO. 500 (1993 REVISION) .

续表

```
= = = = = = = = = = = = = = = = = = = =END OF CREDIT= = = = = = = = = = = = = = = = = = = =
```
For The Development Bank of Singapore Limited, Shanghai Branch

GEORGE BROWN

FORM SERIAL NO. : BR 173720

2. 汇票（见表 14-6）

表 14-6   汇 票

No. 7502580124

Exchange for   US $418, 925. 52   Malaysia, May 25th, 2013

At   * * * * * * * * * * * * * * * *   sight of this First of exchange（Second of the same tenor and duly unpaid）, pay to the Order of NANKAI WORSTED SPINNING SDN. , BHD the sum of SAY U. S. DOLLARS FOUR HUNDRED EIGHTEEN THOUSAND NINE HUNDRED TWENTY-FIVE AND FIFTY-TWO CENTS ONLY

Drawn under   DBS BANK, SHANGHAI BRANCH

To:

Bank of Commerce Malaysia Berhad   NANKAI WORSTED SPINNING SDN. , BHD.

Kuala Lumpur Branch   LOT 20051, GONG BADAK INDUSTRIAL ESTATE

15 Lebuh Pantai   21300 KUALA LUMPUR, MALAYSIA

10300 Kuala Lumpur

Malaysia

3. 商业发票（见表 14-7）

表 14-7   商业发票

NANKAI WORSTED SPINNING SDN. , BHD.

LOT 20051, GONG BADAK INDUSTRIAL ESTATE 21300 KUALA LUMPUR, MALAYSIA TEL: 60-36-74855703 FAX: 60-36-74855724 E-MAIL ADDR: nankai@ hotmail. com	INVOICE	
	NO.	NK-CN063
CONSIGNED TO/FOR ACCOUNT RISK OF:	DATED AT KUALA LUMPUR: May 10th, 2013	
LIDA TRADING COMPANY LIMITED ADD: NO. 1267 EAST NANJING ROAD SHANGHAI, CHINA FAX: 021-64042588	REF. NO.	CONTRACT NO. YN-NK942
	TERMS: FOB KELANG	CREDIT NO. : 0016100293496
SHIPPED PER:	FROM: KELANG, MALAYSIA	TO: SHANGHAI, CHINA

MARKS & NOS.	DESCRIPTION OF GOODS	QUANTITY:	UNIT PRICE:	AMOUNT:
	100% Wool Hosiery Yarn			
NK (in diamond)	Art. No.		FOB	KELANG
SHANGHAI	2/48 NM, raw white in hank	6 480 KGS	@ US $ 11.20	US $ 72 576.00
MADE IN MALAYSIA	2/32 NM, raw white in hank	4 560 KGS	@ US $ 10.32	US $ 47 059.20
0016100293496-1	1/40 NM, raw white in cone	2 040 KGS	@ US $ 10.05	US $ 20 502.00
C/NO. 1-298			TOTAL:	US $ 140 137.20

WEIGHT & MEASUREMENT

CONDITION WEIGHT: 13 080 KGS

GROSS WEIGHT: 13 676 KGS

COMMERCIAL MOISTURE REGAIN: 10%

TOTAL MEASUREMENT * 54.166 M^3

ISSUED BY:

NANKAI WORSTED SPINNING SDN., BHD.

PLS REMIT TO OUR ACCOUNT

USD   140 137.20

A/C NO.:   2345678612345670

AT BANK OF COMMERCE MALAYSIA BERHAD

4. 装箱单（见表14-8）

表14-8   **装箱单**

NANKAI WORSTED SPINNING SDN. , BHD.

LOT 20051, GONG BADAK INDUSTRIAL ESTATE 21300 KUALA LUMPUR, MALAYSIA TEL：60-36-74855703 FAX：60-36-74855724 E-MAIL ADDR：nankai@hotmail.com	PACKING LIST
	NO. NK-CN063

CONSIGNED TO/FOR ACCOUNT RISK OF:	DATED AT KUALA LUMPUR: May 10th, 2001	
LIDA TRADING COMPANY LIMITED ADD：NO.1267 EAST NANJING ROAD SHANGHAI, CHINA FAX：021-64042588	REF. NO.	CONTRACT NO. YN-NK942
	TERMS: FOB KELANG	CREDIT NO. : 0016100293496
SHIPPED PER : s. s. BIN BO V. 911	FROM: KELANG, MALAYSIA	TO: SHANGHAI, CHINA

MARKS & NOS.	CARTON NO.	ITEMS:	QUANTITY:	GROSS WEIGHT:	NET WEIGHT:	MEASUREMENT:
NK SHANGHAI MADE IN MALAYSIA 0016100293496 C/NO. 1-298	1-135 136-230 231-298 298 CARTONS	2/48 NM 2/32 NM 1/40 NM	6480 KGS 4560 KGS 2040 KGS 13080 KGS	6750 KGS 4750 KGS 2176 KGS 13676 KGS	6480 KGS 4560 KGS 2040 KGS 13080 KGS	24.538 M^3 17.268 M^3 12.360 M^3 54.166 M^3

SIZE OF CARTONS: LENGTH：66CM；WIDTH：51CM；HEIGHT：54CM SPECIAL CONDITION OF PACKING：	SIGNED BY: NANKAI WORSTED SPINNING SDN. , BHD. MANAGER Paul N. Ayars
	Authorized signature

5. 提单（见表 14-9）

表 14-9 海运提单

BILL OF LADING FOR COMBINED TRANSPORT SHIPMENT OR PORT TO PORT SHIPMENT

Shipper： NANKAI WORSTED SPINNING SDN. , BHD. LOT 20051, GONG BADAK INDUSTRIAL ESTATE 21300 KUALA LUMPUR, MALAYSIA	B/L NO. : 3456789007 **MISC** Carrier： MALAYSIA INTERNATIONAL SHIPPING CORPORATION BERHAD
Consignee： TO ORDER OF DBS BANK SHANGHAI BRANCH	
Notify Party/Address LIDA TRADING COMPANY LIMITED ADD：NO. 1267 EAST NANJING ROAD SHANGHAI, CHINA FAX：021-64042588	Place of Receipt： (Applicable only when this document is used as a Combined Transport Bill of Lading) KUALA LUMPUR
Vessel and Voy. No. s. s. BIN BO V. 911	Place of Delivery： (Applicable only when this document is used as a Combined Transport Bill of Lading) SHANGHAI, CHINA
Port of Loading： PORT KELANG Port of Discharge： SHANGHAI	

Marks and Nos.	Number and kind of Packages；Description of Goods 100% Wool Hosiery Yarn 298 CARTONS	Gross Weight	Measurement
◇ NK ◇ SHANGHAI MADE IN MALAYSIA 0016100293496-1 C/NO. 1-298	FREIGHT PREPAID	13676 KGS	54. 166 M^3

SIZE/TYPE/CONTAINER # /TARE WGHT./GROSS WGHT./SEAL NUMBER / QUANTITY / STATUS

ON BOARD

ABOVE PARTICULARS AS DECLARED BY SHIPPER

* Total No. of Containers/Packages received by the Carrier ONE 40′FCL	RECEIVED by the Carrier from the Shipper in apparent good order and condition (unless other wise noted herein) the total number or quantity of Containers or other packages or units indicated*, stated by the Shipper to comprise the Goods specified above, for Carriage subject to all the terms hereof (INCLUDING THE TERMS OF THE CARRIER'S APPLICABLE TARIFF) from the Place of Receipt or the Port of Loading, whichever is applicable, to the Port of Discharge or the Place of Delivery, whichever is applicable. One original Bill of Lading must be surrendered duly endorsed in exchange for the Goods. In accepting this Bill of Lading the Merchant expressly accepts and agrees to all its terms, conditions and exceptions, whether printed, stamped or written, or otherwise incorporated, notwithstanding the non-signing of this Bill of Lading by the Merchant
* Movement	
* Freight and Charges (indicate whether prepaid or collect)：	
* Origin Inland Haulage Charge	
* Origin Terminal Handling/LCL Service Charge	Freight payable at： Place and Date of issue：

* Ocean Freight	Number of Original B/L: THREE（3）	May 22nd, 2013, KELANG
* Destination Terminal Handling/LCL Service Charge	For the Carrier: MISC AGENCIES SDN BND AS AGENT FOR THE CARRIER MALAYSIA INTERNATIONAL SHIPPING CORPORATION BERHAD As Agent（s）only	

6. 原产地证明书（见表 14-10）。

表 14-10 原产地证明书

Exporter（Name & Address） NANKAI WORSTED SPINNING SDN BHD LOT 20051, GONG BADAK INDUSTRIAL ESTATE 21300 KUALA LUMPUR, MALAYSIA	MTMA Certificate of Origin No. 28357202 CERTIFICATE OF ORIGIN
Consignee（Name, Address & Country） LIDA TRADING COMPANY LIMITED ADD: NO. 1267 EAST NANJING ROAD SHANGHAI, CHINA FAX: 021-64042588	
Notify Party（Name & Address） LIDA TRADING COMPANY LIMITED ADD: NO. 1267 EAST NANJING ROAD SHANGHAI, CHINA FAX: 021-64042588	ISSUED BY MALAYSIAN TEXTILE MANUFACTURERS ASSOCIATION

Vessel/Aircraft s. s. BIN BO V. 911	B/L Number/AWB Number 3 Originals+3 copies	Box #42, Wisma Selangor Dredging, 9th Floor, West Block. 142C, Jalan Ampang, 50450 Kuala Lumpur, Malaysia
Port of Loading Kelang	Date of Departure May 22nd, 2013	
Port/Airport of Discharge		
Final Destination Shanghai, China		Country of Origin of Goods: MALAYSIA

续表

Marks and Number of Packages	Description of Goods: number and kind of packages	H. S. Code	Quantity or Weight	No. and Date of Invoices
◇ NK				
	100% Wool Hosiery Yarm			
SHANGHAI MADE IN MALAYSIA 0016100293496-1 C/NO. 1-298	289 CARTONS ＊ ＊ ＊ ＊ ＊ ＊ ＊ ＊	5107. 1000	13 080 KGS	Invoice No. NK-CN063 dated May 10th, 2013

Certification: We hereby certify that the above, to the best of our knowledge and belief, to be correct and without prejudice.	Declaration by Exporter: The exporter of the abovementioned merchandise, hereby certify that I have the means of knowing and certify that the goods described in this certificate are of Malaysia origin.
Signature of Authorised Officer TAN CHENG CHOOL	Signature Paul Ayars
For & on behalf of Malaysian Textile Manufacturers Association	Signatory's Company
Designation Adm Executive	
Place, Date and Seal/Stamp of Certifying Authority KUALA LUMPUR May 11st, 2013	Place, Date and Seal/Stamp of the COMPANY KUALA LUMPUR May 10th, 2013

7. 检验证书（见表 14-11）

表 14-11   检验证书   No. : 05394098

Consignor: NANKAI WORSTED SPINNING SDN BHD LOT 20051, GONG BADAK INDUSTRIAL ESTATE 21300 KUALA LUMPUR, MALAYSIA	Issued by: MALAYSIA TEXTILE INSPECTION BUREAU Box # 40, Wisma Selangor Dredging, 6th Floor, West Block. 142C, Jalan Ampang, 50450 Kuala Lumpur, Malaysia CERTIFICATE OF INSPECTION
Consignee: LIDA TRADING COMPANY LIMITED ADD: NO. 1267 EAST NANJING ROAD SHANGHAI, CHINA FAX: 021-64042588	
Ship/Airline s. s. BIN BON V. 911	Date of departure: May 22nd, 2013
Port of loading: KELANG	Port of discharge: SHANGHAI

Marks & Brands	Number & kind of packages	Description of goods:	Net weight:
NK SHANGHAI MADE IN MALAYSIA 0016100293496-1 C/NO. 1-298	298 CARTONS	100% Wool Hosiery Yarn	13080KGS

I hereby certify that ____ the goods ____ specified above has/have been examined and found to the best of my knowledge.

Signature ____ Vivian Chin Jier ____ Authorized Officer

Date: May 14th, 2013

Producer:
Remarks:

（二）任务要求

在议付行审核你所提交的出口单据期间，新加坡发展银行大连分行转来信用证（0016100293496）项下的进口单据一套，系公司与马来西亚客户 NANKAI WORSTED SPINNING SND. BHD 达成的一笔进口业务的单据，请你本着"单证一致，单单相符"的原则，对这套单据进行认真的审核，写出你的审单意见。

（三）参考答案

经过单据审核，新加坡发展银行大连分行转来的信用证（0016100293496）项下的结汇单据存在如下问题：所有单据均未显示出该批货物系分批装运的第一批。此外，还有：

1. 汇票

（1）金额错误，应为该批金额，即 139 641.84 美元。

（2）金额大写错误，应为"SAY US DOLLARS ONE HUNDRED THIRTY NINE THOUSAND AND SIX HUNDRED FOURTY ONE ONLY"。

（3）收款人错误，应为议付银行，即"BANK OF COMMERCE MALAYSIA BERHAD，KUALA LUMPUR BRANCH"。

（4）出票条款中未按信用证要求显示信用证号码。

（5）受票人错误，应为开证行，即"DBS BANK DALIAN BRANCH"。

（6）未经出票人签字。

2. 商业发票

（1）货物描述不完整，缺少"as per Contract No. YN-NK942 dated April 1st, 2008"词句。

（2）未按信用证要求显示承运船名，即"S. S. BIN BO V. 911"。

（3）未按信用证要求显示出分批序号。

（4）货号 1/40NM 单价与信用证不符，应为 10.05 美元，而非 10.50 美元。

（5）未按信用证要求由受益人签署。

（6）2/32NM 的数量错误，此单货物的总金额错误，正确的数量是 4 512KGS，总金额是 USD139 641.84。

3. 装箱单

（1）合同号码与信用证及其他单据不符，应为"YN-NK942"，而非"YNN-NK942"。

（2）唛头与信用证及其他单据不符，应为"0016100293496-1"，而非"0016100293496"。

（3）价格术语与其他单据不符，应为"FOB KELANG"而非"FOB KELAN"。

（4）未按信用证要求显示每件包装（纸箱）的毛净重。

（5）2/32NM 的总数量、总净重错误，应为 4 512KGS。

4. 提单

（1）收货人有误，应为"To Order"，而非凭开证行指示。

（2）运费条款与信用证不符，应为"Freight Payable at Destination"，而非"Freight Prepaid"。

（3）未按信用证要求作相应的空白背书。

（4）未按信用证要求显示船公司在大连代理的名称、地址、联系方式。

5. 原产地证书

（1）货物描述与信用证及其他单据不符，应为"YARN"，而非"YARM"。

（2）包装件数与其他单据不符，应为 298 箱，而非 289 箱。

（3）总数量、总重量应为"13 032KGS"。

6. 检验证书

（1）承运船名与其他单据不符，应为"BIN BO"，而非"BIN BON"。

（2）净重与其他单据不符，应为 13 032KGS，而非 13 676KGS。

7. 其他

未按信用证要求出具受益人寄单证明。

五、实训考核方法

（一）根据相关信息编制、填制信用证分析单

（二）根据相关信息编制、填制出口货物信息明细表

（三）根据相关信息编制、填制已填制单据信息表

（四）根据相关信息编制信用证审单记录表

（五）审单并根据信用证不符点填制信用证审单记录表

综合实训 金喆公司出口案例

一、建交函写作

1. 基础资料

金喆公司（地址：中国大连中山路 1267 号，Address：NO. 1267 ZHONGSHAN ROAD, DALIAN, CHINA；电话（Tel）：0086 - 0411 - 84042525；传真（Fax）：0086 - 0411 - 84042588）于 1952 年成立，专营玩具和工艺品，现在已经成为中国重要的进出口公司之一。由于公司的产品质量高、价格优惠，因此在世界各地的客户中享有很高声誉。2013 年 2 月，公司从国际互联网上得知美国的 DRAGON TOY CO., LTD. 欲求购中国产的遥控赛车（Telecontrol Racing Car）。该美国公司的联系方式如下：

DRAGON TOY CO., LTD.

1180 CHURCH ROAD, NEW YORK,

PA 19446 U. S. A.

TEL：215-393-3920

FAX：215-393-3921

2. 任务要求

请参照上述基本情况，给对方发一封建立业务关系的正式信函，要求格式完整、正确，内容包括公司介绍、产品介绍等，并另寄产品目录及表达想与对方建立业务往来的热切愿望等（注意不要只是简单翻译）。

信函日期：2013 年 3 月 2 日。

二、出口报价核算

1. 基础资料

商品：遥控赛车；货号：18812。其具体内容见表1。

表1   **商品具体资料**

商品大类 玩具		
货号	品名	包装方式
18812	Telecontrol Racing Car	12 辆/纸箱
包装尺码	包装重量（毛/净）	含税采购成本
72cm×36cm×48cm	12kgs/9kgs	150 元/辆

出口退税率：9%。

国内费用：出口包装费15 元/纸箱；仓储费5 元/纸箱；一个20 英尺集装箱的其他国内费用：国内运杂费400 元，商检费550 元，报关费50 元，港口费600 元，其他费用1 400 元。

保险：按发票金额加成10%投保一切险和战争险，费率分别为0.6%和0.3%。

预期利润：报价的10%，付款方式是即期信用证。

2. 任务要求

请根据上述条件分别算出 FOBC3、CFRC3 及 CIFC3 的美元价格并列出详尽的计算过程（注意：计算过程中的数据保留四位小数，报价结果保留两位小数，1 美元=8.25 元人民币）。

三、草拟发盘函

1. 基础资料（询盘函）

DRAGON TOY CO., LTD.

1180 CHURCH ROAD, NEW YORK,

PA 19446 U. S. A.

TEL：215-393-3920   FAX：215-393-3921

DATE：02 March，2013
JINZHE TRADING CO.，LTD.
NO. 1267 ZHONGSHAN ROAD
DALIAN，CHINA
FAX：0411-84042588

Dear Sirs，

We have received your letter together with your catalogs. Having thoroughly studied the catalogs，we find that your Telecontrol Racing Cars Art. No. 18812，18814，18817 and 18819 are quite suitable for our market. We may need one 20′ FCL each for May，2009 delivery. Please kindly inform us if you are able to supply and quote us your most favorable price for the above goods on the basis of CIFC3 NEW YORK with details，including packing，shipment，insurance and payment.
Your immediate attention will be highly appreciated.
With best regards.

Yours faithfully，
DRAGON TOY CO.，LTD.
MANAGER
THEOBALD. TIAN

2. 任务要求

请根据客户来函要求，写一封发盘函，详细回答客户提出的问题，告知对方交易的基本条件，并敦促对方尽快做出决定，发盘有效期为3天。

交易的基本条件：

（1）保险：按发票金额加成10%投保一切险和战争险。

（2）支付方式：即期信用证。

（3）装运时间：5月底装运。

信函日期：2013年3月12日。

四、出口还价核算

根据 DRAGON TOY CO.，LTD. 的还价（见下面的"五、拟写还盘函"）计算

（小数请保留至 4 位，小于 1 时保留至 5 位，计算结果取小数点后 2 位）：

　　（1）货号 18812 出口的总利润额为多少元人民币？

　　（2）如果接受对方的价格，且公司又必须有 5% 的利润，在其他条件均无变化的前提下，我公司能接受的货号 18812 国内最高供货价格为每辆多少元人民币？

　　（3）再次报价：经与生产厂商协调，货号 18812 的供货价格下调至每辆 145 元，请根据新的供货价格再次报出货号 18812 的 CIFC3 价格，报价利润率是 8%。

五、拟写还盘函

1. 基础资料（还盘函）

DRAGON TOY CO. , LTD.

1180 CHURCH ROAD, NEW YORK, U. S. A.

TEL：215-393-3920　FAX：215-393-3921

DATE：12 March, 2013

JINZHE TRADING CO. , LTD.

NO. 1267 ZHONGSHAN ROAD

DALIAN, CHINA

FAX：0411-84042588

Dear Sirs,

We write to thank you for your offer of March 12, 2013. However after a careful study of your quotation, we find that your price seems to be on the high side. It will leave us with almost no profit to accept your price.

We appreciate the quality of your products and are glad to have the opportunity to do business with you. We suggest that you make some allowance on your price. For your reference, the highest prices we can accept are as follows：

ART. NO. 18812 USD19. 40 /PIECE CIFC3 NEW YORK 2 400 PIECES

ART. NO. 18814 USD20. 50 /PIECE CIFC3 NEW YORK 2 000 PIECES

ART. NO. 18817 USD21. 80 /PIECE CIFC3 NEW YORK 2 000 PIECES

ART. NO. 18819 USD22. 60 /PIECE CIFC3 NEW YORK 2 400 PIECES

Please take it into serious consideration and your early reply will be appreciated. Best regards！

Yours faithfully,

DRAGON TOY CO. , LTD.

MANAGER

THEOBALD. TIAN

2. 任务要求

根据客户的还盘以及所作的还价核算，草拟还盘函，主要内容如下：

（1）经与生产商多次联络，得知其供货价格已为最优惠价格。

（2）建议对方考虑我方产品的质量。

（3）对方的还盘无法接受，但出于开拓市场的考虑，首笔交易将尽力配合给予最优惠的报价。

（4）该发盘有效期 8 天。

信函日期：2013 年 3 月 22 日。

六、出口成交核算

请根据你与国外客户最终达成的交易条件，进行详细的出口核算，其中包括：

（1）购货总成本；

（2）实际采购成本；

（3）总退税收入；

（4）费用细目及总额（包括国内费用、海运费、保险费、佣金）；

（5）成交利润额和成交利润率。

注意：计算过程保留四位小数，最后结果保留两位小数。

七、出口合同签订

1. 基础资料（接受函）

DRAGON TOY CO. , LTD.

1180 CHURCH ROAD, NEW YORK, U. S. A.

TEL：215-393-3920　FAX：215-393-3921

DATE：27 March, 2013

JINZHE TRADING CO., LTD.

NO. 1267 ZHONGSHAN ROAD

DALIAN, CHINA

FAX：0411-84042588

Dear Sirs,

Your quotation of March 22 has been accepted and we are glad to place our order NO. Dragon 9701 as follows：

ART. NO. 18812 USD19. 88 /PIECE CIFC3 NEW YORK

ART. NO. 18814 USD20. 66 /PIECE CIFC3 NEW YORK

ART. NO. 18817 USD21. 94 /PIECE CIFC3 NEW YORK

ART. NO. 18819 USD23. 06 /PIECE CIFC3 NEW YORK

Other terms and conditions are the same as we agreed before.

As this is the very first transaction we have concluded, your cooperation would be very much appreciated. Please send us your sales confirmation in duplicate for counter-signing.

Best regards.

Yours faithfully,

DRAGON TOY CO., LTD.

MANAGER

THEOBALD. TIAN

2. 任务要求

（1）给国外客户寄出成交签约函，感谢对方的订单，说明随寄销售确认书，催促迅速会签合同，并希望信用证在 4 月 25 日前开到。

（2）请根据出口合同基本条款的要求和双方在信中确定的条件制作销售确认书，要求条款内容全面、具体。

合同日期：2013 年 4 月 1 日。

信函日期：2013 年 4 月 1 日。

合同号码：JZ-DRGSC01。

八、审核信用证

1. 基础资料

（1）会签函。

DRAGON TOY CO. , LTD.
1180 CHURCH ROAD, NEW YORK, U. S. A.
TEL: 215-393-3920   FAX: 215-393-3921

DATE: April 6, 2013

JINZHE TRADING CO. , LTD.

NO. 1267 ZHONGSHAN ROAD

DALIAN, CHINA

FAX: 0411-84042588

Dear Sirs,

We have duly received and signed your Sales Confirmation NO. JZ-DRGSC01 and are sending back one copy for your file as requested.

Meanwhile the relevant L/C has been opened through Chemical Bank New York and we are certain that it will reach you in a few days. Please arrange shipment upon receipt of it. We hope the first transaction between us will turn out to be successful.

Best regards.

Yours faithfully,

DRAGON TOY CO. , LTD.

MANAGER

THEOBALD. TIAN

（2）会签合同。

SALES CONFIRMATION

S/C No. : JZ-DRGSC01

Date: April 1, 2013

The Seller: JINZHE TRADING CO. , LTD.

Address: NO. 1267 ZHONGSHAN ROAD

          DALIAN, CHINA

The Buyer: DRAGON TOY CO. , LTD.

Address: 1180 CHURCH ROAD

          NEW YORK PA 19446 U. S. A.

Item No.	Commodity & Specifications	Unit	Quantity	Unit Price (USD)	AMOUNT (USD)
TELECONTROL RACING CAR				CIFC3 NEW YORK	
1	ART. 18812	PIECE	2 400	19. 88	47 712. 00
2	ART. 18814	PIECE	2 000	20. 66	41 320. 00
3	ART. 18817	PIECE	2 000	21. 94	43 880. 00
4	ART. 18819	PIECE	2 400	23. 06	55 344. 00
TOTAL					188 256. 00

TOTAL CONTRACT VALUE:
SAY US DOLLARS ONE HUNDRED EIGHTY-EIGHT THOUSAND TWO HUNDRED AND FIFTY-SIX ONLY.

PACKING:	ART. NO. 18812 & 18819 TO BE PACKED IN CARTONS OF 12 PIECES EACH ART. NO. 18814 & 18817 TO BE PACKED IN CARTONS OF 20 PIECES EACH ALL PRODUCTS IN FOUR 20′ CONTAINERS.
TERMS OF SHIPMENT:	SHIPMENT IN MAY 2013 AFTER RECEIVING THE RELEVANT LETTER OF CREDIT WITH PARTIAL SHIPMENT AND TRANSSHIPMENT ALLOWED.
PORT OF LOADING & DESTINATION:	FROM DALIAN CHINA TO NEW YORK U. S. A.
PAYMENT:	THE BUYER SHALL OPEN AN IRREVOCABLE L/C IN FAVOR OF THE SELLER BEFORE APR. 15TH, 2009. THE SAID L/C SHALL BE AVAILABLE BY DRAFT AT SIGHT FOR FULL INVOICE VALUE AND REMAIN VALID FOR NEGOTIATION IN CHINA FOR 15 DAYS AFTER SHIPMENT.
INSURANCE:	TO BE COVERED BY THE SELLER FOR 110% OF TOTAL INVOICE VALUE AGAINST ALL RISKS AND WAR RISK AS PER THE OCEAN MARINE CARGO CLAUSES OF THE PEOPLE′S INSURANCE COMPANY OF CHINA, DATED JAN. 1ST, 1981.

Confirmed by:

THE SELLER THE BUYER
JINZHE TRADING CO. , LTD. DRAGON TOY CO. , LTD.
GRACE ZHANG THEOBALD. TIAN

Remarks:

1. The Buyer shall have the covering letter of credit which should reach the Seller 30 days before shipment, failing which the Seller reserves the right to rescind without further notice, or to regard as still valid whole or any part of this contract not fulfilled by the Buyer, or to lodge a claim for losses thus sustained, if any.

2. In case of any discrepancy in Quality/Quantity, claim should be filed by the Buyer

within 30 days after the arrival of the goods at port of destination; while for quantity discrepancy, claim should be filed by the Buyer within 15 days after the arrival of the goods at port of destination.

3. For transactions concluded on C. I. F. basis, it is understood that the insurance amount will be for 110% of the invoice value against the risks specified in the Sales Confirmation. If additional insurance amount or coverage is required, the Buyer must have the consent of the Seller before Shipment, and the additional premium is to be borne by the Buyer.

4. The Seller shall not hold liable for non-delivery or delay in delivery of the entire lot or a portion of the goods hereunder by reason of natural disasters, war or other causes of Force Majeure. However, the Seller shall notify the Buyer as soon as possible and furnish the Buyer within 15 days by registered airmail with a certificate issued by the China Council for the Promotion of International Trade attesting such event (s).

5. All deputies arising out of the performance of, or relating to this contract, shall be settled through negotiation. In case no settlement can be reached through negotiation, the case shall then be submitted to the China International Economic and Trade Arbitration Commission for arbitration in accordance with its arbitral rules. The arbitration shall take place in DALIAN. The arbitral award is final and binding upon both parties.

6. The Buyer is requested to sign and return one copy of this contract immediately after receipt of the same. Objection, if any, should be raised by the Buyer within it is understood that the Buyer has accepted the terms and conditions of this contract.

7. Special conditions: These shall prevail over all printed terms in case of any conflict.

（3）跟单信用证通知书。

ADDRESS: 50 HUQIU ROAD.　　　　中国银行
CABLE: CHUNG KUO　　　　　　BANK OF CHINA
TELEX: 3062 BOCSH E CN

跟单信用证通知书

SWIFT: BKCHCMBJ30　　　　Notification of Documentary Credit

DATE: 2013/04/20

To: 致: JINZHE TRADING CO., LTD NO. 1267 ZHONGSHAN ROAD, DALIAN, CHINA	WHEN CORRESPONDING PLEASE QUOTE OUR REF. NO. :
ISSUING BANK Chemical Bank New York. 55 Wall Street, Room 1702, New York, New York 10041 U. S. A	Transmitting through 转递行

续表

L/C NO. 信用证号 DRG-JZLC01 DATE 开证日期 APRIL 14TH 2013	Amount 金额 USD 188 256. 00

Dear sirs，敬启者

We have pleasure in advising you that we have received from the a/m bank a（n）

兹通知贵公司，我行已收自上述银行开来的

（ ） pre-advising of	预先通知	（ ） mail confirmation of	证实书
（ ） telex issuing	电传开立	（ ） ineffective	未生效
（x） original	正本	（ ） duplicate	副本

Letter of credit， contents of which are as per attached sheet（s）. This advice and the attached sheet（s）must accompany the relative documents when presented for negotiation.

信用证一份，现随附通知。贵公司交单时，请将本通知书及随附的单据一并提示。

（x） Please note that this advice does not constitute our confirmation of the above L/C nor does it convey any engagement or obligation on our part.

本通知书不构成我行对此信用证之保兑及其他任何责任。

（ ） Please note that we have added our confirmation to the above L/C，negotiation is restricted to ourselves only.

上述信用证已由我行加具保兑，并限向我行交单。

This L/C consists of two sheets，including the covering letter and attachment.

本信用证连同面函及附件共 2 张。

If you find any terms and conditions in the L/C which you are unable to comply with and（or）any error（s），it is suggested that you contact applicant directly for necessary amendment（s）as to avoid any difficulties which may arise when documents are presented. 如本信用证中有无法办到的条款及/或错误，请直接与开证申请人联系，进行必要的修改，以排除交单时可能发生的问题。	FOR BANK OF CHINA, DALIAN BRANCH 中国银行大连分行 信用证通知章 Yours faithfully

（4）信用证。

34127 B BOCSH CN

6229

1705 03/25 04803089 TCH0063

0325004658

ZCZC

FROM：CHEMICAL BANK NEW YORK

OUR REF. ：NY980520004658001T01

TO：BANK OF CHINA DALIAN BRANCH

　　　50 HUQIU ROAD, DALIAN

　　　THE PEOPLE'S REP. OF CHINA

FOR USD 188 256.00 ON DATE 14/04/2013

PLEASE ADVISE BENEFICIARY OF THE FOLLOWING IRREVOCABLE LETTER OF CREDIT

ISSUED BY US IN THEIR FAVOR SUBJECT TO UCP600：

DOCUMENTARY CREDIT NUMBER：DRG-JZLC01

DATE AND PLACE OF EXPIRY：June 10th 2013, IN U.S.A.

APPLICANT：DRAGON TOY CO. , LTD. 1180 CHURCH ROAD, NEW YORK, PA 19446 U.S.A.

BENEFICIARY：JINZHE　CO. , LTD. NO. 1267　ZHONGSHAN　ROAD, DALIAN, CHINA

AMOUNT：USD 188 256.00

SAY UNITED STATES DOLLARS ONE HUNDRED AND EIGHTY EIGHT THOUSAND TWO HUNDRED AND FIFTY SIX ONLY.

AVAILABLE WITH：ANY BANK

BY：NEGOTIATION OF BENEFICIARY'S DRAFT（S）AT 30 DAYS' SIGHT DRAWN ON CHEMICAL BANK NEW YORK, ACCOMPANIED BY THE DOCUMENTS INDICATED HEREIN.

COVERING SHIPMENT OF：

COMMODITY ART. NO. QUANTITY

TELECONTROL RACING CAR

18812　　2 000 PIECES

18814　　2 000 PIECES

18817　　2 000 PIECES

18818　　2 000 PIECES

SHIPPING TERMS：CIF NEW YORK

SHIPPING MARK：JZ-DRGSC01/DRAGON TOY/NEW YORK/NO. 1-UP

DOCUMENTS REQUIRED：

— 3 COPIES OF COMMERCIAL INVOICE SHOWING VALUE IN U. S. DOLLARS AND INDICATING L/C NO. AND CONTRACT NO.

— 2COPIES OF PACKING LIST SHOWING GROSS/NET WEIGHT AND MEASUREMENT OF EACH CARTON.

— CERTIFICATE OF ORIGIN IN TRIPLICATE ISSUED BY CHINA CHAMBER OF INTERNATIONAL COMMERCE.

— 2 COPIES OF INSURANCE POLICY OR CERTIFICATE ENDORSED IN BLANK FOR THE INVOICE VALUE OF THE GOODS PLUS 110% COVERING ALL RISKS AND WAR RISK AS PER AND SUBJECT TO OCEAN MARINE CARGO CLAUSES OF THE PEOPLE'S INSURANCE COMPANY OF CHINA DATED 1/1/1981.

— 3/3 SET AND ONE COPY OF CLEAN ON BOARD OCEAN BILLS OF LADING MADE OUT TO ORDER OF SHIPPER AND BLANK ENDORSED MARKED FREIGHT PREPAID AND NOTIFY APPLICANT.

PARTIAL SHIPMENTS：PERMITTED

TRANSSHIPMENTS：PERMITTED

SHIPMENT FROM：DALIAN，CHINA　　TO：NEW YORK，U. S. A

NOT LATER THAN：MAY 31，2013

DOCUMENTS MUST BE PRESENTED WITHIN 15 DAYS AFTER SHIPMENT，BUT WITHIN VALIDITY OF THE LETTER OF CREDIT.

INSTRUCTIONS TO THE PAYING/ACCEPTING /NEGOTIATING BANK

NEGOTIATING BANK IS TO FORWARD ALL DOCUMENTS IN ONE AIRMAIL TO CHEMICAL BANK NEW YORK，55 WALL STREET，ROOM 1702 ，NEW YORK，NEW YORK 10041 U. S. A. ATTN：LETTER OF CREDIT DEPARTMENT.

END OF MESSAGE

NN/

62814 CBC VW

（WRU）

34127 B BOCSH CN

NNNN

2. 任务要求

请根据审证的一般原则和方法对收到的信用证进行认真细致的审核，列明信用证存在的问题并陈述要求改证的理由。

九、修改信用证

根据你的审证结果草拟改证函,要求列明不符点,并清晰告知客户如何进行修改。信函日期:2013 年 4 月 25 日。

十、托运订舱

1. 基础资料(改证函)

DRAGON TOY CO. , LTD.

1180 CHURCH ROAD , NEW YORK , U. S. A.

TEL:215-393-3920   FAX:215-393-3921

DATE:28 April,2013

JINZHE TRADING CO. , LTD.

NO. 1267 ZHONGSHAN ROAD ,

DALIAN , CHINA

FAX:0411-84042588

Dear Sirs,

We have received your letter of L/C amendment. We are sorry to hear that the relevant L/C contains several discrepancies. Anyhow, after careful study of your letter, we have instructed our bank to make the necessary amendment accordingly. We think you will receive the L/C Amendment in due time, and we are sure that you will have fully prepared for the shipment.

We are looking forward to receiving your shipping advice.

Yours faithfully,

DRAGON TOY CO. , LTD.

MANAGER

THEOBALD. TIAN

跟单信用证修改通知书

中国银行

BANK OF CHINA DALIAN BRANCH

ADDRESS：50 HUQIU ROAD

CABLE：CHUNG KUO

TELEX：33062 BOCSH E CN

SWIFT：BKCHCMBJ300

FAX：0411-83232071

YEAR/MONTH/DAY

跟单信用证修改通知书

Notification of Amendment to Documentary Credit

2013/04/29

ISSUING BANK Chemical Bank New York 55 Wall Street，Room 1702，New York，U. S. A.	DATE OF THE AMENDMENT APRIL 28，2013
BENEFICIARY JINZHE TRADING CO. ，LTD NO. 1267 ZHONGSHAN ROAD DALIAN，CHINA	APPLICANT DRAGON TOY CO. ，LTD. 1180 CHURCH ROAD NEW YORK，PA 19446 U. S. A

L/C NO. DRG-JZLC01	DATED APRIL 14TH 2013	THIS AMENDMENT IS TO BE CONSIDERED AS PART OF THE ABOVE MENTIONED CREDIT AND MUST BE ATTACHED THERETO.

Dear sirs,

We have pleasure in advising you that we have received from the above mentioned bank an amendment to Documentary Credit No. DRG-JZLC01 contents of which are as follows：

-The place of expiry：In China，instead of"In U. S. A. ".

-The date of the expiry should be June 15，2013，instead of"June 10，2013".

-The draft(s)should be sight draft(s)instead of"at 30 days sight".

-The article number of the goods is"18819"instead of"18818".

-The insurance value should be total invoice value plus 10% instead of"plus 110%".

-The quantity of ART NO. 18812 & 18819 should be"2 400 pieces"instead of"2 000 pieces".

-The beneficiary should be JINZHE TRADING CO. ，LTD. ，instead of JINZHE CO. LTD.

ALL OTHER TERMS AND CONDITIONS REMAIN UNCHANGED.

THE ABOVE MENTIONED DOCUMENTARY CREDIT IS SUBJECT TO THE UNIFORM CUSTOMS AND PRACTICE FOR DOCUMENTARY CREDITS（2006 REVISION，INTERNATIONAL CHAMBER OF COMMERCE，PUBLICATION NO. 600）

PLEASE ADVISE THE BENEFICIARY：	ADVISING BANK'S NOTIFICATIONS：
JINZHE TRADING CO. ，LTD	CHU KONG HOU

2. 任务要求

在收到跟单信用证修改通知书后,公司即开始安排出口货物的装运事宜,首先要向船公司订舱。订舱文件主要包括出口货物订舱委托书、商业发票、装箱单(请根据订舱单据的填制要求认真填写)。

公司编号	公司开户银行	银行账号	INVOICE NO.
BH01LD	中国人民银行	4784939302	JZ-DRGINV01

出口货物订舱委托书日期:5 月 9 日。

商业发票日期:5 月 9 日。

十一、出口报关

1. 基础资料(配舱回单)

配舱回单见表 2。

表 2 　　　　　　　　　　　　　　配舱回单

Shipper(发货人)JINZHE TRADING CO.,LTD. NO.1267 ZHONGSHAN ROAD, DALIAN,CHINA		D/R No.(编号) JZ-DRGBL01
Consignee(收货人) TO ORDER		
Notify Party(通知人) DRAGON TOY CO.,LTD. 1180 CHURCH ROAD,NEW YORK, PA 19446 U.S.A.		配舱回单
Pre-carriage by (前程运输)	Place of Receipt (收货地点) DALIAN CY	
Vessel (船名) CHENG FEN	Voy. No. (航次) V.208	Port of Loading (装货港) DALIAN
Port of Discharge (卸货港) NEW YORK	Place of Delivery (交货地点)	Final Destination for the Merchant's Reference(目的地)

续表

Container No. （集装箱号）	Marks & Nos. （标志与号码）	Nos. and Kinds of Packages （包装件数与种类）	Description of Goods （货名）	Gross Weight（kg） 毛重（千克）	Measurements（m³） 尺码（立方米）
57233331 57233332 57233333 57233334	JZ–DRGSC01 DRAGON TOY NEW YORK NO. 1–600	4 CONTAINERS 600 CTNS	TELECO- NTROL RACING CAR	9 200KGS	99. 533m³

| Total Number of Containers or Packages（In Words）
集装箱数或件数合计（大写） | SAY SIX HUNDRED CARTONS ONLY | | | | |

Freight & Charges （运费与附加费）		Revenue Tons （运费吨）	RATE （运费率）	Prepaid （运费预付）	Collect （运费到付）
Ex. Rate： （兑换率）	Prepaid at（预付地点） DALIAN Total Prepaid（预付总额） USD3 900		Payable at （到付地点）	Place of Issue（签发地点） DALIAN	
			No. of Original B（s）/L（正本提单份数） THREE		

Service Type on Receiving CY	Service Type on Delivery CY	提单签发：
可否转船：YES	可否分批：YES	
装期：31–May–13	效期：15–Jun–13	孙浩博
金额：USD 188 256. 00		
制单日期：11–May–13		COSCO DALIAN SHIPPING CO. ,LTD.

2. 任务要求

出口商在订妥舱位收到配舱回单后，必须向海关办理货物的申报出口手续。报关文件主要包括出口货物报关单、商业发票和装箱单。

请根据出口货物报关单的填制要求认真填写。

出口日期：5月20日。

申报及出单日期：5月12日。

十二、投保装船

1. 基础资料（装货单）

装货单见表3。

表3 <center>装货单</center>

Shipper（发货人） JINZHE TRADING CO., LTD. NO. 1267 ZHONGSHAN ROAD, DALIAN, CHINA	D/R No.（编号） JZ-DRGBL01
Consignee（收货人） TO ORDER	装货单
Notify Party（通知人） DRAGON TOY CO., LTD. 1180 CHURCH ROAD, NEW YORK, PA 19446 U. S. A.	

Pre-carriage by （前程运输）	Place of Receipt （收货地点） DALIAN CY		

Vessel （船名） CHENG FEN	Voy. No. （航次） V. 208	Port of Loading （装货港） DALIAN	

Port of Discharge （卸货港） NEW YORK	Place of Delivery （交货地点）	Final Destination for the Merchant's Reference（目的地）

Container No. （集装箱号）	Marks & Nos. （标志与号码）	Nos. and Kinds of Packages （包装件数与种类）	Description of Goods （货名）	Gross Weight （kg） 毛重（千克）	Measurements （m³） 尺码（立方米）
57233331 57233332	JZ-DRGSC01	4 CONTAINERS 600 CTNS		9 200KGS	99. 533m³
57233333	DRAGON TOY		TELECO- NTROL RACING CAR		
57233334	NEW YORK NO. 1-600		实际装船日 （On board date）		2013-5-20

Total Number of Containers or Packages(In Words) 集装箱数或件数合计(大写)	SAY SIX HUNDRED CARTONS ONLY				
	Freight & Charges （运费与附加费）	Revenue Tons （运费吨）	RATE （运费率）	Prepaid （运费预付）	Collect （运费到付）
Ex. Rate： （兑换率）	Prepaid at(预付地点) DALIAN Total Prepaid(预付总额) USD3 900		Payable at (到付地点)	Place of Issue(签发地点) DALIAN	
			No. of Original B(s)/L(正本提单份数) THREE		
Service Type on Receiving CY	Service Type on Delivery CY	中华人民共和国海关 验讫放行			
可否转船：YES	可否分批：YES				
装期：31-May-13	效期：15-Jun-13				
金额：USD 188 256.00					
制单日期：16-May-13					

2. 任务要求

（1）投保。以 CIF 条件成交的出口货物订妥舱位（收到配舱回单后）、向海关申报出口的同时，应向保险公司办理投保手续。请你根据投保单的基本规定认真填写出口货物投保单。

（2）拟写装船通知。出口货物在海关验讫放行（即收到盖有海关验讫放行章的装货单）后，即可办理货物的装运手续；与此同时，你作为出口商应向进口商发出货物装运的通知。装运通知的内容主要包括：合同号码、货物名称、货物金额、货物数量、包装件数、承运船名、运输航次、提单号码。

如果信用证中对装船通知有具体规定，则应根据信用证规定的时间和内容及时发出。

投保日期：2013 年 5 月 15 日。

信函日期：2013 年 5 月 15 日。

十三、出口单据制作

1. 基础资料（海运出口货物承保回执）

海运出口货物承保回执见表 4。

表4

海运出口货物承保回执

(1) 保险人: 中国人民保险公司	(2) 被保险人: JINZHE TRADING CO., LTD.
(3) 保单号次: JZ-DRGBD01	(4) 保单日期: 18-May-13

(5) 标记: AS PER INV. JZ-DRGINV01	(6) 包装及数量: 600 CARTONS	(7) 保险货物项目: TELECONTROL RACING CAR	(8) 保险货物金额: USD 207 082. 00

(9) 总保险金额(大写):

SAY US DOLLARS TWO HUNDRED AND SEVEN THOUSAND AND EIGHTY TWO ONLY.

(10) 运输工具(船名、航次): CHENG FEN V. 208	(11) 装运港: DALIAN	(12) 目的港: NEW YORK

(13) 投保险别: ALL RISKS AND WAR RISKS AS PER CIC OF P. I. C. C. DATED1/1/1981	(14) 保险代理: GODWIN INSURANCE COMPANY P. O. BOX 17764 NEW YORK, U. S. A. FAX: 215-393-8576
(15) 赔付地点: DESTINATION IN U. S. A.	中国人民保险公司大连分公司 THE PEOPLE'S INSURANCE COMPANY OF CHINA DALIAN BRANCH 郭 昕 General Manager
(16) 应缴保费: 1 863. 73(美元)	

2. 任务要求

根据出口单据制作的要求及国外银行开来的信用证和修改书中的具体规定,缮制全套出口单据。

十四、单据审核

1. 基础资料

信用证见表5。

表5   信用证

DBS BANK   ORIGINAL

SHANGHAI BRANCH

Suite 2301, JF News Tower, 300 Han Kou Road, Shanghai 200001 People's Republic of China Tel: 86-21-5618838 Telex: 30436 DBSSH CN Fax: 86-21-5618711	IRREVOCABLE　　　　　　　NUMBER DOCUMENTARY CREDIT　　0016100293496 PLACE AND DATE OF ISSUE: Shanghai, April 10th, 2013 DATE AND PLACE OF EXPIRY Aug. 15th, 2001, Malaysia
APPLICANT LIDA TRADING COMPANY LIMITED ADD: NO. 1267 EAST NANJING ROAD 　　　SHANGHAI, CHINA FAX: 021-64042588	BENEFICIARY NANKAI WORSTED SPINNING SDN. , BHD. ADD: LOT 20051, GONG BADAK 　　　INDUSTRIAL ESTATE 21300 　　　KUALA LUMPUR, MALAYSIA
ADVISING BANK: BANK OF COMMERCE MALAYSIA BERHAD KUALA LUMPUR BRANCH 15 LEBUH PANTAI 10300 KUALA LUMPUR MALAYSIA	AMOUNT: *** USD ******** 418, 925. 52 **** * SAY US DOLLARS FOUR HUNDRED AND EIGHTEEN THOUSAND NINE HUNDRED AND TWENTY FIVE POINT FIFTY-TWO * CREDIT AVAILABLE WITH: BANK OF COMMERCE MALAYSIA BERHAD * BY: NEGOTIATION
PARTIAL SHIPMENTS:　　ALLOWED TRANSSHIPMENT:　　ALLOWED SHIPPED FROM:　　KELANG, MALAYSIA SHIPPED TO:　　SHANGHAI, CHINA LATEST SHIPMENT　　July 31st, 2013	AGAINST PRESENTATION OF THE DOCUMENTS DETAILED HEREIN AND OF YOUR DRAFTS IN DUPLICATE　　AT SIGHT DRAWN ON: DBS BANK, SHANGHAI BRANCH * BEARING OUR DOCUMENTARY CREDIT NO.

DOCUMENTS REQUIRED:

01 FULL SET OF CLEAN ON BOARD BILLS OF LADING MADE OUT TO ORDER, ENDORSED IN BLANK MARKED 'FREIGHT PAYABLE AT DESTINATION' AND NOTIFY APPLICANT.

02 PACKING LIST IN 3 ORIGINAL/S AND 3 COPY/IES, INDICATING CONTRACT NUMBER, SHIPPING MARKS, TOTAL PACKAGES, GROSS AND NET WEIGHT OF EACH PACKAGE AND PACKAGE NUMBER FOR EACH SPECIFICATION OR ITEM.

03 YOUR SIGNED COMMERCIAL INVOICE IN 3 ORIGINAL/S AND 3 COPY/IES, INDICATING CONTRACT NUMBER, SHIPPING MARKS, NAME OF CARRYING VESSEL, NUMBER OF THE L/C AND SHIPMENT NUMBER IN CASE OF PARTIAL SHIPMENT.

04 CERTIFICATE OF INSPECTION IN TRIPLICATE ISSUED BY MALAYSIA TEXTILE INSPECTION BUREAU.

05 CERTIFICATE OF ORIGIN ISSUED BY GOVERNMENT AUTHOR ITY.

MERCHANDISE DESCRIPTION:

100% Wool Hosiery Yarn Art. No. 2/48nm, raw white in hank 19440kgs@ US＄11.20 Art. No. 2/32 nm, raw white in hank 13536kgs@ US＄10.32 Art. No. 1/40nm, raw white in cone 6120kgs@ US ＄10.05. as per Contract No. YN-NK942 dated April 1st, 2013

The goods are dispatched in three equal monthly lots during May/June/July, documents of which should be the same.

SPECIAL INSTRUCTIONS:

1) ALL BANK CHARGES OUTSIDE CHINA INCLUDING REIMBURSEMENT COMMISSIONS ARE FOR BENEFICIARY'S ACCOUNT.

2) USD35.00 WILL BE CHARGED FOR EACH SET OF DISCREPANT DOCUMENTS PRESENTED. THIS DISCREPANCY FEE WILL ALWAYS BE FOR ACCOUNT OF THE BENEFICIARY.

3) B/L MUST INDICATE NAME, ADDRESS AND TEL. NO. OF SHIPPING COMPANY AGENT IN SHANGHAI.

4) ONE SET OF NON-NEGOTIABLE DOCUMENTS MUST BE FAXED TO APPLICANT WITHIN 24 HOURS AFTER SHIPMENT. A CERTIFICATE TO THIS EFFECT IS REQUIRED.

INSTRUCTIONS TO NEGOTIATING/PAYING BANK:

1. UPON RECEIPT OF DOCUMENTS CONFORMING TO THE TERMS OF THIS CREDIT, WE WILL REMIT PROCEEDS AS PER YOUR INSTRUCTIONS.

2. DOCUMENTS MUST BE DISPATCHED DIRECTLY TO US AT DBS SHANGHAI BRANCH, Suite 2301, JF News Tower, 300 Han Kou Road, Shanghai 200001, China ATTN. TRADE SERVICES (IMPORT LC) IN TWO CONSECUTIVE REGISTERED AIRMAILS.

WE HEREBY ISSUE THIS DOCUMENTARY CREDIT IN YOUR FAVOUR. WE AGREE WITH DRAWERS, ENDORSERS, AND BONA FIDE HOLDERS OF DRAFTS DRAWN UNDER AND IN COMPLIANCE WITH THE TERMS AND CONDITIONS OF THIS CREDIT THAT THE SAME WOULD BE DULY HONORED IF NEGOTIATED/PAID WITHIN THE VALIDITY DATE OF THIS CREDIT. THE NEGOTIATING/PAYING BANK MUST ENDORSE THE AMOUNT NEGOTIATED/ PAID ON THE REVERSE OF THIS CREDIT.

THIS CREDIT IS SUBJECT TO THE UNIFORM CUSTOMS AND PRACTICES FOR DOCUMENTARY CREDITS ICC PUBLICATION NO. 600 (2006 REVISION).

═══════════════ END OF CREDIT ═══════════════

For The Development Bank of Singapore Limited, Shanghai Branch

GEORGE BROWN

FORM SERIAL NO.: BR 173720

汇票见表6。

表6   汇票

　　　No. 7502580124

Exchange for　　　　US＄418，925.52　　　　　　　　Malaysia，May 25th，2013

　　At　　＊＊＊＊＊＊＊＊＊＊＊＊＊＊＊＊　sight of this First of exchange（Second of the

same tenor and duly unpaid），pay to the Order of NANKAI WORSTED SPINNING SDN.，BHD the sum

of SAY US DOLLARS FOUR HUNDRED AND EIGHTEEN THOUSAND NINE HUNDRED TWENTY-

FIVE AND FIFTY-TWO CENTS ONLY.

Drawn under　　DBS BANK，SHANGHAI BRANCH

To：

Bank of Commerce Malaysia Berhad　　NANKAI WORSTED SPINNING SDN.，BHD.

Kuala Lumpur Branch　　　　　　　　LOT 20051，GONG BADAK INDUSTRIAL ESTATE

15 Lebuh Pantai　　　　　　　　　　21300 KUALA LUMPUR，MALAYSIA

10300 Kuala Lumpur

Malaysia

商业发票见表7。

表7   商业发票

　　　　　NANKAI WORSTED SPINNING SDN.，BHD.

LOT 20051，GONG BADAK INDUSTRIAL ESTATE 21300

KUALA LUMPUR，MALAYSIA

TEL：60-36-74855703　　FAX：60-36-74855724

E-MAIL ADDR：nankai@ hotmail. com

	INVOICE	
	NO.　　NK-CN063	
CONSIGNED TO/FOR ACCOUNT RISK OF：	DATED AT KUALA LUMPUR： May 10th，2013	
LIDA TRADING COMPANY LIMITED	REF. NO.	CONTRACT NO.
ADD：NO. 1267 EAST NANJING ROAD		YN-NK942
SHANGHAI，CHINA	TERMS：	CREDIT NO. ：
FAX：021-64042588	FOB KELANG	0016100293496
	FROM：	TO：
SHIPPED PER：		
	KELANG，MALAYSIA	SHANGHAI，CHINA

续表

MARKS & NOS.	DESCRIPTION OF GOODS	QUANTITY	UNIT PRICE	AMOUNT
NK	100% Wool Hosiery Yarn Art. No.		FOB	KELANG
SHANGHAI	2/48 NM, raw white in hank	6 480 KGS	@ US $ 11.20	US $ 72 576.00
MADE IN MALAYSIA	2/32 NM, raw white in hank	4 560 KGS	@ US $ 10.32	US $ 47 059.20
0016100293496-1	1/40 NM, raw white in cone	2 040 KGS	@ US $ 10.05	US $ 20 502.00
C/NO. 1-298			TOTAL:	US $ 140 137.20

WEIGHT & MEASUREMENT CONDITION WEIGHT: 13 080 KGS GROSS WEIGHT: 13 676 KGS COMMERCIAL MOISTURE REGAIN: 10% TOTAL MEASUREMENT: 54.166 M³	ISSUED BY: NANKAI WORSTED SPINNING SDN., BHD.
PLS REMIT TO OUR ACCOUNT USD 140 137.20 A/C NO.: 2345678612345670 AT BANK OF COMMERCE MALAYSIA BERHAD	

装箱单见表8。

表 8   装箱单

NANKAI WORSTED SPINNING SDN. , BHD.

LOT 20051，GONG BADAK INDUSTRIAL ESTATE 21300

KUALA LUMPUR，MALAYSIA

TEL：60-36-74855703   FAX：60-36-74855724

E-MAIL ADDR：nankai@ hotmail. com

	PACKING LIST
	NO. NK-CN063

CONSIGNED TO/FOR ACCOUNT RISK OF:	DATED AT KUALA LUMPUR： May 10th, 2013	

LIDA TRADING COMPANY LIMITED
ADD：NO. 1267 EAST NANJING ROAD
   SHANGHAI, CHINA
   FAX：021-64042588
	REF. NO.	CONTRACT NO.
		YN-NK942

	TERMS： FOB KELANG	CREDIT NO. : 0016100293496
SHIPPED PER： s. s. BIN BO V. 911	FROM： KELANG, MALAYSIA	TO： SHANGHAI, CHINA

MARKS & NOS.	CARTON NO.	ITEMS	QUANTITY	GROSS WEIGHT	NET WEIGHT	MEASUREMENT
◇ NK ◇ SHANGHAI MADE INMALAYSIA 0016100293496 C/NO. 1-298	1-135 136-230 231-298 298 CARTONS	2/48 NM 2/32 NM 1/40 NM	6 480 KGS 4 560 KGS 2 040 KGS 13 080 KGS	6 750 KGS 4 750 KGS 2 176 KGS 13 676 KGS	6 480 KGS 4 560 KGS 2 040 KGS 13 080 KGS	24. 538 M^3 17. 268 M^3 12. 360 M^3 54. 166 M^3

SIZE OF CARTONS： LENGTH：66CM；WIDTH：51CM；HEIGHT：54CM SPECIAL CONDITION OF PACKING：	SIGNED BY： NANKAI WORSTED SPINNING SDN. , BHD. MANAGER Paul N. Ayars
	Authorized signature

海运提单见表9。

表9　　　　　　　　　海运提单

BILL OF LADING FOR COMBINED TRANSPORT SHIPMENT OR PORT TO PORT SHIPMENT

Shipper： NANKAI WORSTED SPINNING SDN. , BHD. LOT 20051, GONG BADAK INDUSTRIAL ESTATE 21300 KUALA LUMPUR, MALAYSIA	B/L NO. ：　　　3456789007 MISC
Consignee： TO ORDER OF DBS BANK SHANGHAI BRANCH	Carrier： MALAYSIA INTERNATIONAL SHIPPING CORPORATION BERHAD
Notify Party/Address LIDA TRADING COMPANY LIMITED ADD：NO. 1267 EAST NANJING ROAD 　　　SHANGHAI, CHINA 　　　FAX：021-64042588	Place of Receipt： (Applicable only when this document is used as a Combined Transport Bill of Lading) 　　　KUALA　LUMPUR
Vessel and Voy.　No. 　　　s. s. BIN BO V. 911	Place of Delivery： (Applicable only when this document is used as a Combined Transport Bill of Lading)
Port of Loading：　Port of Discharge： PORT KELANG　　　SHANGHAI	SHANGHAI, CHINA

Marks and Nos.	Number and kind of Packages；Description of Goods	Gross Weight	Measurement
◇ NK ◇ SHANGHAI MADE IN MALAYSIA 0016100293496-1 C/NO. 1-298	100%　Wool Hosiery Yarn 298 CARTONS FREIGHT PREPAID	13 676 KGS	54. 166 M³

SIZE/TYPE/CONTAINER # /TARE WGHT. /GROSS WGHT. /SEAL NUMBER / QUANTITY / STATUS

ON BOARD

ABOVE PARTICULARS AS DECLARED BY SHIPPER

＊Total No. of Containers/Packages received by the Carrier ONE40' FCL	RECEIVED by the Carrier from the Shipper in apparent good order and condition (unless otherwise noted herein) the total number or quantity of Containers or other packages or units indicated＊, stated by the Shipper to comprise the Goods specified above, for Carriage subject to all the terms hereof (INCLUDING THE TERMS OF THE CARRIER'S APPLICABLE TARIFF) from the Place of Receipt or the Port of Loading, whichever is applicable, to the Port of Discharge or the Place of Delivery, whichever is applicable. One original Bill of Lading must be surrendered duly endorsed in exchange for the Goods. In accepting this Bill of Lading the Merchant expressly accepts and agrees to all its terms, conditions and exceptions, whether printed, stamped or written, or otherwise incorporated, not withstanding the non-signing of this Bill of Lading by the Mercharnt
＊ Movement	
＊ Freight and Charges (indicate whether prepaid or collect)：	
＊ Origin Inland Haulage Charge	
＊ Origin　Terminal　Handling/ LCL Service Charge	Freight payable at：　　　　　Place and Date of issue：
＊ Ocean Freight	Number of Original B/L： THREE (3)　　　　　　　May 22nd 2013, KELANG
＊Destination Terminal Handling/LCL Service Charge	For the Carrier： 　　　MISC AGENCIES SDN BND AS AGENT FOR THE CARRIER MALAYSIA INTERNATIONAL SHIPPING CORPORATION BERHAD 　　　As Agent (s) only

原产地证书见表 10。

表 10   原产地证书

Exporter (Name & Address) NANKAI WORSTED SPINNING SDN BHD LOT 20051, GONG BADAK INDUSTRIAL ESTATE 21300 KUALA LUMPUR, MALAYSIA		MTMA Certificate of Origin No. 28357202 CERTIFICATE OF ORIGIN		

MTMA Certificate of Origin No.
28357202
CERTIFICATE OF ORIGIN

ISSUED BY

MALAYSIAN TEXTILE MANUFACTURERS
ASSOCIATION

Box #42, Wisma Selangor Dredging, 9th Floor, West Block. 142C, Jalan Ampang, 50450 Kuala Lumpur, Malaysia

Exporter (Name & Address)
NANKAI WORSTED SPINNING SDN BHD
LOT 20051, GONG BADAK INDUSTRIAL ESTATE
21300 KUALA LUMPUR, MALAYSIA

Consignee (Name, Address & Country)
LIDA TRADING COMPANY LIMITED
ADD: NO. 1267 EAST NANJING ROAD
　　　SHANGHAI, CHINA
　　　FAX: 021-64042588

Notify Party (Name & Address)
LIDA TRADING COMPANY LIMITED
ADD: NO. 1267 EAST NANJING ROAD
　　　SHANGHAI, CHINA
　　　FAX: 021-64042588

Vessel/Aircraft s. s. BIN BO V. 911	B/L Number/AWB Number 3 Originals+3 copies
Port of Loading Kelang	Date of Departure May 22nd, 2013

Port/Airport of Discharge

Final Destination
Shanghai, China

Country of Origin of Goods:
MALAYSIA

Marks and Number of packages	Description of goods: number and kind of packages	H. S. Code	Quantity or weight	No. and date of invoices
NK SHANGHAI MADE IN MALAYSIA 0016100293496-1 C/NO. 1-298	100% Wool Hosiery Yarn 298 CARTONS ********************	5107. 1000	13 080 KGS	Invoice No. NK-CN063 dated May 10th, 2013

Certification：	Declaration by Exporter：
We hereby certify that the above, to the best of our knowledge and belief, to be correct and without prejudice. Signature of Authorised Officer 　　TAN CHENG CHOOL --------------------------------------- For & on behalf of Malaysian Textile Manufacturers Association Designation　　　　Adm. Executive Place, Date and Seal/Stamp of Certifying Authority 　　　　　　　KUALA LUMPUR 　　　　　　　May 11st, 2013	The exporter of the abovementioned merchandise, hereby certify that I have the means of knowing and certify that the goods described in this certificate are of 　　Malaysia　　origin. ----------------------------- Signature 　　　　　　　　　Paul Ayars Signatory's Company Place, Date and Seal/Stamp of the COMPANY 　　　　　　　KUALA LUMPUR 　　　　　　　May 10th, 2013

检验证书见表 11。

表 11　　　　　　　　　　　　检验证书

No.：05394098

Consignor： NANKAI WORSTED SPINNING SDN BHD LOT 20051, GONG BADAK INDUSTRIAL ESTATE 21300 KUALA LUMPUR, MALAYSIA	
Consignee： LIDA TRADING COMPANY LIMITED ADD：NO. 1267 EAST NANJING ROAD 　　　SHANGHAI, CHINA 　　　FAX：021-64042588	Issued by： 　　MALAYSIA TEXTILE INSPECTION 　　　　　　　BUREAU Box #40, Wisma Selangor Dredging, 6th Floor, West Block. 142C, Jalan Ampang, 50450 Kuala Lumpur, Malaysia CERTIFICATE OF INSPECTION
Ship/Airline s. s. BIN BOV. 911	Date of departure May 22nd, 2013
Port of loading KELANG	Port of discharge SHANGHAI

Marks & Brands	Number & kind of packages	Description of goods	Net weight
NK SHANGHAI MADE IN MALAYSIA 0016100293496-1 C/NO. 1-298	298 CARTONS	100% Wool Hosiery Yarn	13 080KGS

I hereby certify that _____ the goods _____ specified above has/have been examined and found to the best of my knowledge.

Signature _____
Authorized Officer

Date：   May 14th，2013

Producer：

Remarks：

2. 任务要求

（1）在议付行审核你所提交的出口单据期间，新加坡发展银行大连分行转来信用证（0016100293496）项下的进口单据一套，系公司与马来西亚客户 NANKAI WORSTED SPINNING SND. BHD 达成的一笔进口业务的单据；请你本着"单证一致，单单相符"的原则，对这套单据进行认真的审核，写出你的审单意见。

（2）请根据开证银行的反馈信息，给国外客户发一封善后函。

附录一 单证常用英文缩略语表

A

a (@)	At	按
abt.	about	大约
A/C	for account of	代、代表
acc	acceptance	承兑、接受
A/C, acct.	account	账（账户）
ADB	Asian Development Bank	亚洲开发银行
add.	address	地址
AIR	all in rate	包干费率
a. m.	ante meridiem（L.）	上午（拉丁文）
A/M	above mentioned	上述
amt.	amount	金额
A/O	account of…	入某人账内
a. p. l.	as per list	按照表列
app.	appendix	附表
approx.	approximately	大约
A. R.	All Risks	一切险
art.	article	条款、货品
Art. No.	Article Number	货号
A/S	after sight = at sight	见票后（即付）
asst.	assortment	搭配
Asst.	assistant	助理
A. T. L.	actual total loss	实际全损
att.	attached	附
Attn.	Attention	注意，通知
Aug.	August	八月
A. V.	Ad Valorem	从价
AV.	Average	海损
AWB	airway bill	航空运单

B

b/–b/s	bale (s), bag (s)	包、袋
BAF	bunker adjustment factor	燃油附加费
bal.	balance	余额、平衡
B. B. Clause	both to blame collision clause	船舶互撞条款
B/C	Bill for Collection	托收汇票
bdle.	bundle	把、捆
B/E	Bill of Exchange	汇票
b/f	brought forward	承前页
bg.	bag	袋
BIMCO	Baltic and International Maritime Council	波罗的海国际海事协会
Bk.	bank	银行
bkt	basket	篮、筐
bl.	bale	包
B/L	Bill of Lading	提单
bldg.	building	大厦
B/N	booking note	托运单
BOC	Bank of China	中国银行
B. O.	branch office	分公司
bot.	bottle	瓶
br.	branch	分行、分支机构
brl.	barrel	桶
Bros.	Brothers	兄弟（公司）
b/s	bales, bags	包、袋（复数）
BS	bunker surcharge	燃油附加费
B. P.	Bill Purchased	银行议付汇票
btl.	bottle	瓶
BTN	Brussels Tariff Nomenclature	布鲁塞尔税则目录
Bx (s)	Box (es)	箱、盒

C

c/–, c/–s	case (s)	箱
C/A	cable address	电挂
CAF	currency adjustment factor	货币贬值附加费
CAD	cash against delivery	货到付款
canc.	cancelled, cancellation	取消
Capt	Captain	船长

Caricom	Caribbean Community	加勒比共同体
cat.	catalogue	目录
	category	类别
C. C.	carbon copy	抄本、复写本
CCCN	Customs Co-operative Council Nomenclature	海关合作理事会税则目录
CCIB	China Commodity Inspection Bureau	中国商品检验局
CCIC	China Commodity Inspection Corporation	中国商品检验公司
CCPIT	China Council for Promotion of International Trade	中国国际贸易促进委员会
C. C. V. O	Combined Certificate of Value and Origin	价值、产地联合证明书
c/f	carried forward	续后页
CFR	cost and freight	成本加运费价
CFS	Container Freight Station	集装箱货运站
cft.	cubic feet	立方英尺
ch.	cheque	支票
chg.	charge	费用
C/I	Certificate of Inspection	检验证书
	Certificate of Insurance	保险证书
CIC	China Insurance Clause	中国保险条款
CIF	cost, insurance, freight	成本、保险加运费价
CIFC	cost, insurance, freight, commission	成本、保险、运费加佣金价
C. I. O	cash in order	订货时付款
CIP	freight or carriage & insurance paid to…	运费、保险费付至……
CISS	Comprehensive Import Supervision Scheme	进口商品全面监督计划
ck.	check	支票
ct	centiliter	厘升
CL	container load	集装箱装载
CLP	container load plan	集装箱装载单
cm	centimeter	公分、厘米
CMI	Committee Maritime International	国际海事委员会
C/N	Credit Note	贷项账单（贷记通知单）
CNFTTC	China National Foreign Trade Transportation Corp.	中国外贸运输公司
CNY	Chinese Yuan	人民币
Co.	Company	公司
C/O	Certificate of Origin	产地证书
	care of	转交
	Cash Order	本票

COA	contract of affreightment	租船契约
COC	carrier's own container	承运人集装箱
C. O. D	cash on delivery or collection on delivery	货到付款
comm.	commission	佣金
Cont.	contract	合同
contd.	continued	继续
Co-op	co-operation	合作经营，合作社
Corp.	corporation	公司
COSCO	China Ocean Shipping Company	中国远洋运输公司
C/P	Charter Party	租船合同
C. Q. D.	customary quick dispatch	按港口习惯快速装卸（尽快装卸）
Cr.	Credit	贷方
C/R	cargo receipt	货物承运收据
crt.	crate	板条箱
c/s	cases	箱
C. T. B/L	Combined Transport Bill of Lading	联合运输提单
C. T. D.	Combined Transport Documents	联合运输单据
C. T. L.	Constructive Total Loss	推定全损
ctn	carton	纸箱
C. T. O.	combined transport operator	多式联运经营人
cu.	cubic	立方
cu. ft.	cubic feet	立方英尺
cu. m	cubic meter	立方米
cur. /cy	currency	币制
C. W. O.	cash with order	订货时付款
CY	container yard	集装箱堆场
CY to CY	container yard to container yard	集装箱堆场至集装箱堆场
C. Z.	canal zone	运河地带

D

D/A	Documents against Acceptance	承兑交单
D/C	Documentary Credit	跟单信用证
DCP	freight or carriage paid to...	运费付至……
D/D	Demand Draft	即期汇票
dd.	dated	日期
DDC	destination delivery charge	目的地交货费
Dec.	December	十二月
dept	department	部、处、科

D/F	dead freight	亏舱费
DHL	DHL International Ltd.	敦豪公司（信使传递）
diam.	diameter	直径
disc.	discount	折扣、贴现息
D/N	debit note	借项账单
do.	ditto = the same	同上、同前
doc.	document	单据、单证
D/O，D. O.	Delivery Order	提货单
Dol.	dollar	元
Doz.（DZ.）	dozen	打
D/P	Documents against Payment	付款交单
DPP	damage protection plan	损害修理条款
D. P. V.	duty paid value	完税价格
d/s	days	天数
Dt.	debit	借方
dr.	drum	桶
D/R	dock receipt	集装箱场站收据
dup.	duplicate	副本、复本

E

EATA	Europe-Asia Trade Agreement	欧亚贸易协定
EBS	emergency bunker surcharge	紧急燃油附加费
EIR	equipment interchange receipt	设备交接单
EMS	Express Mail Service	特快专递
encl.	enclosure	附件
E. & O. E.	errors & omissions excepted	错漏当查
EPZ	Export Processing Zone	出口加工区
Equip/R	equipment receipt	设备交接单
eq.（equiv.）	equivalent	等于
ERC	equipment reposition charge	空箱调运费
Est.	establishment	机构、企业、商店
ETA	estimated time of arrival	预计到达时间
etc.	et cetera（and so on）	等等
ETD	estimated time of departure	预计离港时间
ex.	example	举例
exc.	excepted	除外
exch.	exchange	兑换，汇票
Ex Facie	in accordance with the documents	按照单证

exp.	export	出口
EXQ	Ex quay	码头交货价
EXS	Ex ship	目的港船上交货价
EXW	Ex work	工厂交货价
FAF	Fuel adjustment factor	燃油附加费

F

F. A. Q.	fair average quality	大路货、中等货
F. A. S.	Free Alongside Ship	船边交货
F. B.	Freight Bill	运费账单
Feb.	February	二月
FCA	Free Carrier（named place）	货交承运人
Fch.	franchise	特许经营权
F. C. L.	full container load	整箱货
F. C. T. B/L.	FIATA Combined Transport B/L	国际运输商协会联合会联合运输提单
FEFC	Far East Freight Conference	远东（欧洲）运费工会
FEU	forty-foot equivalent unit	40 英尺集装箱
FIATA	Federation Internationale des Associations de Transitaires et Assimiles（International Federation of Forwarding Agents Associations）	国际运输商协会联合会（简称"菲亚塔"）
F. I.	free in	船方不负担装货费用
F. I. O.	free in and out	船方不负担装卸费用
F. I. O. S.	free in and out and stowed	船方不负担装卸及理舱费
F. I. O. S. T.	free in and out and stowed and trimmed	船方不负担装卸及理舱、平舱费用
F. I. O. T.	free in and out and trimmed	船方不负担装卸及平舱费用
F. I. W.	free into wagons	车上交货
F. M. V.	fair market value	公平市场价
F. O.	free out	船方不负担卸货费用
F. O. B.	Free on Board	装运港船上交货
F. O. C.	free of charge	免费
F. O. I.	free of interest	免息
F. P. A.	free from particular average	平安险
FR	flat rack container	框架集装箱
F. R. E. C.	fire risks extension clauses	火险扩展条款
Fri.	Friday	星期五

frt.	freight	运费
FRWD	Fresh & Rain Water Damage	淡水雨淋险
F/T	freight ton	运费吨
Ft.	Feet	英尺

G

GA	General Average	共同海损
gal.	gallon	加仑
GATT	General Agreement on Tariffs & Trade	关税及贸易总协定
G. M. Q.	good merchantable quality	上好可销品质
G. M. T.	Greenwich Mean Time	格林威治时间
GPC	general purpose container	通用集装箱
G. P. O.	General Post Office	邮政总局
gr.	Gross	一罗（十二打）
grm.	Gram	克
GRI	general rate increase	整体费率上调
G. R. T.	gross registered tonnage	注册总吨（总登记吨）
gr. wt.	gross weight	毛重
GSP	Generalized System of Preferences	普惠制
GSP C/O	Generalized System of Preferences Certificate of Origin	普惠制产地证
GSP Form A	Generalized System of Preferences Form A	普惠制格式 A

H

HAWB	House Airway Bill	航空分运单
H/H	house to house	集装箱门到门
H. O.	Head Office	总行
HOUSE B/L	House Bill of Lading	仓至仓提单
h. p.	horse power	马力
H/P	house to pier	从厂、库到码头
Hrs.	hours	钟点（小时）
HSBC	HongKong & Shanghai Banking Corporation	汇丰银行
ht.	height	高度
hund.	Hundred	百

I

ICC	International Chamber of Commerce	国际商会
	Institute Cargo Clause	伦敦保险协会货物条款

ICS	International Chamber of Shipping	国际航运公会
I/D	Import Declaration	进口申请书
i. e.	id est（L. ）= that is	即是
I/E	import/export	进口/出口
IGO	inter-government organization	政府间国际组织
IMDG Code	International Maritime Dangerous Goods Code	国际海运危险货物规则
IMO	International Maritime Organization	国际海事组织
I/L	Import Licence	进口许可证
In.	inch	英寸
Inc.	Incorporated	组成公司的
ind.	indent	代购单
incl.	including，inclusive	包括
INCOTERMS	International Rules for the Interpretation of Trade Terms	国际贸易术语解释通则
Ins.	insurance	保险
inst.	instant	本月的
inv.	invoice	发票
I/O	instead of	代替
I/P	Insurance Policy	保险单
I. O. P.	irrespective of percentage	无免赔率
I. Q.	Import Quota	进口配额
I. O. U.	I owe you	借据
ISO	International Standard Organization	国际标准化组织

J

Jan.	January	一月
Jul.	July	七月
Jun.	June	六月

K

| Kg. /kilo | Kilogram | 千克 |
| Km. | Kilometer | 千米、公里 |

L

LASH	lighter-aboard-ship	载驳船、子母船
Lb（s）	pound（s）	磅
L/C	Letter of Credit	信用证
LCL	less than container（cargo）load	拼箱集装箱货
ldg	loading	装载

L/G	Letter of Guarantee	保函
LIBOR	London interbank offered rate	伦敦银行同业拆放利率
L/L	Loading List	装货清单
L/T	long ton	长吨
Ltd.	Limited（company）	有限（公司）
ltg.	Lighterage	驳运费

M

Mar.	March	三月
MAWB	Master Airway Bill	总航空运单
max.	maximum	最大量、最高额
M. D.	malicious damage	恶意破坏所造成的损失
mdse	merchandise	货物、商品
med.	medium	中等
memo	memorandum	备忘录、便签
Messrs.	Messieurs	公司名称前的尊称
Mfg	manufacturing	制造中、生产
M/F	manifest	载货清单（单）
MFN	Most Favoured Nation	最惠国
Mfr	manufacturer	制造商
min.	minimum	最小量、最低额
M. L. B.	Mini-Land-Bridge	小陆桥
M/L cls.	More or less clause	溢短装条款
mm.	millimeter	毫米
Mon.	Monday	星期一
M. P. H.	miles per hour	时速……英里
M/R	mate's receipt	收货单（大副收据）
M/S	motor ship	内燃机轮、货轮
M/T	mail transfer	信汇
M/T	metric ton	公吨
M. V.	motor vessel	内燃机轮
M. T. O.	Multi-modal Transport Operation	多式联运
M/W	measurement/weight	体积或重量

N

N/A	not applicable	不适用
N/Arr.	Notice of Arrival	到货通知书
N. B	note below	注意
N. C. V	no commercial value	无商业价值

NGO	non-government organization	非政府间国际组织
N/M	no mark	无唛头
N. N. B/L	non-negotiable, not negotiable B/L	副本提单
No.	number	号码
non. d.	non delivery	提货不着
N. O. E.	not otherwise enumerated	除非另有列举
N. O. P. F.	not otherwise provided for	除非另有规定
N. O. S.	not otherwise specified	除非另有指定
Nov.	November	十一月
N. P.	notary public	公证人
N/R	Notice of Readiness	装卸准备就绪通知书
NRT	net registered tonnage	净登记吨
N/S	not sufficient	不足
NVOCC	non-vessel operating common carrier	无船承运人
N. Wt.	net weight	净重
NYPE	New York Produce Exchange	纽约土产交易所

O

O/A	on account	赊账
O/A	on account of	代表
O/B	on behalf of	代表
O/C	open cover	预约承保书
OC	Outward Collection	出口托收
OCP	Overland Common Point	内陆转运点
Oct.	October	十月
OG (I) L	Open General (Import) Licence	开放配额（进口）许可证
OMCC	Ocean Marine Cargo Clause	海洋运输货物保险条款
O/O	(by) order of	送交
O. P	Open Policy	预约保单
OPT	outward processing trade	对外加工贸易
OT	open-top container	敞顶集装箱
ORC	original receiving charge	原产地接货费
Orig.	original	正本、原件
Oz (s)	ounce (s)	英两、盎司
OSS	Ourselves	我们自己

P

PAM & C	Processing of given material, Assembling provided components,	三来一补

	Made to order against buyer's sample,	
	& Compensation trade	
P. A.	particular average	单独海损
p. a.	per annual	按年（计息）
P. &I. Club	Protection & Indemnity Club	保障赔偿协会
payt	payment	付款
p. c.	per cent	百分之
pc/pce（s）	piece（s）	件、个、只、块、张
pct.	percent	百分之
pd.	paid	付讫
p. d.	per day	按日（计息）
PICC	The People's Insurance Company of China	中国人民保险公司
pkg.	package	件、包
pls.	please	请
p. m.	post meridiem（L.）	下午（拉丁文）
	per month	按月（计息）
P. O.	post office	邮局
	purchase order	购货订单
P. O. B.	Post Office Box	邮政信箱
P. O. D.	payment on delivery/	付款交货
	Proof of Delivery	交付凭证
p. p.	per procuration	代表、代签
pr（s）	pair（s）	双、付
pro rata	proportionally	按比例
P. R. C.	the People's Republic of China	中华人民共和国
prem.	premium	保险费
prox.	proximo	下月的
P. S.	postscript	附言、再启
P. T. O.	please turn over	请阅背面
Pte.	private	私人
P. V. C.	Polyvinyl chloride	聚氯乙烯

Q

qr	Quarter	四分之一
Q. V.	quod vide（which see）	请查阅
qnty.	quantity	数量
qlty.	Quality	品质

R

Re/ref	Reference	参考、关于
Ref. No.	Reference Number	参考号、发文编号
Reg.	registered	注册、挂号的
rep.	representation	代表
retd.	returned	退回的
RF	refrigerator	冷藏库
R. F. W. D.	Rain &/or Fresh Water Damage	雨淋、淡水险
Rm	ream	令（500 张纸）
RO/RO	roll on/roll off ship	滚上滚下船
Ry.	Railway	铁路

S

s. or sh.	Shilling	先令
Sat.	Saturday	星期六
S/C	Sales Confirmation	售货确认书
	Service Contract	协议运价（服务合同）
SCI	Special Customs Invoice	（美国）特别海关发票
SDR	special drawing right	特别提款权
Sect.	section	部分、组、部
Sep.	September	九月
SF	stowage factor	（货物）积载因素
SGS	Switzerland General Surveyor	瑞士通用鉴定公司
sk	sack	布袋
shpt	shipment	装运
SINOTRANS	China National Foreign Trade Transportation Corporation	中国外贸运输公司
SML.	small/medium/large	小、中、大
S/N	Shipping Note	装货通知单
S/O	Shipping Order	装货单、下货单
SOC	shipper's own container	货主箱
S. O. L.	shipowner's liability	船东责任
spec.	specification	规格
sq. in.	square inch	平方英寸
sq. ft	square foot	平方英尺
sq. yd	square yard	平方码
S. R.	strike risks	罢工险
S. S.	steam ship	汽轮

S/T	short ton	短吨
S. T. C.	said to contain	包括、据称
Std.	standard	标准
Stg.	Sterling	英镑
Sun.	Sunday	星期日
S. W.	shipping weight	装货重量
SWB	Sea Way Bill	海运单
SWIFT	Society for Worldwide Interbank Financial Telecommunication	环球同业银行金融电讯协会

T

T.	tare, ton	皮重，吨
T/A	transshipment allowed	允许转运
	transshipment additional	转船附加费
	train/air	陆/空（联运）
TAT	train-air-truck	陆空陆（联运）
TBD	To Be Declared Policy	待报保险单
TCT	time charter on trip basis	航次期租
tdg.	trading	贸易
TEU	twenty-feet equivalent unit	20 英尺标准集装箱
tgm	telegram	电报
THC	terminal handling charge	码头作业费（操作费）
Thur.	Thursday	星期四
TK	tank container	罐式集装箱
Tlx.	Telex	电传
T. L. O.	Total Loss Only	全损险
TM	telegram multiple	同文电报、分送电报
tonn.	tonnage	吨位
TPDA	Trans-Pacific Discussion Agreement	越太平洋航线协商协定
T. P. N. D.	theft, pilferage&non-delivery	偷窃、提货不着险
tr. wt.	tare weight	皮重
T/R	Trust Receipt	信托收据
tr	tare	皮重
TSA	Trans-Pacific Stabilization Agreement	越太平洋航线稳定协议
T/T	Telegraphic Transfer	电汇
TTL.	Total	总计
Tues.	Tuesday	星期二

U

UCP	Uniform Customs&Practice	统一惯例
U. K. Ports	United Kingdom Ports	英国港口
UL	Underwriter Laboratory Mark	美国 UL 公司对产品生产符合其规定经过跟踪检验的认证的标记
ult.	ultimo	上月的
U/T	unlimited transshipment	无限制转船
U/M	Under-mentioned	下述

V

V.	Vide	参阅
val.	value	价值
via	by way of	经由
viz.	videlicet（L.）namely	即是
voy.	voyage	航次
VV	vice versa（L.）	反之亦然

W

Wed.	Wednesday	星期三
Whse	warehouse	仓库
W/M	weight/measurement	重量或体积
W. O.	washing overboard	浪击落海
W. P. A.	With Particular Average	水渍险
W. R.	War Risks	战争险
Wt.	weight	重量
W/T	with transshipment	转船、转运
wtd.	warranted	保证
wty.	warranty	保证书
W/W	Warehouse to Warehouse Clause	仓至仓条款
WWD	Weather working day	晴天工作日

X

Xl	extra large	特大
XP	Express	快递
xs	Excess	超过

Y

Y. A. R.	York–Antwerp Rule	约克-安特卫普规定（国际共同海损理算规则）
Yd.	Yard	码

附录二　国际货物买卖合同参考案例

1. 国际货物买卖标准合同

InternationalSale Contract
（Manufactured Goods Intended for Resale）

A. SPECIFIC CONDITIONS

These Specific Conditions have been prepared in order to permit the parties to agree the particular terms of their sale contract by completing the spaces left open or choosing （as the case may be） between the alternatives provided in this document. Obviously this does not prevent the parties from agreeing other terms or further details.

SELLER＿＿＿（name and address）＿＿＿　　BUYER＿＿＿（name and address）＿＿＿

CONTACT PERSON（name and address）CONTACT PERSON（name and address）

The present contract of sale will be governed by these Specific Conditions （to the extent that the relevant boxes have been completed） and by the ICC General Conditions of Sale （Manufactured Goods Intended for Resale） which constitute part B of this document.

SELLER＿＿＿＿＿＿＿＿＿＿＿＿　　BUYER＿＿＿＿＿＿＿＿＿＿＿＿

　　　　（Signature）　　　　　　　　　　（signature）

Place＿＿＿＿＿Date＿＿＿＿＿　　Place＿＿＿＿＿Date＿＿＿＿＿

A-1 GOODS SOLD

DESCRIPTION OF THE GOODS

If there is insufficient space, parties may use an annex.

A-2 CONTRACT PRICE （ART. 4）

Currency：

amount in numbers：　　　　　　　　　　amount in letters：

A-3 DELIVERY TERMS

RecommendedTerms （according to INCOTERMS 2010）：

EXW Ex Works named place：

FCA Free Carrier named place：

CPT Carriage Paid To named place of destination：

CIP Carriage and Insurance Paid to named place of destination:

DAT   delivered at terminal

DAP   delivered at place

DDP Delivered Duty Paid named place of destination:

OtherTerms (according to INCOTERMS 2010)

FAS Free Alongside Ship named port of shipment:

FOB Free On Board named port of shipment:

CFR Cost and Freight named port of destination:

CIF Cost, Insurance and Freight named port of destination:

Other Delivery Terms

CARRIER (where applicable)

NAME AND ADDRESS. CONTACT PERSON

A-4 TIME OF DELIVERY

Indicate here the date or period (e. g. week or month) at which or within which the Seller must perform his delivery obligations according to clause A. 4 of the respective Incoterm (see Introduction, § 6)

A-5 INSPECTION OF THE GOODS BY BUYER (ART. 3)

Before shipment: _____ Place of inspection: _____

Other: _____

A-6 RETENTION OF TITLE (ART. 7)

YES

NO

A-7 PAYMENT CONDITIONS (ART. 5)

Payment on open account (ART. 5. 1)

Time for payment (if different from art. 5. 1) _____ days from date of invoice.

Other: _____

____ Open account backed by demand guarantee or standby letter of credit (ART. 5. 5)

Payment in advance (ART. 5. 2)

Date (if different from art. 5. 2): _____ Total price _____% of the price

Documentary Collection (ART. 5. 5)

_____ D/P Documents against payment

_____ D/A Documents against acceptance

Irrevocable documentary credit (ART. 5. 3) ____ Confirmed ____ Unconfirmed

Place of issue (if applicable): _____ Place of confirmation (if applicable): _____

Credit available: Partial shipments:

Transhipment:

_____ By payment at sight   _____ Allowed   _____ Allowed

_____ By deferred payment at: _____ days.   _____ Not allowed   _____ Not allowed

_____ By acceptance of drafts at: _____ days

_____ By negotiation

Date on which the documentary credit must be notified to seller (if different from ART. 5. 3)

_____ days before date of delivery. _____ other: _____

Other: _____

(e. g. cheque, bank draft, electronic funds transfer to designated bank account of seller)

A-8 DOCUMENTS

Indicate here documents to be provided by Seller. Parties are advised to check the Incoterm they have selected under A-3 of these Specific Conditions.

_____ Transport documents: indicate type of transport document required _____

_____ Commercial Invoice

_____ Certificate of Origin

_____ PackingList

_____ Certificate of Inspection

_____ Insurance Document

_____ Other: _____

A-9 CANCELLATION DATE

TO BE COMPLETED ONLY IF THE PARTIES WISH TO MODIFY ARTICLE 10. 3.

If the goods are not delivered for any reason whatsoever (including force majeure) by (date) _____ the Buyer will be entitled to CANCEL THE CONTRACT IMMEDIATELY BY NOTIFICATION TO THE SELLER

A-10 LIABILITY FOR DELAY (ART. 10. 1, 10. 4 AND 11. 3)

TO BE COMPLETED ONLY IF THE PARTIES WISH TO MODIFY ART. 10. 1, 10. 4 OR 11. 3.

Liquidated damages for delay in delivery shall be:

_____ % (of price of delayed goods) per week, with a maximum of _____ % (of price of delayed goods)

or:

_____ (specify amount)

In case of termination for delay, Seller's liability for damages for delay is limited to _____ % of the price of the non-delivered goods.

A-11 LIMITATION OF LIABILITY FOR LACK OF CONFORMITY （ART. 11. 5）

TO BE COMPLETED ONLY IF THE PARTIES WISH TO MODIFY ART. 11. 5.

Seller's liability for damages arising from lack of conformity of the goods shall be:

_____ limited to proven loss （including consequential loss, loss of profit, etc. ） not exceeding _____% of the contract price;

or:

_____ as follows （specify）:

A-12 LIMITATION OF LIABILITY WHERE NON-CONFORMING GOODS ARE RETAINED BY THE BUYER （ART. 11. 6）

TO BE COMPLETED ONLY IF THE PARTIES WISH TO MODIFY ART. 11. 6.

The price abatement for retained non-conforming goods shall not exceed:

_____ % of the price of such goods

or:

_____ （specify amount）

A-13 TIME-BAR （ART. 11. 8）

TO BE COMPLETED ONLY IF THE PARTIES WISH TO MODIFY ART. 11. 8.

Any action fornon-conformity of the goods （as defined in article 11. 8） must be taken by the Buyer not later than _____ from the date of arrival of the goods at destination.

A-14 （a）, A-14 （b） APPLICABLE LAW （ART. 1. 2）

TO BE COMPLETED ONLY IF THE PARTIES WISH TO SUBMIT THESALE CONTRACT TO A NATIONAL LAW INSTEAD OF CISG. The solution hereunder is not recommended.

（a） This sales contract is governed by the domestic law of _____ （country）.

To be completed if the parties wish to choose a law other than that of the seller for questions not covered by CISG.

（b） Any questions not covered by CISG will be governed by the law of _____ （country）.

A-15 RESOLUTION OF DISPUTES （ART. 14）

The two solutions hereunder （arbitration or litigation before ordinary courts） are alternatives: parties cannot choose both of them. If no choice is made, ICC arbitration will apply, according to ART. 14.

_____ ARBITRATION _____ LITIGATION （ordinary courts）

_____ ICC （according to ART. 14. 1） In case of dispute the courts of

Place of arbitration _____ （place）

_____ Other _____ （specify） shall have jurisdiction.

A-16 OTHER

InternationalSale Contract

(Manufactured Goods Intended for Resale)

B. GENERAL CONDITIONS

ART. 1 GENERAL

1.1　These General Conditions are intended to be applied together with the Specific Conditions (part A) of the International Sale Contract (Manufactured Goods Intended for Resale), but they may also be incorporated on their own into any sale contract. Where these General Conditions (Part B) are used independently of the said Specific Conditions (Part A), any reference in Part B to Part A will be interpreted as a reference to any relevant specific conditions agreed by the parties. In case of contradiction between these General Conditions and any specific conditions agreed upon between the parties, the specific conditions shall prevail.

1.2　Any questions relating to this Contract which are not expressly or implicitly settled by the provisions contained in the Contract itself (i. e. these General Conditions and any specific conditions agreed upon by the parties) shall be governed:

A. by the United Nations Convention on Contracts for the International Sale of Goods (Vienna Convention of 1980, hereafter referred to as CISG), and

B. to the extent that such questions are not covered by CISG, by reference to the law of the country where the Seller has his place of business.

1.3　Any reference made to trade terms (such as EXW, FCA, etc.) is deemed to be made to the relevant term of Incoterms published by the International Chamber of Commerce.

1.4　Any reference made to a publication of the International Chamber of Commerce is deemed to be made to the version current at the date of conclusion of the Contract.

1.5　No modification of the Contract is valid unless agreed or evidenced in writing. However, a party may be precluded by his conduct from asserting this provision to the extent that the other party has relied on that conduct.

ART. 2 CHARACTERISTICS OF THE GOODS

2.1　It is agreed that any information relating to the goods and their use, such as weights, dimensions, capacities, prices, colours and other data contained in catalogues, prospectuses, circulars, advertisements, illustrations, price – lists of the Seller, shall not take effect as terms of the Contract unless expressly referred to in the Contract.

2.2　Unless otherwise agreed, the Buyer does not acquire any property rights in software, drawings, etc. which may have been made available to him. The Seller also remains the exclusive owner of any intellectual or industrial property rights relating to the goods.

ART. 3 INSPECTION OF THE GOODS BEFORE SHIPMENT

If the parties have agreed that the Buyer is entitled to inspect the goods before shipment, the Seller must notify the Buyer within a reasonable time before the shipment that the goods are ready for inspection at the agreed place.

ART. 4 PRICE

4. 1   If no price has been agreed, the Seller's current list price at the time of the conclusion of the Contract shall apply. In the absence of such a current list price, the price generally charged for such goods at the time of the conclusion of the Contract shall apply.

4. 2   Unless otherwise agreed in writing, the price does not include VAT, and is not subject to price adjustment.

4. 3   The price indicated under A-2 (contract price) includes any costs which are at the Seller's charge according to this Contract. However, should the Seller bear any costs which, according to this Contract, are for the Buyer's account (e. g. for transportation or insurance under EXW or FCA), such sums shall not be considered as having been included in the price under A-2 and shall be reimbursed by the Buyer.

ART. 5 PAYMENT CONDITIONS

5. 1   Unless otherwise agreed in writing, or implied from a prior course of dealing between the parties, payment of the price and of any other sums due by the Buyer to the Seller shall be on open account and time of payment shall be 30 days from the date of invoice. The amounts due shall be transferred, unless otherwise agreed, by teletransmission to the Seller's bank in the Seller's country for the account of the Seller and the Buyer shall be deemed to have performed his payment obligations when the respective sums due have been received by the Seller's bank in immediately available funds.

5. 2   If the parties have agreed on payment in advance, without further indication, it will be assumed that such advance payment, unless otherwise agreed, refers to the full price, and that the advance payment must be received by the Seller's bank in immediately available funds at least 30 days before the agreed date of delivery or the earliest date within the agreed delivery period. If advance payment has been agreed only for a part of the contract price, the payment conditions of the remaining amount will be determined according to the rules set forth in this article.

5. 3   If the parties have agreed on payment by documentary credit, then, unless otherwise agreed, the Buyer must arrange for a documentary credit in favour of the Seller to be issued by a reputable bank, subject to the Uniform Customs and Practice for Documentary Credits published by the International Chamber of Commerce, and to be notified at least 30 days before the agreed date of delivery or at least 30 days before the earliest date within the agreed delivery period. Unless otherwise agreed, the documentary

credit shall be payable at sight and allow partial shipments and transshipments.

5.4　If the parties have agreed on payment by documentary collection, then, unless otherwise agreed, documents will be tendered against payment (D/P) and the tender will in any case be subject to the Uniform Rules for Collections published by the International Chamber of Commerce.

5.5　To the extent that the parties have agreed that payment is to be backed by a bank guarantee, the Buyer is to provide, at least 30 days before the agreed date of delivery or at least 30 days before the earliest date within the agreed delivery period, a first demand bank guarantee subject to the Uniform Rules for Demand Guarantees published by the International Chamber of Commerce, or a standby letter of credit subject either to such Rules or to the Uniform Customs and Practice for Documentary Credits published by the International Chamber of Commerce, in either case issued by a reputable bank.

ART. 6 INTEREST IN CASE OF DELAYED PAYMENT

6.1　If a party does not pay a sum of money when it falls due the other party is entitled to interest upon that sum from the time when payment is due to the time of payment.

6.2　Unless otherwise agreed, the rate of interest shall be 2% above the average bank short-term lending rate to prime borrowers prevailing for the currency of payment at the place of payment, or where no such rate exists at that place, then the same rate in the State of the currency of payment. In the absence of such a rate at either place the rate of interest shall be the appropriate rate fixed by the law of the State of the currency of payment.

ART. 7 RETENTION OF TITLE

If the parties have validly agreed on retention of title, the goods shall remain the property of the Seller until the complete payment of the price, or as otherwise agreed.

ART. 8 CONTRACTUAL TERM OF DELIVERY

Unless otherwise agreed, delivery shall be "Ex Works" (EXW) .

ART. 9 DOCUMENTS

Unless otherwise agreed, the Seller must provide the documents (if any) indicated in the applicable Incoterm or, if no Incoterm is applicable, according to any previous course of dealing.

ART. 10 LATE-DELIVERY, NON-DELIVERY AND REMEDIES THEREFORE

10.1　When there is delay in delivery of any goods, the Buyer is entitled to claim liquidated damages equal to 0.5% or such other percentage as may be agreed of the price of those goods for each complete week of delay, provided the Buyer notifies the Seller of the delay. Where the Buyer so notifies the Seller within 15 days from the agreed date of delivery, damages will run from the agreed date of delivery or from the last day within the agreed period of delivery. Where the Buyer so notifies the Seller after 15 days of the agreed date of delivery, damages will run from the date of the notice. Liquidated damages for delay shall not exceed 5% of the price of the delayed goods or such other maximum amount as may be agreed.

10. 2   If the parties have agreed upon a cancellation date in Box A-9, the Buyer may terminate the Contract by notification to the Seller as regards goods which have not been delivered by such cancellation date for any reason whatsoever (including a force majeure event).

10. 3   When article 10. 2 does not apply and the Seller has not delivered the goods by the date on which the Buyer has become entitled to the maximum amount of liquidated damages under article 10. 1, the Buyer may give notice in writing to terminate the Contract as regards such goods, if they have not been delivered to the Buyer within 5 days of receipt of such notice by the Seller.

10. 4   In case of termination of the Contract under article 10. 2 or 10. 3 then in addition to any amount paid or payable under article 10. 1, the Buyer is entitled to claim damages for any additional loss not exceeding 10% of the price of the non-delivered goods.

10. 5   The remedies under this article are exclusive of any other remedy for delay in delivery or non-delivery.

ART. 11 NON-CONFORMITY OF THE GOODS

11. 1   The Buyer shall examine the goods as soon as possible after their arrival at destination and shall notify the Seller in writing of any lack of conformity of the goods within 15 days from the date when the Buyer discovers or ought to have discovered the lack of conformity. In any case the Buyer shall have no remedy for lack of conformity if he fails to notify the Seller thereof within 12 months from the date of arrival of the goods at the agreed destination.

11. 2   Goods will be deemed to conform to the Contract despite minor discrepancies which are usual in the particular trade or through course of dealing between the parties but the Buyer will be entitled to any abatement of the price usual in the trade or through course of dealing for such discrepancies.

11. 3   Where goods are non-conforming (and provided the Buyer, having given notice of the lack of conformity in compliance with article 11. 1, does not elect in the notice to retain them), the Seller shall at his option:

(a) replace the goods with conforming goods, without any additional expense to the Buyer, or

(b) repair the goods, without any additional expense to the Buyer, or

(c) reimburse to the Buyer the price paid for the non-conforming goods and thereby terminate the Contract as regards those goods.

The Buyer will be entitled to liquidated damages as quantified under article 10. 1 for each complete week of delay between the date of notification of the non-conformity according to article 11. 1 and the supply of substitute goods under article 11. 3 (a) or repair under article 11. 3 (b) above. Such damages may be accumulated with damages (if any) payable under article 10. 1 , but can in no case exceed in the aggregate 5% of the price of those goods.

11. 4   If the Seller has failed to perform his duties under article 11. 3 by the date on which the Buyer becomes entitled to the maximum amount of liquidated damages according to that article, the Buyer may give notice in writing to terminate the Contract as regards the non-conforming goods unless the supply of replacement goods or the repair is effected within 5 days of receipt of such notice by the Seller.

11. 5   Where the Contract is terminated under article 11. 3 (c) or article 11. 4, then in addition to any amount paid or payable under article 11. 3 as reimbursement of the price and damages for any delay, the Buyer is entitled to damages for any additional loss not exceeding 10% of the price of the non-conforming goods.

11. 6   Where the Buyer elects to retain non-conforming goods, he shall be entitled to a sum equal to the difference between the value of the goods at the agreed place of destination if they had conformed with the Contract and their value at the same place as delivered, such sum not to exceed 15% of the price of those goods.

11. 7   Unless otherwise agreed in writing, the remedies under this article 11 are exclusive of any other remedy for non–conformity.

11. 8   Unless otherwise agreed in writing, no action for lack of conformity can be taken by the Buyer, whether before judicial or arbitral tribunals, after 2 years from the date of arrival of the goods. It is expressly agreed that after the expiry of such term, the Buyer will not plead non-conformity of the goods, or make a counter-claim thereon, in defence to any action taken by the Seller against the Buyer for non-performance of this Contract.

ART. 12 COOPERATION BETWEEN THE PARTIES

12. 1   The Buyer shall promptly inform the Seller of any claim made against the Buyer by his customers or third parties concerning the goods delivered or intellectual property rights related thereto.

12. 2   The Seller will promptly inform the Buyer of any claim which may involve the product liability of the Buyer.

ART. 13 FORCE MAJEURE

13. 1   A party is not liable for a failure to perform any of his obligations in so far as

he proves:

(a) that the failure was due to an impediment beyond his control, and

(b) that he could not reasonably be expected to have taken into account the impediment and its effects upon his ability to perform at the time of the conclusion of the Contract, and

(c) that he could not reasonably have avoided or overcome it or its effects.

13. 2   A party seeking relief shall, as soon as practicable after the impediment and its effects upon his ability to perform become known to him, give notice to the other party of such impediment and its effects on his ability to perform. Notice shall also be given when the ground of relief ceases. Failure to give either notice makes the party thus failing liable in damages for loss which otherwise could have been avoided.

13. 3   Without prejudice to article 10. 2, a ground of relief under this clause relieves the party failing to perform from liability in damages, from penalties and other contractual sanctions, except from the duty to pay interest on money owing as long as and to the extent that the ground subsists.

13. 4   If the grounds of relief subsist for more than six months, either party shall be entitled to terminate the Contract with notice.

ART. 14 RESOLUTION OF DISPUTES

14. 1   Unless otherwise agreed in writing, all disputes arising in connection with the present Contract shall be finally settled under the Rules of Arbitration of the International Chamber of Commerce by one or more arbitrators appointed in accordance with the said Rules.

14. 2   An arbitration clause does not prevent any party from requesting interim or conservatory measures from the courts.

2. 普通货物买卖合同

SALES CONTRACT

Contract No: _____   Date: _____   Place: _____

The Seller: _____

TEL: _____   FAX: _____   E-MAIL: _____

The Buyer: _____

TEL: _____   FAX: _____   E-MAIL: _____

The Seller agrees to sell and the Buyer agrees to buy the under-mentioned commodity according to the terms and conditions stated below:

(1) NAME OF COMMODITY AND SPECIFICATION

(2) QUANTITY

(3) UNIT PRICE

(4) TOTAL AMOUNT

(5) TERMS OF DELIVERY

FOB/CFR/CIF. The terms "FOB", "CFR" or "CIF" shall be subject to the INCOTERMS 2010 provided by International Chamber of Commerce (ICC) unless otherwise stipulated herein.

(6) STANDARD OF PRODUCTION

(7) PACKING

(8) SHIPPING MARK

(9) TIME OF SHIPMENT

(10) PORT OF SHIPMENT

(11) PORT OF DESTINATION

(12) INSURANCE

If the term of delivery is on FOB or CFR basis, insurance shall be effected by the Buyer. If the term of delivery is on CIF basis, insurance shall be covered by the Seller for 110% of the invoice value against all risks.

(13) TERMS OF PAYMENT

13.1 Letter of Credit

The Buyer shall, _____ days prior to the time of shipment/ after the Contract came into effect, open an irrevocable Letter of Credit by Telex/Mail in favor of the Seller in Bank. The L/C shall expire _____ days after the completion of loading of the shipment in the locality of the beneficiary.

13.2 Collection

13.2.1 After shipment, the Seller shall draw a sight bill of exchange on the Buyer and deliver the documents through Seller's bank and the bank to the Buyer against payment, i.e D/P. The Buyer shall effect the payment immediately upon the first presentation of the bill of exchange.

13.2.2 After shipment, the Seller shall draw a bill of exchange, payable _ _ _ _ _ _ days after _____ on the Buyer and deliver the documents through Seller's bank and Bank to Buyer against acceptance (D/A _____ days). The Buyer shall make payment on the maturity date of the bill of exchange.

(14) DOCUMENTS REQUIRED

The Seller shall present the following documents to the negotiating bank:

(A) Full set of clean on board ocean Bills of Lading and blank endorsed marked freight prepaid/to collect;

(B) Commercial Invoice;

(C) Under the term of CIF: Insurance policy/Insurance Certificate;

(D) Quality Certificate;

(E) Packing List;

(F) Certificate of Origin.

(15) TERMS OF SHIPMENT

15. 1　On the FOB basis, the Buyer shall book shipping space in accordance with the date of shipment stipulated in the Contract. The seller shall _____ days before the date of shipment stipulated in the Contract advise the Buyer by Telex/Fax of the Contract number, the name of commodity, quantity, total amount, package numbers, total weight, and volume and the date from which goods are ready for loading at the port of shipment. The buyer shall _____ days before the date of shipment stipulated in the Contract, notify the Seller of name of the vessel, the estimated date of loading and the Contract number for the Seller to effect shipment. In case the carrying vessel of the date of arrival has to be changed, the Buyer or its shipping agent shall advise the Seller in time. Should the vessel fail to arrive at the port of shipment within days after the arrival date advised by the Buyer, the Buyer shall bear the storage expense calculated from the days thereafter.

15. 2　On FOB, CFR and CIF basis, the Seller shall immediately upon completion of loading of the goods, give a shipping notice to the Buyer by Telex/Fax. The notice shall include the Contract number, name of commodity, quantity, gross weight, measurement, invoice value, bill of lading number, sailing date. The IMDG code number of inflammable and dangerous goods, if any shall also be included.

15. 3　Partial shipment and the transshipment are/are not allowed.

15. 4　With _____% more or less both in amount and quantity allowed at the Seller's option.

(16) QUALITY/QUANTITY DISCREPANCY AND CLAIM

In case the quality and/or quantity/ weight of the goods found by the Buyer are not in conformity with the Contract after arrival of the goods at the port of destination, the Buyer may lodge claim with the Seller supported by survey report issued by an inspection organization agreed by both parties, with the exception, however, of those claims for which the insurance company and/of the shipping company are to be held responsible. Claim for quality discrepancy should be filed by the Buyer within 30 days after arrival of the goods at the port of destination, while for quantity/weight discrepancy, claim should be filed by the Buyer within 15 days after arrival of the goods at the port of destination. The Seller shall reply to the Buyer no later than 30 days after receipt of the claim requirement.

(17) FORCE MAJEURE

The Seller shall not be held responsible for failure or delay to perform all or any part of the Contract due to flood, fire, earthquake, drought, war, or any other event which could not be predicted at the time of the conclusion of the Contract, and could not be controlled, avoided or overcome by the Seller. However, the Seller shall inform the other party of its occurrence in written as soon as possible and thereafter send a certificate of the Event issued by the relevant authority to the other party but no later than 15 days after its occurrence. If the Force Majeure Event last over 120 days, both parties shall negotiate the performance or the termination of the Contract.

(18) ARBITRATION

All disputes arising from the Contract, should be settled through friendly negotiations. Should no settlement be reached through negotiation, the case shall then be submitted for arbitration to the China International Economic and Trade Arbitration Commission (Beijing) and arbitration rules of this Commission shall be applied. The award of the arbitration shall be final and binding upon both parties. The arbitration fee shall be borne by the losing party unless otherwise awarded by the arbitration organization.

(19) SPECIAL PROVISIONS

In witness thereof, this Contract shall come into effect immediately after it is signed by both parties in twooriginal copies and each party holds one copy.

The Seller _____ The Buyer _____

附录三 综合实训参考答案

一、建交函写作

金 喆 贸 易 有 限 公 司

JINZHE TRADING COMPANY LIMITED

地址：中国大连中山路 1267 号

电话：0411-84042525 传真：0411-84042588

ADD：NO. 1267 ZHONGSHAN ROAD, DALIAN, CHINA

TEL：0411-84042525 FAX：0411-84042588

March 2nd 2013

TO：DRAGON TOY CO., LTD.

1180 CHURCH ROAD, NEWYORK,

PA 19446 U.S.A.

Dear Sirs,

We have your name and address from the Internet and are glad to learn that you are seeking for Chinese telecontrol racing car.

Our company was founded in 1952 and has grown to be one of the leading Imp. & Exp. Companies in China, dealing in toys and handicrafts. As the commodities we supply are of good quality and fair price, we have won a very good reputation from our clients all over the world.

After a careful study of your market, we find that our commodities are suitable for children aged from six to fourteen, as they will make the children be more interested in science and technology. And that is why we are filled with confidence that there is a promising market in your country.

We take the liberty of writing to you with a view to establish business relations with you and are sending you by separate post our illustrated catalogs for your reference.

We look forward to your early reply and trust that through our cooperation we shall be able to conclude some transactions with you in the near future.

With best regards.

Yours faithfully,

JINZHE TRADING CO. , LTD.

×××,

Sale Manager

二、出口报价核算

（1）实际成本＝采购成本－退税收入＝150－150×9%÷（1＋17%）＝138.4615（元/辆）

（2）20英尺集装箱装箱量＝25÷（0.72×0.36×0.48）＝200.9388（箱）（取整数，为200箱）

报价数量＝200×12＝2 400（辆）

（3）国内费用＝［400＋550＋50＋600＋1 400＋（15＋5）×200］÷2 400＝2.9167（元/辆）

（4）出口运费＝2 200×8.25÷2 400＝7.5625（元/辆）

（5）出口报价：

①FOBC3＝（实际成本＋国内费用）÷（1－佣金率－预期利润率）

＝（138.4615＋2.9167）÷（1－3%－10%）÷8.25＝19.70（美元/辆）

②CFRC3＝（实际成本＋国内费用＋出口运费）÷（1－佣金率－预期利润率）

＝（138.4615＋2.9167＋7.5625）÷（1－3%－10%）÷8.25＝20.75（美元/辆）

③CIFC3＝$\left(\begin{matrix}\text{实际}\\\text{成本}\end{matrix}+\begin{matrix}\text{国内}\\\text{费用}\end{matrix}+\begin{matrix}\text{出口}\\\text{运费}\end{matrix}\right)$÷$\left[1-\text{佣金率}-\begin{matrix}\text{预期}\\\text{利润率}\end{matrix}-（1+\text{加成率}）×\text{保费率}\right]$

＝（138.4615＋2.9167＋7.5625）÷（1－3%－10%－110%×0.90%）÷8.25

＝20.99（美元/辆）

三、草拟发盘函

金喆贸易有限公司

JINZHE TRADING COMPANY LIMITED

地址：中国大连中山路1267号

电话：0411-84042525　　传真：0411-84042588

ADD：NO.1267 ZHONGSHAN ROAD, DALIAN, CHINA

TEL：0411-84042525　　FAX：0411-84042588

March 12th 2013

DRAGON TOY CO. , LTD.

1180 CHURCH ROAD, NEWYORK,

PA 19446 U. S. A.

Dear Sirs,

Thank you for your enquiry of March 7th, 2013. We are very glad to learn that you are interested in our products. Recently we have received a large number of orders from our clients and it seems that the demand is still increasing. We hope the same thing will happen in your market and are very glad to quote as follows:

Commodity: Telecontrol Racing Car

ART. NO. 18812 USD20. 99 /PIECE CIFC3 NEW YORK

ART. NO. 18814 USD22. 45 /PIECE CIFC3 NEW YORK

ART. NO. 18817 USD23. 75 /PIECE CIFC3 NEW YORK

ART. NO. 18819 USD24. 89 /PIECE CIFC3 NEW YORK

Packing: ART. NO. 18812 & 18819 to be packed in cartons of 12 pieces each /ART. NO. 18814 & 18817 to be packed in cartons of 20 pieces each one 20' FCL for each Art. No.

Shipment: Shipment is to be effected within 30 days on the receipt of the relevant L/C, but not later than May 31, 2013.

Insurance: To be covered by the seller for 110% of total invoice value against all risks and war risks.

Payment: By irrevocable sight letter of credit for full amount of the invoice value.

This quotation is valid for 3 days and we are looking forward to receiving your order.

Best regards!

Yours faithfully,

JINZHE TRADING CO. , LTD.

×××

MANAGER

四、出口还价核算

（1）利润核算

货号 18812 客户还价 USD19. 40 CIFC3

总利润额 = 19. 40× （1−110%×0. 90% −3% ） ×8. 25×2 400− （138. 4615+2. 9167+7. 5625） ×2 400

= 11 335. 92 （元）

（2）成本核算（货号 18812）

实际成本 $= 19.40 \times$（$1-110\% \times 0.90\% -3\% -5\%$）$\times 8.25-7.5625-2.9167$

$\qquad = 19.40 \times 0.9101 \times 8.25-7.5625-2.9167$

$\qquad = 135.1823$（元/辆）

采购成本 $= 135.1823 \div [1-9.00\% \div (1+17.00\%)]$

$\qquad = 135.1823 \div 0.9231$

$\qquad = 146.44$（元/辆）

（3）再次报价

出口运费及国内费用不变，分别为 7.5625 元/辆和 2.9167 元/辆（货号 18812）

实际成本 $= 145 \times [1-9.00\% \div (1+17.00\%)]$

$\qquad = 133.8462$（元）

$CIFC3 =$（$133.8462+2.9167+7.5625$）$\div$（$1-110\% \times 0.90\% -3\% -8\%$）$\div 8.25$

$\qquad = 19.88$（美元）

五、拟写还盘函

金喆贸易有限公司

JINZHE TRADING COMPANY LIMITED

地址：中国大连中山路 1267 号

电话：0411-84042525　传真：0411-84042588

ADD：NO. 1267 ZHONGSHAN ROAD, DALIAN, CHINA

TEL：0411-84042525　FAX：0411-84042588

March 22nd 2013

DRAGON TOY CO. , LTD.

1180 CHURCH ROAD, NEW YORK,

PA 19446 U. S. A.

Dear Sirs,

Thank you for your letter of March 17th 2013. We have discussed the matter with our manufacturers and brought them to see eye to eye with the idea of lowering our price, but still your counter-offer seems too high to be accepted.

Carefully you take the quality of our products into consideration, you will find our quotations are reasonable. However since this is the first business between us, we try our best to quote as follows:

TELECONTROL RACING CAR

ART. NO. 18812 USD 19.88 /PIECE CIFC3NEW YORK

ART. NO. 18814 USD 20.66 /PIECE CIFC3NEW YORK

ART. NO. 18817 USD 21. 94 /PIECE CIFC3NEW YORK

ART. NO. 18819 USD 23. 06 /PIECE CIFC3NEW YORK

This quotation is valid for only 8 days. Please take advantage of this chance and send your acceptance to us as soon as possible.

Best regards!

Yours faithfully,

JINZHE TRADING CO. , LTD.

×××

MANAGER

六、出口成交核算

合同核算：

货号　18812/18814/18817/18819　电动遥控玩具赛车

数量　每个货号 1 个 20′集装箱

ART NO. 18812 & 18819 各 2 400 辆，共计 4 800 辆

ART NO. 18814 & 18817 各 2 000 辆，共计 4 000 辆

成交单价（USD）：

ART. NO. 18812 USD 19. 88 /PIECE CIFC3NEW YORK

ART. NO. 18814 USD 20. 66 /PIECE CIFC3NEW YORK

ART. NO. 18817 USD 21. 94 /PIECE CIFC3NEW YORK

ART. NO. 18819 USD 23. 06 /PIECE CIFC3NEW YORK

国内供货价格分别为：145. 00 元、150. 00 元、160. 00 元、170. 00 元

合同金额：USD188 256. 00

总成交金额：188 256×8. 25＝155 3112（元）

（1）购货总成本＝（145+170）×2 400+（150+160）×2 000

$\qquad$ ＝1 376 000（元）

（2）实际采购成本＝［（145+170）×2 400+（150+160）×2 000］×1.08÷1. 17

$\qquad$ ＝1 270 153. 85（元）

（3）总退税收入＝1 376 000－1 270 153. 85

$\qquad$ ＝105 846. 15（元）

（4）费用细目及总额：

国内费用＝（400+600+600+1 400）×4+（100+200）×2×20

$\qquad$ ＝24 000. 00（元）

海运费 = 2 200×4×8.25

$\qquad$ = 72 600.00（元）

保险费 = 188 256×8.25×110% ×0.90%

$\qquad$ = 15 375.81（元）

佣金 = 188 256×8.25×3%

$\qquad$ = 46 593.36（元）

（5）$\dfrac{成交}{利润额}$ = 188 256×8.25-1 376 000+105 846.15-24 000-72 600.00-15 375.81-46 593.36

$\qquad$ = 124 388.98（元）

成交利润率 = 124 388.98÷188 256÷8.25

$\qquad$ = 8.01%

七、出口合同签订

(1) 成交签约函

金 喆 贸 易 有 限 公 司

JINZHE TRADING COMPANY LIMITED

地址：中国大连中山路 1267 号

电话：0411-84042525　传真：0411-84042588

ADD：NO.1267 ZHONGSHAN ROAD, DALIAN, CHINA

TEL：0411-84042525　FAX：0411-84042588

April 1st 2013

DRAGON TOY CO. , LTD.

1180 CHURCH ROAD, NEWYORK,

PA 19446 U. S. A.

Dear Sirs,

Thank you for your order of March 22nd 2013. We are pleased to do business with you and are sending you our signed Sales Confirmation No. JZ-DRGSC01 in duplicate. Please return one copy with your counter-signature for our file.

You can be assured that we will try our best to execute the order, and that the good quality of our commodities will meet your request. As the shipment date is approaching, please open the relevant L/C as soon as possible so that we can effect shipment on time.

With best regards.

Yours faithfully,

JINZHE TRADING CO. , LTD.

×××

MANAGER

（2）销售确认书

SALES CONFIRMATION

S/C No. : JZ-DRGSC01

Date：April 1st 2013

The Seller：JINZHE TRADING CO. , LTD.	The Buyer：DRAGON TOY CO. , LTD.
Address： NO. 1267 ZHONGSHAN ROAD, DALIAN，CHINA	Address：1180 CHURCH ROAD, NEW YORK PA 19446U. S. A.

Item No.	Commodity & Specifications	Unit	Quantity	Unit Price (USD)	AMOUNT (USD)
TELECONTROL RACING CAR				CIFC3 NEWYORK	
1	ART. NO. 18812	PIECE	2 400	19. 88	47 712. 00
2	ART. NO. 18814	PIECE	2 000	20. 66	41 320. 00
3	ART. NO. 18817	PIECE	2 000	21. 94	43 880. 00
4	ART. NO. 18819	PIECE	2 400	23. 06	55 344. 00
TOTAL					188 256. 00

TOTAL CONTRACT VALUE：

SAY US DOLLARS ONE HUNDRED EIGHTY-EIGHT THOUSAND TWO HUNDRED AND FIFTY-SIX ONLY.

PACKING：ART. NO. 18812 & 18819 TO PACKED IN CARTONS OF 12 PIECES EACH

ART. NO. 18814 & 18817 TO PACKED IN CARTONS OF 20 PIECES EACH

ALL PRODUCTS IN FOUR 20′ CONTAINERS.

TERMS OF SHIPMENT：SHIPMENT IN MAY 2013 AFTER RECEIVING THE RELEVANT LETTER OF CREDIT, WITH PARTIAL SHIPMENT AND TRANSSHIPMENT ALLOWED.

PORT OF LOADING & DESTINATION：FROM DALIAN, CHINA TO NEW YORK, USA

PAYMENT：THE BUYER SHALL OPEN AN IRREVOCABLE L/C IN FAVOR OF THE SELLER BEFORE APR. 15TH, 2009. THE SAID L/C SHALL BE AVAILABLE BY DRAFT AT SIGHT FOR FULL INVOICE VALUE AND REMAIN VALID FOR NEGOTIATION IN CHINA FOR 15 DAYS AFTER SHIPMENT.

INSURANCE：TO BE COVERED BY THE SELLER FOR 110% OF TOTAL INVOICE VALUE AGAINST ALL RISKS AND WARRISK AS PER THE OCEAN MARINE CARGO CLAUSES OF THE PEOPLE′S INSURANCE COMPANY OF CHINA, DATED JAN. 1ST, 1981.

Confirmed by:

THE SELLER　　　　　　　　　　THE BUYER

JINZHE TRADING CO. , LTD.

GRACE ZHANG

Remarks:

1. The buyer shall have the covering letter of credit which should reach the Seller 30 days before shipment, failing which the Seller reserves the right to rescind without further notice, or to regard as still valid whole or any part of this contract not fulfilled by the Buyer, or to lodge a claim for losses thus sustained, if any.

2. In case of any discrepancy in Quality/Quantity, claim should be filed by the Buyer within 30 days after the arrival of the goods at port of destination; while for quantity discrepancy, claim should be filed by the Buyer within 15 days after the arrival of the goods at port of destination.

3. For transactions concluded on C. I. F. basis, it is understood that the insurance amount will be for 110% of the invoice value against the risks specified in the Sales Confirmation. If additional insurance amount or coverageis required, the Buyer must have the consent of the Seller before Shipment, and the additional premium is to be borne by the Buyer.

4. The Seller shall not hold liable for non-delivery or delay in delivery of the entire lot or a portion of the goods hereunder by reason of natural disasters, war or other causes of Force Majeure, However, the Seller shall notify the Buyer as soon as possible and furnish the Buyer within 15 days by registered airmail with a certificate issued by the China Council for the Promotion of International Trade attesting such event (s) .

5. All deputies arising out of the performance of, or relating to this contract, shall be settled through negotiation. In case no settlement can be reached through negotiation, the case shall then be submitted to the China International Economic and Trade Arbitration Commission for arbitration in accordance with its arbitral rules. The arbitration shall take place in DALIAN. The arbitral award is final and binding upon both parties.

6. The Buyer is requested to sign and return one copy of this contract immediately after receipt of the same. Objection, if any, should be raised by the Buyer within 15 days otherwise it is understood that the Buyer has accepted the terms and conditions of this contract.

7. Special conditions: (These shall prevail over all printed terms in case of any conflict.)

八、审核信用证

金喆贸易有限公司

JINZHE TRADING COMPANY LIMITED

地址：中国大连中山路 1267 号

电话：0411-84042525　　传真：0411-84042588

ADD：NO. 1267 ZHONGSHAN ROAD，DALIAN，CHINA

TEL：0411-84042525　FAX：0411-84042588

审证意见：

信用证存在的问题	需要修改的理由
1. 国外到期	易产生逾期交单
2. 两个品种数量有误	少于合同规定数量
3. 投保加成错误	增加保费支出
4. 受益人公司名称有误	会出现单、证不符
5. 一个品种货号有误	与实际出运货号不符
6. 付款期限不妥	超出合同规定期限
7. 信用证到期日提前	易产生逾期交单

审核人：×××

九、修改信用证

金 喆 贸 易 有 限 公 司

JINZHE TRADING COMPANY LIMITED

地址：中国大连中山路 1267 号

电话：0411-84042525　传真：0411-84042588

ADD：NO. 1267 ZHONGSHAN ROAD，DALIAN，CHINA

TEL：0411-84042525　FAX：0411-84042588

April 25th 2013

DRAGON TOY CO. ，LTD.

1180 CHURCH ROAD，NEW YORK，

PA 19446 U. S. A.

Dear Sirs，

We are very glad to receive your L/C No. DRG-JZLC01，but we are quite sorry to find that it contains some discrepancies with the S/C. Please instruct your bank to amend the L/C as quickly as possible.

The L/C is to be amended as follows：

-The place of expiry should be in China，instead of "In U. S. A. ".

–The date of the expiry should be June 15th 2013, instead of "June 10th 2013".

–The draft (s) should be sight draft (s) instead of "at 30 days sight".

–Thearticle number of the goods is "18819" in stead of "18818".

–The insurance value should be total invoice value plus 10% insteadof "plus 110%".

–The quantity of ART. NO. 18812 & 18819 should be "2 400 pieces" instead of "2 000 pieces".

–The beneficiary should be JINZHE TRADING CO. LTD., instead of JINZHE CO. LTD.

With best regards!

Yours faithfully,

JINZHE TRADING CO., LTD

×××

MANAGER

十、托运订舱

(1) 出口货物订舱委托书

出口货物订舱委托书

日期：9-May-13

(1) 发货人 JINZHE TRADING CO., LTD. NO. 1267ZHONGSHAN ROAD, DALIAN, CHINA	(4) 信用证号码　DRG-JZLC01	
	(5) 开证银行　CHEMICAL BANK NEW YORK	
	(6) 合同号码　JZ-DRGSC01	(7) 成交金额 USD 188 256.00
	(8) 装运口岸　DALIAN	(9) 目的港　NEW YORK
(2) 收货人 TO ORDER	(10) 转船运输　YES	(11) 分批装运 YES
	(12) 信用证效期 15-Jun-13	(13) 装船期限 31-May-13
	(14) 运费　PREPAID	(15) 成交条件 CIF NEW YORK
	(16) 公司联系人　×××	(17) 电话/传真 0411-84042588
(3) 通知人 DRAGON TOY CO., LTD. 1180 CHURCH ROAD, NEW YORK, PA 19446 U.S.A.	(18) 公司开户行 Bank of China	(19) 银行账号 4784939302
	(20) 特别要求	

续表

(21) 标记、唛码	(22) 货号规格	(23) 包装件数	(24) 毛重	(25) 净重	(26) 数量	(27) 单价	(28) 总价
		TELECONTROL RACING CAR				CIFNEW YORK	
JZ-DRGSC01	18812	200CTNS	2 400KGS	1 800KGS	2 400PCS	USD19.88	USD47 712.00
DRAGON TOY	18814	100CTNS	2 200KGS	1 800KGS	2 000PCS	USD20.66	USD41 320.00
NEW YORK	18817	100CTNS	2 200KGS	1 800KGS	2 000PCS	USD21.94	USD43 880.00
C/NO. 1~600	18819	200CTNS	2 400KGS	1 800KGS	2 400PCS	USD23.06	USD55 344.00

(29) 总件数	(30) 总毛重	(31) 总净重	(32) 总尺码	(33) 总金额
600 CTNS	9 200KGS	7 200KGS	99.533m³	USD 188 256.00

(34) 备注

(2) 商业发票

COMMERCIAL INVOICE

(1) SELLER JINZHE TRADING CO., LTD.	(3) INVOICE NO. JZ-DRGINV01	(4) INVOICE DATE 9-May-13
Address: NO. 1267 ZHONGSHAN ROAD, DALIAN, CHINA	(5) L/C NO. DRG-JZLC01	(6) DATE 14-Apr-13
	(7) ISSUED BY CHEMICAL BANKNEW YORK	
(2) BUYER DRAGON TOY CO., LTD.	(8) CONTRACT NO. JZ-DRGSC01	(9) DATE 1-Apr-13
Address: 1180 CHURCH ROAD, NEW YORK, PA 19446 U.S.A.	(10) FROM DALIAN	(11) TO NEW YORK
	(12) SHIPPED BY	(13) PRICE TERM CIFNEW YORK

(14) MARKS	(15) DESCRIPTION OF GOODS	(16) QTY.	(17) UNIT PRICE	(18) AMOUNT
JZ-DRGSC01 DRAGONTOY	TELECONTROL RACING CAR		CIF NEW YORK	

续表

NEW YORK	ART. NO.			
NO. 1-600	18812	2 400 PCS	USD 19. 88	USD 47 712. 00
	18814	2 000 PCS	USD 20. 66	USD 41 320. 00
	18817	2 000 PCS	USD 21. 94	USD 43 880. 00
	18819	2 400 PCS	USD 23. 06	USD 55 344. 00

TOTAL: USD 188 256. 00

AS PER SALES CONFIRMATION NO. JZ-DRGSC01   DATED APRIL 1ST, 2013

AS PER L/C NO. DRG-JZLC01 DATED APRIL 14, 2013

ART NO. 18812 AND 18819 PACKED IN 400 CARTONS OF 12 PIECES EACH AND THEN TO TWO
20'FCL CONTAINERS

ART NO. 18814 AND 18817 PACKED IN 200CARTONS OF 20 PIECES EACH AND THEN TO TWO
20'FCL CONTAINERS

TOTAL NUMBER OF PACKAGE: 600 CTNS

TOTAL GROSS WEIGHT: 9 200KGS

(19) TOTAL VALUE

SAY US DOLLARS ONE HUNDRED AND EIGHTY-EIGHT THOUSAND TWO HUNDRED AND
FIFTY-SIX ONLY.

(20) ISSUED BY

JINZHE TRADING CO. , LTD.

(21) SIGNATURE

×××

3 COPIES

(3) 装箱单

PACKING LIST

(1) SELLER	(3) INVOICE NO.	(4) INVOICE DATE
JINZHE TRADING CO. , LTD.	JZ-DRGINV01	2013-5-9

Address: NO. 1267ZHONGSHAN ROAD, DALIAN, CHINA	(5) FROM DALIAN	(6) TO NEW YORK
	(7) TOTAL PACKAGES (IN WORDS) SAY SIX HUNDRED CARTONS ONLY	
(2) BUYER DRAGON TOY CO. , LTD. Address: 1180 CHURCH ROAD, NEW YORK, PA 19446U. S. A.	(8) MARKS & NOS. JZ-DRGSC01 DRAGON TOY NEW YORK NO. 1-600	

(9) C/NOS.	(10) NOS. & KINDS OF PKGS	(11) ITEM.	(12) QTY. (PCS.)	(13) G. W. (kg)	(14) N. W. (kg)	(15) MEAS (m³)
	TELECONTROL RACING CAR					
1-200	200 CTNS	18812	2 400	2 400	1 800	24. 8832
201-300	100 CTNS	18814	2 000	2 200	1 800	24. 8832
301-400	100 CTNS	18817	2 000	2 200	1 800	24. 8832
401-600	200 CTNS	18819	2 400	2 400	1 800	24. 8832
TOTAL	600 CTNS		8 800	9 200	7 200	99. 533

SHIPPING MARKS　　　　WEIGHT AND MEAS. PER EXPORT CARTON:

JZ-DRGSC01	ART. NO.	G. W. (KGS.)	N. W. (KGS.)	MEAS. (m³)
DRAGON TOY	18812	12	9	0. 124
NEW YORK	18814	22	18	0. 249
NO. 1-600	18817	22	18	0. 249
	18819	12	9	0. 124

(16) ISSUED BY

JINZHE TRADING CO. , LTD.

(17) SIGNATURE

×××

2 COPIES

十一、出口报关

(1) 出口货物报关单

中华人民共和国海关出口货物报关单

预录入编号：		海关编号：	
出口口岸 大连海关	备案号	出口日期 2013.05.20	申报日期 2013.05.12
经营单位 金喆贸易有限公司	运输方式 水路运输	运输工具名称 CHENG FEN/V. 208	提运单号 JZ-DRGBL01
发货单位 金喆贸易有限公司	贸易方式 一般贸易	征免性质	结汇方式 信用证
许可证号	运抵国（地区） U. S. A.	指运港 NEW YORK	境内货源地 大连
批准文号	成交方式 CIF	运费 502/8 800.00 /3	保费 142/15 375.81 /3	杂费 142/24 000.00/3
合同协议号 JZ-DRGSC01	件数 600	包装种类 CARTONS	毛重（千克） 9 200	净重（千克） 7 200
集装箱号 TE57233331/20/2275	随附单据		生产厂家 金喆贸易有限公司

标记、唛码及备注

JZ-DRGSC01

DRAGON TOY

NEW YORK

NO.1-600

项号	商品编号	商品名称、规格、型号	数量及单位	最终目的国（地区）	单价	总价	币制	征免
01	9503.8000	遥控赛车	USD	美国				照章征税
		TELECONTROL RACING CAR						
	18812		2 400SETS		19.88	47 712.00		
	18814		2 000SETS		20.66	41 320.00		
	18817		2 000SETS		21.94	43 880.00		
	18819		2 400SETS		23.06	55 344.00		
						188 256.00		

录入员 录入单位	兹声明以上申报无讹并承担法律责任	海关审单批注及放行日期（签章）	
报关员 孙子武		审单	审价
单位地址 中国大连中山路 1267 号	申报单位（签章） 金喆贸易有限公司	征税	统计
邮编××× 电话 84042525 填制日期 2013-5-12		查验	放行

（2）商业发票

COMMERCIAL INVOICE

(1) SELLER JINZHE TRADING CO., LTD.	(3) INVOICE NO. JZ-DRGINV01	(4) INVOICE DATE 9-May-13
Address： NO. 1267ZHONGSHAN ROAD, DALIAN, CHINA	(5) L/C NO. DRG-JZLC01	(6) DATE 14-Apr-13
	(7) ISSUED BY CHEMICAL BANK NEW YORK	
(2) BUYER DRAGON TOY CO., LTD.	(8) CONTRACT NO. JZ-DRGSC01	(9) DATE 1-Apr-13
Address： 1180 CHURCH ROAD, NEW YORK, PA 19446U. S. A.	(10) FROM DALIAN	(11) TO NEW YORK
	(12) SHIPPED BY	(13) PRICE TERM CIF NEW YORK

(14) MARKS (15) DESCRIPTION OF GOODS (16) QTY.   (17) UNIT PRICE (18) AMOUNT

JZ-DRGSC01	TELECONTROL RACING CAR		CIF NEW YORK	
DRAGON TOY				
NEW YORK	ART. NO.			
NO. 1-600	18812	2 400 PCS	USD 19. 88	USD 47 712. 00
	18814	2 000 PCS	USD 20. 66	USD 41 320. 00
	18817	2 000 PCS	USD 21. 94	USD 43 880. 00
	18819	2 400 PCS	USD 23. 06	USD 55 344. 00

TOTAL：USD 188 256. 00

续表

AS PER SALES CONFIRMATION NO. JZ-DRGSC01 DATED APRIL 1ST, 2013

AS PER L/C NO. DRG-JZLC01 DATED APRIL 14, 2013

ART NO. 18812 AND 18819 PACKED IN 400 CARTONS OF 12 PIECES EACH AND THEN TO TWO 20′FCL CONTAINERS

ART NO. 18814 AND 18817 PACKED IN 200 CARTONS OF 20 PIECES EACH AND THEN TO TWO 20′ FCL CONTAINERS

TOTAL NUMBER OF PACKAGE：600 CTNS

TOTAL GROSS WEIGHT：9 200KGS

---

(19) TOTAL VALUE

SAY US DOLLARS ONE HUNDRED AND EIGHTY-EIGHT THOUSAND TWO HUNDRED AND

FIFTY-SIX ONLY.

(20) ISSUED BY

JINZHE TRADING CO. , LTD.

(21) SIGNATURE

×××

3 COPIES

（3）装箱单

PACKING LIST

(1) SELLER JINZHE TRADING CO. , LTD.	(3) INVOICE NO. JZ-DRGINV01	(4) INVOICE DATE 2013-5-9
Address： NO. 1267 ZHONGSHAN ROAD, DALIAN, CHINA	(5) FROM DALIAN	(6) TO NEW YORK
	(7) TOTAL PACKAGES (IN WORDS) SAY SIX HUNDRED CARTONS ONLY	
(2) BUYER DRAGON TOY CO. , LTD.	(8) MARKS & NOS. JZ-DRGSC01	
Address： 1180 CHURCH ROAD, NEW YORK, PA 19446U. S. A.	DRAGON TOY NEW YORK NO. 1-600	

续表

(9) C/NOS.	(10) NOS. & KINDS OF PKGS	(11) ITEM	(12) QTY. (PCS.)	(13) G.W. (kg)	(14) N.W. (kg)	(15) MEAS (m³)
	TELECONTROL RACING CAR					
1-200	200 CTNS	18812	2 400	2 400	1 800	24.8832
201-300	100 CTNS	18814	2 000	2 200	1 800	24.8832
301-400	100 CTNS	18817	2 000	2 200	1 800	24.8832
401-600	200 CTNS	18819	2 400	2 400	1 800	24.8832
TOTAL	600 CTNS		8 800	9 200	7 200	99.533

SHIPPING MARKS	WEIGHT AND MEAS. PER EXPORT CARTON:			
JZ-DRGSC01	ART. NO.	G.W. (KGS.)	N.W. (KGS.)	MEAS. (m³)
DRAGON TOY	18812	12	9	0.124
NEW YORK	18814	22	18	0.249
NO. 1-600	18817	22	18	0.249
	18819	12	9	0.124

(16) ISSUED BY

JINZHE TRADING CO., LTD.

(17) SIGNATURE

×××

2 COPIES

十二、投保装船

(1) 出口货物投保单

海运出口货物投保单

(1) 保险人： 中国人民保险公司		(2) 被保险人： JINZHE TRADING CO. , LTD	
(3) 标记 AS PER INV. JZ-DRGINV01	(4) 包装及数量 600 CTNS	(5) 保险货物项目 TELECONTROL RACING CAR	(6) 保险货物金额 USD 207 082. 00
(7) 总保险金额（大写） SAY US DOLLARS TWO HUNDRED AND SEVEN THOUSAND EIGHTY TWO ONLY.			
(8) 运输工具（船名、航次） 　　CHENG FEN　　V. 208		(9) 装运港： DALIAN	(10) 目的港： NEW YORK
(11) 投保险别： ALL RISKS AND WAR RISKS AS PER CIC OF P. I. C. C. DATED1/1/1981		(12) 货物起运日期 20-May-13	

(13) 投保日期：15-May-13　　(14) 投保人签字：JINZHE TRADING CD. , LTD.

(2) 装船通知

金喆贸易有限公司
JINZHE TRADING COMPANY LIMITED
地址：中国大连中山路 1267 号
电话：0411-84042525　传真：0411-84042588
ADD：NO. 1267 ZHONGSHAN ROAD, DALIAN, CHINA
TEL：0411-84042525　FAX：0411-84042588

15th May 2013
DRAGON TOY CO. , LTD
1180 CHURCH ROAD, NEW YORK,
PA 19446U. S. A.

Dear Sirs,

We are very pleased to inform you that the goods（four containers of telecontrol racing cars）under S/C No. JZ–DRGSC01 will be dispatched by S. S. CHENG FEN V. 208 on May 20th 2013 and it will arrive in New York in May 30th 2013. The B/L number is JZ–DRGBL01 and the total invoice value is USD 188 256. 00.

With best regards.

Yours faithfully,

JINZHE TRADING CO. , LTD

×××

MANAGER

十三、出口单据制作

（1）汇票

BILL OF EXCHANGE

No.   JZ–DRGINV01

For USD 188 256. 00	DALIAN 27–May–13
（amount in figure）	（place and date of issue）

At   *************   sight of this   FIRST   Bill of exchange（SECOND being unpaid）

pay to   BANK OF CHINA, DALIAN BRANCH   or order the sum of

SAY UNITED STATES DOLLARS ONE HUNDRED AND EIGHTY EIGHT THOUSAND AND TWO HUNDRED AND FIFTY SIX ONLY.

（amount in words）

Value received for	600 SETS Of	TELECONTROL RACING CAR
	（quantity）	（name of commodity）

Drawn under   CHEMICAL BANK NEW YORK

续表

| L/C No. | DRG-JZLC01 | dated | 14-Apr-13 |

To：　CHEMICAL BANK NEW YORK

　　　55 WALL STREET, ROOM 1702,

　　　NEW YORK 10041

For and on behalf of

JINZHE TRADING CO. , LTD.

×××

（Signature）

（2）海运提单

BILL OF LADING

(1) SHIPPER JINZHE TRADING CO. , LTD	(10) B/L NO. JZ-DRGBL01
Address： NO. 1267 ZHONGSHAN ROAD, DALIAN, CHINA	CARRIER
(2) CONSIGNEE TO ORDER	COSCO 中国远洋运输（集团）总公司
(3) NOTIFY PARTY DRAGON TOY CO. , LTD. 1180 CHURCH ROAD, NEW YORK, PA 19446 U. S. A	CHINA OCEAN SHIPPING（GROUP）CO. ORIGINAL

(4) PLACE OF RECEIPT DALIAN CY	(5) OCEAN VESSEL CHENG FEN	COMBINED TRANSPORT BILL OF LADING
(6) VOYAGE NO. V. 208	(7) PORT OF LOADING DALIAN	
(8) PORT OF DISCHARGE NEW YORK	(9) PLACE OF DELIVERY NEW YORK CY	

(11) MARKS	(12) NOS. & KINDS OF PKGS.	(13) DESCRIPTION OF GOODS	(14) G. W. （kg）	(15) MEAS（m³）
JZ-DRGSC01 DRAGON TOY NEW YORK NO. 1-600	600 CARTONS	TELECONTROL RACING CAR	9 200	99. 533

续表

FREIGHT PREPAID

L/C NO. DRG-JZLC01

(16) TOTAL NUMBER OF CONTAINERS OR PACKAGES (IN WORDS)		SAY SIX HUNDRED CARTONS ONLY
FREIGHT & CHARGES	REVENUE TONS	RATE /PER /PREPAID /COLLECT
PREPAID AT	PAYABLE AT	(17) PLACE AND DATE OF ISSUE DALIAN 20-May-13
TOTAL PREPAID	(18) NUMBER OF ORIGINAL B (S) L THREE	(20) LOADING ON BOARD THE VESSEL 郭 复 北 COSCO DALIAN SHIPPING CO. , LTD. AS AGENT FOR THE CARRIER CHINA
(19) DATE 20-May-13		

ENDORSEMENT：JINZHE TRADING CO. , LTD

　　　　×××　　　　　　20-May-13

3 COPIES

（3）商业发票

COMMERCIAL INVOICE

(1) SELLER JINZHE TRADING CO. , LTD.	(3) INVOICE NO. JZ-DRGINV01	(4) INVOICE DATE 9-May-13
Address： NO. 1267 ZHONGSHAN ROAD, DALIAN, CHINA	(5) L/C NO. DRG-JZLC01	(6) DATE 14-Apr-13
	(7) ISSUED BY CHEMICAL BANKNEW YORK	
(2) BUYER DRAGON TOY CO. , LTD.	(8) CONTRACT NO. JZ-DRGSC01	(9) DATE 1-Apr-13
Address： 1180 CHURCH ROAD, NEW YORK, PA 19446U. S. A.	(10) FROM DALIAN	(11) TO NEW YORK
	(12) SHIPPED BY	(13) PRICE TERM CIF NEW YORK

(14) MARKS	(15) DESCRIPTION OF GOODS	(16) QTY.	(17) UNIT PRICE	(18) AMOUNT

续表

JZ-DRGSC01	TELECONTROL RACING CAR			CIF NEW YORK	
DRAGON TOY					
NEW YORK	ART. NO.				
NO. 1-600	18812		2 400 PCS	USD 19. 88	USD 47 712. 00
	18814		2 000 PCS	USD 20. 66	USD 41 320. 00
	18817		2 000 PCS	USD 21. 94	USD 43 880. 00
	18819		2 400 PCS	USD 23. 06	USD 55 344. 00
				TOTAL:	USD 188 256. 00

PACKING: AS PER SALES CONFIRMATION NO. JZ-DRGSC01 DATED APRIL 1ST, 2013

AS PER L/C NO. DRG-JZLC01 DATED APRIL 14, 2013

ART NO. 18812 AND 18819 PACKED IN 400 CARTONS OF 12 PIECES EACH AND THEN TO TWO

20'FCL CONTAINERS

ART NO. 18814 AND 18817 PACKED IN 200 CARTONS OF 20 PIECES EACH AND THEN TO TWO

20' FCL CONTAINERS

TOTAL NUMBER OF PACKAGE: 600 CTNS

TOTAL GROSS WEIGHT: 9 200KGS

(19) TOTAL VALUE

SAY US DOLLARS ONE HUNDRED AND EIGHTY-EIGHT THOUSAND TWO HUNDRED AND
FIFTY-SIX ONLY.

(20) ISSUED BY

JINZHE TRADING CO. , LTD.

(21) SIGNATURE

×××

3 COPIES

（4）装箱单

PACKING LIST

(1) SELLER JINZHE TRADING CO. , LTD.	(3) INVOICE NO. JZ-DRGINV01	(4) INVOICE DATE 2013-5-9
Address： NO. 1267 ZHONGSHAN ROAD, DALIAN, CHINA	(5) FROM DALIAN	(6) TO NEW YORK
	(7) TOTAL PACKAGES（IN WORDS) SAY SIX HUNDRED CARTONS ONLY	
(2) BUYER DRAGON TOY CO. , LTD.	(8) MARKS & NOS. JZ-DRGSC01	
Address： 1180 CHURCH ROAD, NEW YORK, PA 19446U. S. A.	DRAGON TOY NEW YORK NO. 1-600	

(9) C/NOS.	(10) NOS. & KINDS OF PKGS	(11) ITEM.	(12) QTY. （PCS.）	(13) G. W. （kg）	(14) N. W. （kg）	(15) MEAS （m³）
		TELECONTROL RACING CAR				
1-200	200 CTNS	18812	2 400	2 400	1 800	24. 8832
201-300	100 CTNS	18814	2 000	2 200	1 800	24. 8832
301-400	100 CTNS	18817	2 000	2 200	1 800	24. 8832
401-600	200 CTNS	18819	2 400	2 400	1 800	24. 8832
TOTAL	600 CTNS		8 800	9 200	7 200	99. 533

SHIPPING MARKS JZ-DRGSC01 DRAGON TOY NEW YORK NO. 1-600	WEIGHT AND MEAS. PER EXPORT CARTON：			
	ART. NO.	G. W. （KGS.)	N. W. （KGS.)	MEAS. （m³）
	18812	12	9	0. 124
	18814	22	18	0. 249
	18817	22	18	0. 249
	18819	12	9	0. 124

(16) ISSUED BY

JINZHE TRADING CO. , LTD.

(17) SIGNATURE

×××

2 COPIES

（5）保险单

中 国 人 民 保 险 公 司

THE PEOPLE'S INSURANCE COMPANY OF CHINA

总公司设于北京　　　　一九四九年创立

Head office：BEIJING　　　　Established in 1949

保险单 INSURANCE POLICY	保险单号次 POLICY NO.　JZ–DRGBD01

中国人民保险公司（以下简称本公司）

THIS POLICY OF INSURANCE WITNESSES THAT THE PEOPLE'S INSURANCE COMPANY OF CHINA（HEREINAFTER CALLED "THE COMPANY"）

根据金喆贸易有限公司

AT THE REQUEST OF JINZHE TRADING CO．，LTD

（以下简称被保险人）的要求，由被保险人

（HEREINAFTER CALLED "THE INSURED"）AND IN CONSIDERATION OF THE AGREED PREMIUM

向本公司缴付约定的保险费，

PAID TO THE COMPANY BY THE INSURED，UNDERTAKES TO INSURE THE UNDERMENTIONED

按照本保险单承保险别和背面所载条款与

GOODS IN TRANSPORTATION SUBJECT TO THE CONDITIONS OF THIS POLICY AS PER THE

下列特款承保下述货物运输保险，特立本保险单

CLAUSES PRINTED OVERLEAF AND OTHER SPECIAL CLAUSES ATTACHED HEREON.

标记 MARKS& NOS	数量 QUANTITY	保险货物项目 DESCRIPTION OF GOODS	保险金额 AMOUNT INSURED
JZ–DRGSC01 DRAGON TOY NEW YORK NO 1–600	8 800 PIECES	TELECONTROL RACING CAR	USD 207 082. 00

总保险金额

TOTAL AMOUNT INSURED

SAY US DOLLARS TWO HUNDRED AND SEVEN THOUSAND EIGHTY TWO ONLY.

保费 PREMIUM	费率 RATE	装载运输工具 PER CONVEYANCE S. S.
AS ARRANGED	AS ARRANGED	CHENG FEN V. 208

开航日期 SLG. ON OR ABT.　　　　　　　自　　　　　　至

AS PER BILL OF LADING　　　　　　　FROM DALIAN　　TO NEW YORK

承保险别：

CONDITIONS COVERING ALL RISKS AND WAR RISK AS PER AND SUBJECT TO OCEAN MARINE CARGO CLAUSES OF PICC DATED 1/1/1981

所保货物，如遇出险，本公司凭本保险单及其他有关证件给付赔款。

CLAIMS, IF ANY, PAYABLE ON SURRENDER OF THIS POLICY TOGETHER WITH OTHER RELEVANT DOCUMENTS.

所保货物，如发生本保险单项下负责赔偿的损失或事故，

IN THE EVENT OF ACCIDENT WHEREBY LOSS OR DAMAGE MAY RESULT IN A CLAIM UNDER THIS POLICY.

应立即通知本公司下述代理人查勘。

IMMEDIATELY NOTICE APPLYING FOR SURVEY MUST BE GIVEN TO THE COMPANY'S AGENT AS MENTIONED HEREUNDER.

GODWIN INSURANCE COMPANY

P. O. BOX 17764

NEW YORK, U. S. A.

FAX：215-393-8576

赔款偿付地点

CLAIM PAYABLE AT/IN DALIAN IN CHINA

日 期   大连

DATE   18-May-13   DALIAN

地址：中国大连中山路 1267 号

Address：NO. 1267 ZHONGSHAN ROAD, DALIAN, CHINA

ENDORSEMENT：JINZHE TRADING CO. , LTD.

中国人民保险公司大连分公司

THE PEOPLE'S INSURANCE CO. OF CHINA

DALIAN BRANCH

孙博

General Manager

×××   18-May-13   2 COPIES

（6）原产地证书

ORIGINAL

1. Exporter（full name and address） JINZHE TRADING CO. , LTD. NO. 1267 ZHONGSHAN ROAD, DALIAN, CHINA	Certificate No. JZ-DRGORG01 CERTIFICATE OF ORIGIN OF THE PEOPLE'S REPUBLIC OF CHINA
2. Consignee（full name, address, country） DRAGON TOY CO. , LTD. 1180 CHURCH ROAD, NEW YORK, PA 19446 U. S. A.	
3. Means of transport and route FROM DALIAN TO NEW YORK BY SEA	5. For certifying authority use only
4. Destination port NEW YORK, U. S. A	

续表

6. Marks and numbers of packages	7. Description of goods/number and kind of packages	8. H. S. Code	9. Quantity or weight	10. Number and date of invoices
JZ-DRGSC01 DRAGON TOY NEW YORK NO. 1-600	600 CARTONS (SAY SIX HUNDRED CARTONS ONLY) TELECONTROL RACING CAR	9503. 8000	9 200KGS	JZ-DRGINV01 09-May-13

****

11. Declaration by the exporter	12. Certification
The undersigned hereby declares that the above details and statements are correct; that all the goods were produced in China and that they comply with the Rules of Origin of the People's Republic of China. JINZHE TRADING CO. , LTD. DALIAN	It is hereby certified that the declaration by the exporter is correct. 郭哲昕 DALIAN
Date：MAY 14, 2013 signature and stamp of authorized signatory	Date：MAY 16, 2013 signature and stamp of certifying authority

China Council for the Promotion of International Trade is China Chamber of International Commerce.

2 COPIES

十四、单据审核

1. 单据审核

新加坡发展银行大连分行信用证 0016100293496 项下的结汇单据存在如下问题：所有单据均未显示出该批货物系分批装运的第一批。此外，还有：

1）汇票

（1）金额错误，应为该批金额，即 139 641.84 美元。

（2）金额大写错误，应为"SAY US DOLLARS ONE HUNDRED THIRTY NINE THOUSAND SIX HUNDRED FORTY-ONE AND EIGHTY-FOUR CENTS ONLY"。

（3）收款人错误，应为议付银行，即"BANK OF COMMERCE MALAYSIA BERHAD, KUALA LUMPUR BRANCH"。

（4）出票条款中未按信用证要求显示信用证号码。

（5）受票人错误，应为开证行，即"DBS BANK, DALIAN BRANCH"。

（6）未经出票人签字。

2）发票

（1）货物描述不完整，缺少"as per Contract No. YN-NK942 dated April 1st, 2013"词句。

（2）未按信用证要求显示承运船名，即"S. S. BIN BO V. 911"。

（3）未按信用证要求显示出分批序号。

（4）货号1/40nm单价与信用证不符，应为10.05美元，而非10.50美元。

（5）未按信用证要求由受益人签署。

（6）2/32NM的数量错误，此单货物的总金额也有错误。

3）装箱单

（1）合同号码与信用证及其他单据不符，应为"YN-NK942"，而非"YNN-NK942"。

（2）唛头与信用证及其他单据不符，应为"0016100293496-1"，而非"0016100293496"。

（3）价格术语与其他单据不符，应为"FOB KELANG"，而非"FOB KELAN"。

（4）未按信用证要求显示每件包装（纸箱）的毛净重。

（5）2/32NM的总数量、总净重错误。

4）提单

（1）收货人有误，应为"To Order"，而非凭开证行指示。

（2）运费条款与信用证不符，应为"Freight Payable at Destination"，而非"Freight Prepaid"。

（3）未按信用证要求作相应的空白背书。

（4）未按信用证要求显示船公司在大连代理的名称、地址、联系电话。

5）产地证

（1）货物描述与信用证及其他单据不符，应为"YARN"，而非"YARM"。

（2）包装件数与其他单据不符，应为298箱，而非289箱。

（3）总数量、总重量应为13 032KGS。

6）检验证书

（1）承运船名与其他单据不符，应为"BIN BO"，而非"BIN BON"。

（2）净重与其他单据不符，应为13 032kg，而非13 676kg。

7）其他

未按信用证要求出具受益人寄单证明。

2. 善后函

金 喆 贸 易 有 限 公 司

JINZHE TRADING COMPANY LIMITED

地址：中国大连中山路 1267 号

电话：0411-84042525　　传真：0411-84042588

ADD：NO. 1267 ZHONGSHAN ROAD, DALIAN, CHINA

TEL：0411-84042525　FAX：0411-84042588

Date：June 22，2013

DRAGON TOY CO．，LTD

1180 CHURCH ROAD，NEW YORK，

PA 19446U. S. A.

Dear Sirs，

We are very pleased tobe inform by the Bank of China，DALIAN Branch that we have received money from Chemical Bank New York.

Recalling of the whole transaction，we feel really glad to establish business relations with you and it is through our mutual cooperation that this transaction turn out to be successful. As we have had a good beginning，we hope that the development of trade will enhance the friendship between us.

Thank you again for the efforts you have made in the transaction and we are looking forward to another opportunity to do business with you.

With best regards.

Yours faithfully，

JINZHE TRADING CO．，LTD

×××

MANAGER

附录四 各模块实训用样表

模块二

1. 出口许可证

表 2-1

出口许可证

中华人民共和国出口许可证

EXPORT LICENCE OF THE PEOPLE'S REPUBLIC OF CHINA

1. 出口商： Exporter	3. 出口许可证号： Export licence No.
2. 发货人： Consignor	4. 进口国： Export licence expiry date
5. 贸易方式： Terms of trade	8. 出口最终目的国（地区）： Country / Region of purchase
6. 合同号： Contract No.	9. 付款方式： Mode of payment
7. 报关口岸： Place of clearance	10. 运输方式： Mode of transport

11. 商品名称： Description of goods			商品编码： Code of goods			
12. 规格、型号 Specification	13. 单位 Unit	14. 数量 Quantity	15. 单价（USD） Unit price	16. 总值（USD） Amount	17. 总值折美元 Amount in USD	
18. 总计 Total						

19. 备 注： Supplementary details	20. 发证机关盖章： Issuing authority's stamp & signature
输欧或输美许可证号： 类别号：	21. 发证日期： Licence date

第一联（正本）发货人办理海关手续

中华人民共和国商务部监制（2007）

2. 进口许可证

表 2-2 进口许可证

中华人民共和国进口货物许可证
IMPORT LICENCE OF THE PEOPLE'S REPUBLIC OF CHINA

1. 进口商： Importer	3. 进口许可证号： Import license No.
2. 收货人： Consignee	4. 进口许可证有效截止日期： Import license expiry date
5. 贸易方式： Terms of trade	8. 出口国（地区）： Country/Region of exportation
6. 外汇来源： Terms of foreign exchange	9. 原产国（地区）： Country/Region of origin
7. 报关口岸： Place of clearance	10. 商品用途： Use of goods

11. 商品名称：　　　　　　　　　　商品编码：
Description of goods　　　　　　　Code of goods

12. 规格、型号 Specification	13. 单位 Unit	14. 数量 Quantity	15. 单价 Unit Price	16. 总值 Amount	17. 总值折美元 Amount in USD
18. 总 计 Total					

19. 备 注 Supplementary details	20. 发证机关签章： Issuing authority's stamp & signature
	21. 发证日期： License date

中华人民共和国商务部监制（2007）

模块三

1. 商业发票

表 3-1

商业发票

COMMERCIAL INVOICE

(1) SELLER	(3) INVOICE NO.	(4) INVOICE DATE
	(5) L/C NO.	(6) DATE
	(7) ISSUED BY	
(2) BUYER	(8) CONTRACT NO.	(9) DATE
	(10) FROM	(11) TO
	(12) SHIPPED BY	(13) PRICE TERM

(14) MARKS　(15) DESCRIPTION OF GOODS　(16) QTY.　(17) UNIT PRICE　(18) AMOUNT

TOTAL

(19) ISSUED BY

(20) SIGNATURE

3 COPIES

2. 装箱单

表 3-2

装箱单
PACKING LIST

(1) SELLER		(3) INVOICE NO.	(4) INVOICE DATE
		(5) FROM	(6) TO
		(7) TOTAL PACKAGES (IN WORDS)	
(2) BUYER		(8) MARKS & NOS.	

(9) C/NOS.	(10) NOS. & KINDS OF PKGS.	(11) ITEM	(12) QTY. (pcs.)	(13) G. W. (kg)	(14) N. W. (kg)	(15) MEAS. (m³)

TOTAL

(16) ISSUED BY

(17) SIGNATURE

3COPIES

3. 出口货物订舱委托书

表 3-3　　　　　　　　　　出口货物订舱委托书

日期：

（1）发货人	（4）信用证号码	
	（5）开证银行	
	（6）合同号码	（7）成交金额
	（8）装运口岸	（9）目的港
（2）收货人	（10）转船运输	（11）分批装运
	（12）信用证效期	（13）装船期限
	（14）运费	（15）成交条件
	（16）公司联系人	（17）电话/传真
（3）通知人	（18）公司开户行	（19）银行账号
	（20）特别要求	

（21）标记、唛码	（22）货号规格	（23）包装件数	（24）毛重	（25）净重	（26）数量	（27）单价	（28）总价

（29）总件数	（30）总毛重	（31）总净重	（32）总尺码	（33）总金额

（34）备注

模块四

表4-1

商业发票
COMMERCIAL INVOICE

(1) SELLER	(3) INVOICE NO.	(4) INVOICE DATE
	(5) L/C NO.	(6) DATE
	(7) ISSUED BY	
(2) BUYER	(8) CONTRACT NO.	(9) DATE
	(10) FROM	(11) TO
	(12) SHIPPED BY	(13) PRICE TERM

(14) MARKS (15) DESCRIPTION OF GOODS (16) QTY. (17) UNIT PRICE (18) AMOUNT

TOTAL

(19) ISSUED BY

(20) SIGNATURE

3 COPIES

模块五

1. 出境货物检验证书

表 5-1　　　　　　　　　　　**出境货物检验证书**

CCIC Shanghai Co. , Limited.　　　　　　　　ORIGINAL

No. 361 , Zhao Jia Bang Road , Shanghai

P. C： 200032

Tel： 021-63062406/64189367

Fax： 021-63244587

E-mail： shanghai@ ccic. com

Pre-shipment Inspection Certificate for Quantity

Certificate No. ： SH/EXY6170

Date： Sept. 3, 2013

Applicant：

Consignor：

Consignee：

Commodity：

Quantity/Weight Declared：

Invoice No. ：

Letter of Credit No. ：

Shipping Marks：

Results of Inspection：

*　　*　　*　　*

This report is issued without prejudice to the liabilities to the parties concerned.

2. 进口商品检验证书

表 5-2   进口商品检验证书

中华人民共和国上海进出口商品检验局
SHANGHAI IMPORT & EXPORT COMMODITY
INSPECTION BUREAU OF THE PEOPLE'S REPUBLIC
OF CHINA

地址：上海市中山东一路 13 号   检 验 证 书   No. ：

Address：13，Zhongshan Road   INSPECTION CERTIFICATE   日期 Date：

　　　　（E. 1），Shanghai

电话 Tel：8621-32155296

收 货 人：

Consignee：

发 货 人：

Consignor：

品　名：

Commodity：

报验数量/重量：

Quantity/Weight Declared：

运　输：

Transportation：

进口日期：

Date of Arrival：

卸毕日期：

Date of Completion of Discharge：

发 票 号：

Invoice No. ：

合 同 号：

Contract No. ：

标记及号码：

Mark & No. ：

注意：本证书译文如有任何异点，概以中文为主。

（N. B. In case if divergence，the Chinese text shall be regarded as authentic）

模块六

1. 海运出口货物投保单

表 6-1 　　　　　　　　　　　　**海运出口货物投保单**

（1）保险人		（2）被保险人	
（3）标记	（4）包装及数量	（5）保险货物项目	（6）保险货物金额

（7）总保险金额：（大写）

（8）运输工具：　　　　　（船名）　　　　　（航次）

（9）装运港：　　　　　　　　　（10）目的港：

（11）投保险别：　　　　　　　　（12）货物起运日期：

（13）投保日期：　　　　　　　　（14）投保人签字：

2. 保险单

表 6-2 保险单

中 国 人 民 保 险 公 司
THE PEOPLE'S INSURANCE COMPANY OF CHINA

总公司设于北京 一九四九年创立

Head office：BEIJING Established in 1949

保险单 保险单号次

INSURANCE POLICY POLICY NO. JZ-DRGBD01

中国人民保险公司（以下简称本公司）
THIS POLICY OF INSURANCE WITNESSES THAT THE PEOPLE'S INSURANCE COMPANY OF CHINA（HEREINAFTER CALLED "THE COMPANY"）

根据
AT THE REQUEST OF _____

（以下简称被保险人）的要求，由被保险人
（HEREINAFTER CALLED "THE INSURED"）AND IN CONSIDERATION OF THE AGREED PREMIUM 向本公司缴付约定的保险费，PAID TO THE COMPANY BY THE INSURED, UNDERTAKES TO INSURE THE UNDERMENTIONED

按照本保险单承保险别和背面所载条款与 GOODS IN TRANSPORTATION SUBJECT TO THE CONDITIONS OF THIS POLICY AS PER THE

下列特款承保下述货物运输保险，特立本保险单。
CLAUSES PRINTED OVERLEAF AND OTHER SPECIAL CLAUSES ATTACHED HEREON.

标记 MARKS& NOS.	包 装 及 数 量 QUANTITY	保 险 货 物 项 目 DESCRIPTION OF GOODS	保 险 金 额 AMOUNT INSURED

总保险金额：
TOTAL AMOUNT INSURED：_____

保费： 费率： 装载运输工具：
PREMIUM _____ RATE _____ PER CONVEYANCE S. S. _____

开航日期： 自 至
SLG. ON OR ABT. _____ FROM _____ TO _____

承保险别：
CONDITIONS

所保货物，如遇出险，本公司凭本保险单及其他有关证件给付赔款。
CLAIMS, IF ANY, PAYABLE ON SURRENDER OF THIS POLICY TOGETHER WITH OTHER RELEVANT DOCUMENTS.

所保货物，如发生本保险单项下负责赔偿的损失或事故，
IN THE EVENT OF ACCIDENT WHEREBY LOSS OR DAMAGE MAY RESULT IN A CLAIM UNDER THIS POLICY IMMEDIATE,

应立即通知本公司下述代理人查勘
NOTICE APPLYING FOR SURVEY MUST BE GIVEN TO THE COMPANY'S AGENT AS MENTIONED HEREUNDER.

中国人民保险公司上海分公司
赔款偿付地点 THE PEOPLE'S INSURANCE CO. OF CHINA
CLAIM PAYABLE AT/IN _____ SHANGHAI BRANCH

日期 上海
DATE SHANGHAI 郭复北

地址：中国上海中山东一路 23 号
Address：23 Zhongshan Dong Yi Lu, Shanghai, China. General Manager
TEL：63234305 63217466-44 Telex：33128 PICCS CN.
Cable：42001 Shanghai

模块七

1. 一般原产地证明书

表 7-1   CERTIFICATE OF ORIGINAL

1. Exporter（full name and address）	Certificate No.
	CERTIFICATE OF ORIGIN OF THE PEOPLE'S REPUBLIC OF CHINA
2. Consignee（full name, address, country）	
3. Means of transport and route	
4. Country/region of destination	5. For certifying authority use only

6. Marks and numbers of packages	7. Description of goods, number and kind of packages	8. H. S. Code	9. Quantity or weight	10. Number and date of invoices

11. Declaration by the exporter The undersigned hereby declares that the above details and statements are correct; that all the goods were produced in China and that they comply with the Rules of Origin of the People's Republic of China.	12. Certification It is hereby certified that the declaration by the exporter is correct.
Place and date, signature and stamp of authorized signatory	Place and date, signature and stamp of certifying authority

China Council for the Promotion of International Trade is China Chamber of International Commerce.

2. 普惠制原产地证明书

表 7-2　　GENERALIZED SYSTEM OF PREFERENCES CERTIFICATE OF ORIGINAL

1. Goods consigned from (Exporter's business name, address, country)	Reference No. GENERALIZED SYSTEM OF PREFERENCES CERTIFICATE OF ORIGIN (Combined declaration and certificate) FORM A Issued in THE PEOPLE'S REPUBLIC OF CHINA (country) See notes overleaf
2. Goods consigned to (Consignee's name, address, country)	
3. Means of transport and route (as far as known)	4. For official use

5. Item number	6. Marks and numbers of packages	7. Number and kind of packages; description of goods	8. Origin criterion (See notes overleaf)	9. Gross weight or other quantity	10. Number and date of invoices

11. Certification It is hereby certified, on the basis of control carried out, that the declaration by the exporter is correct.	12. Declaration by the exporter The undersigned hereby declares that the above details and statements are correct; that all the goods were produced in _____ (country) and that they comply with the origin requirements specified for those goods in the Generalized System of Preferences for goods exported to _____ (importing country)
Place and date, signature and stamp of certifying authority	Place and date, signature of authorized signatory

模块八

表 8-1 　　　　　　　　　中华人民共和国出口货物报关单

预录入编号：　　　　　　　　　　海关编号：

出口口岸		备案号	出口日期	申报日期
经营单位		运输方式	运输工具名称	提运单号
发货单位		贸易方式	征免性质	结汇方式
许可证号	运抵国（地区）		指运港	境内货源地
批准文号	成交方式	运费	保费	杂费
合同协议号	件数	包装种类	毛重（千克）	净重（千克）
集装箱号	随附单据			生产厂家

标记、唛码及备注

项号 商品编号 商品名称、规格型号 数量及单位 最终目的国（地区）　单价 总价 币制 征免

税费征收情况

录入员　　录入单位	兹声明以上申报无讹并承担法律责任	海关审单、批注及放行日期（签章）	
报关员		审单	审价
单位地址	申报单位（签章）	征税	统计
邮编　　电话	填制日期	查验	放行

模块九

表 9-1　　　　　　　　　　　海运提单

托运人 Shipper		B/L　No.
收货人或指示 Consignee or Order		中 国 对 外 贸 易 运 输 总 公 司 北　京 BEIJING 联　运　提　单 COMBINED TRANSPORT BILL OF LADING
通知地址 Notify Address		RECEIVED the foods in apparent good order and condition as specified below unless otherwise stated herein. Thecarrier, in accordance with the provisions contained in this document,
前段运输 Pre-carriage by	收货地点 Place of Receipt	(1) undertakes to perform or to procure the performance of the entire transport from the place at which the goods are taken in charge to the place designated for delivery in this
海运船只 Ocean Vessel	装货港 Port of Loading	document, and (2) assumes liability as prescribed in this document for such transport one of the bills of lading must be surrendered duty indorsed in exchange for the goods or delivery order.

卸货港 Port of Discharge	交货地点 Place of Delivery	运费支付地 Freight Payable at	正本提单份数 Number of Original Bs/L

标志和号码 Marks and Nos.	件数和包装种类 Number and Kind of Packages	货名 Description of Goods	毛重（千克） Gross Weight （kgs.）	尺码（立方米） Measurement （m³）

以 上 细 目 由 托 运 人 提 供

ABOVE PARTICULARS FURNISHED BY SHIPPER

运杂费 Freight and Charges	In witness whereof the number of original bills of lading stated above have been signed, one of which being accomplished, the other (s) to be void.
	签单地点和日期 Place and Date of Issue
	代表承运人签字 Signed for or on Behalf of the Carrier 代　理 as Agents

模块十

表 10-1   BILL OF EXCHANGE

No._____

For_____   _____

　　(amount in figure)   (place and date of issue)

At_____sight of this FIRST Bill of Exchange (SECOND being unpaid)

pay to_____ or order the sum of

_____

　　　　　　　　　　　　　　(amount in words)

Value received for_____of_____

　　　　　　　　(quantity)　　　　(name of commodity)

Drawn under_____

L/C No._____ dated_____

To：   For and on behalf of

                                            _____

                                                 (Signature)

模块十二

1. 装运通知书

表 12-1　　　　　　　　　　　　　　**装运通知书**

金 喆 进 出 口 有 限 公 司

JINZHE IMP. AND EXP. CO. LTD.

Tel：86-21-64331255　　　　Fax：86-21-64331256

ADD. ：ROOM 302，WORLD TRADE CENTER，277 WU XING ROAD，SHANGHAI，CHINA

TO：　　　　　　　　　DATE：

FROM：　　　　　　　　　　SHIPPING ADVICE

　　　　S/C NO. :

　　　　L/C NO. :

　　　　B/L NO. :

　　　　GOODS：

　　　　VALUE（USD）：

　　　　QUANTITY：

　　　　PACKAGES：

　　　　G. W.（KGS.）：

　　　　N. W.（KGS.）：

　　　　MEAS.（m^3）：

　　　　VESSEL：

　　　　FROM：

　　　　TO：

　　　　ETD：

　　　　ETA：

BEST REGARDS

---

2. 受益人证明

表 12-2　　　　　　　　　　　　　　**受益人证明**

金　喆　进　出　口　有　限　公　司

JINZHE IMP. AND EXP. CO. LTD.

DATE：

ADD. :		TEL：	
		FAX：	
		E-MAIL：	
TO:			

S/C NO. :

L/C NO. :

INVOICE NO. :

B/L NO. :

GOODS：

VALUE：

QUANTITY：

WE CERTIFY THAT SHIPPING SAMPLE HAVE BEEN SENT TO APPLICANT BEFORE SHIPMENT.

模块十三

1. 汇票

表 13-1

汇 票

BILL OF EXCHANGE

No. _____

For _____   _____

    （amount in figure）   （place and date of issue）

At _____ sight of this FIRST Bill of Exchange （SECOND of exchange being unpaid）

pay to _____ or order the sum of

_____

                        （amount in words）

Value received for _____ of _____

                  （quantity）   （name of commodity）

Drawn under _____

L/C No. _____ dated _____

To：   For and on behalf of

                                                    _____

                                                            （Signature）

2. 提单

表 13-2

提 单
BILL OF LADING

(1) SHIPPER:	(10) B/L NO.:
Address:	
(2) CONSIGNEE:	COSCO 中国远洋运输（集团）总公司 CHINA OCEAN SHIPPING（GROUP）CO. ORIGINAL Combined Transport BILL OF LADING
(3) NOTIFY PARTY:	

(4) PLACE OF RECEIPT:	(5) OCEAN VESSEL:
(6) VOYAGE NO.:	(7) PORT OF LOADING:

(8) PORT OF DISCHARGE:	(9) PLACE OF DELIVERY:

(11) MARKS:	(12) NOS. & KINDS OF PKGS.:	(13) DESCRIPTION OF GOODS	(14) G.W.（kg）	(15) MEAS（m³）

(16) TOTAL NUMBER OF CONTAINERS OR PACKAGES（IN WORDS）:

FREIGHT & CHARGES	REVENUE TONS	RATE	PER	PREPAID	COLLECT
PREPAID AT	PAYABLE AT		(17) PLACE AND DATE OF ISSUE:		
TOTAL PREPAID	(18) NUMBER OF ORIGINAL B（S）L:				

LADEN ON BOARD THE VESSEL (21) SIGNED FOR THE CARRIER:

(19) DATE: (20) BY:

ENDORSEMENT:

3. 商业发票

表13-3

商业发票

COMMERCIAL INVOICE

(1) SELLER		(3) INVOICE NO.	(4) INVOICE DATE
Address:		(5) L/C NO.	(6) DATE
		(7) ISSUED BY	
(2) BUYER		(8) CONTRACT NO.	(9) DATE
Address:		(10) FROM	(11) TO
		(12) SHIPPED BY	(13) PRICE TERM
(14) MARKS	(15) DESCRIPTION OF GOODS	(16) QTY.	(17) UNIT PRICE	(18) AMOUNT

TOTAL:

Packing:

(19) TOTAL VALUE:

(20) ISSUED BY

(21) SIGNATURE

3 COPIES

4. 保险单

表 13-4 保险单

中 国 人 民 保 险 公 司
THE PEOPLE'S INSURANCE COMPANY OF CHINA
总公司设于北京 一九四九年创立
Head office：BEIJING Established in 1949

保险单	保险单号次
INSURANCE POLICY	POLICY NO. JZ-DRGBD01

中国人民保险公司（以下简称本公司）
THIS POLICY OF INSURANCE WITNESSES THAT THE PEOPLE'S INSURANCE COMPANY OF CHINA（HEREINAFTER CALLED "THE COMPANY"）

根据
AT THE REQUEST OF
（以下简称被保险人）的要求，由被保险人
（ HEREINAFTER CALLED " THE INSURED "）AND IN CONSIDERATION OF THE AGREED PREMIUM
向本公司缴付约定的保险费，
BEING PAID TO THE COMPANY BY THE INSURED, UNDERTAKES TO INSURE THE UNDERMENTIONED
按照本保险单承保别和背面所载条款与
GOODS IN TRANSPORTATION SUBJECT TO THE CONDITIONS OF THIS POLICY AS PER THE
下列特款承保下述货物运输保险，特立本保险单
CLAUSES PRINTED OVERLEAF AND OTHER SPECIAL CLAUSES ATTACHED HEREON.

标记	数量	保险货物项目	保险金额
MARKS& NOS	QUANTITY	DESCRIPTION OF GOODS	AMOUNT INSURED

总保险金额：
TOTAL AMOUNT INSURED： _____

保费	费率	装载运输工具
PREMIUM ____	RATE ____	PER CONVEYANCE ____
开航日期	自	至
SLG. ON OR ABT. _____	FROM ____	TO ____

承保险别：
CONDITIONS
所保货物，如遇出险，本公司凭本保险单及其他有关证件给付赔款。
CLAIMS, IF ANY, PAYABLE ON SURRENDER OF THIS POLICY TOGETHER WITH OTHER RELEVANT DOCUMENTS.
所保货物，如发生本保险单项下负责赔偿的损失或事故，
IN THE EVENT OF ACCIDENT WHEREBY LOSS OR DAMAGE MAY RESULT IN A CLAIM UNDER THIS POLICY IMMEDIATE
应立即通知本公司下述代理人查勘
NOTICE APPLYING FOR SURVEY MUST BE GIVEN TO THE COMPANY'S AGENT AS MENTIONED HEREUNDER：
所保货物，如遇出险，本公司凭本保险单及其他有关证件给付赔款。

赔款偿付地点
CLAIM PAYABLE AT/IN _____

日 期	大连
DATE _____	DALIAN

地址：中国大连中山东一路 23 号
TEL：83234305 83217466-44 Telex：33128 PICCS CN.
Address：23 Zhongshan Dong Yi Lu Dalian，China.
Cable：42008 Dalian

中国人民保险公司大连分公司
THE PEOPLE'S INSURANCE CO. OF CHINA
DALIAN BRANCH
孙博
General Manager

5. 装箱单

表 13-5

装箱单
PACKINGLIST

(1) SELLER	(3) INVOICE NO. (4) INVOICE DATE
Address:	(5) FROM (6) TO
	(7) TOTAL PACKAGES (IN WORDS)
(2) BUYER	(8) MARKS & NOS.
Address:	

(9) C/NOS.	(10) NOS. & KINDS OF PKGS.	(11) ITEM	(12) QTY. (PCS.)	(13) G. W. (kg)	(14) N. W. (kg)	(15) MEAS. (m³)

TOTAL

SHIPPING MARKS   WEIGHT AND MEAS. PER EXPORT CARTON:

(16) ISSUED BY

(17) SIGNATURE

×××

2COPIES

6. 原产地证明

表 13-6

原产地证明书

CERTIFICATE OF ORIGINAL

1. Exporter (full name and address)	Certificate No.
2. Consignee (full name, address, country)	CERTIFICATE OF ORIGIN OF THE PEOPLE'S REPUBLIC OF CHINA
3. Means of transport and route	5. For certifying authority use only
4. Destination port	

6. Marks and numbers of packages	7. Description of goods/ number and kind of packages	8. H. S. Code	9. Quantity or weight	10. Number and date of invoices

****

11. Declaration by the exporter	12. Certification
The undersigned hereby declares that the above details and statements are correct; that all the goods were produced in China and that they comply with the Rules of Origin of the People's Republic of China.	It is hereby certified that the declaration by the exporter is correct. DATE:
Place and date/signature and stamp of certifying authority	Place and date/signature and stamp of certifying authority

China Council for the Promotion of International Trade is China Chamber of International Commerce.

2 COPIES

附录五 法定检验检疫代码表及海关监管证件代码表

法定检验检疫代码表

代码	含义
M	表示进口商品检验
N	表示出口商品检验
P	表示进境动植物、动植物产品检疫
Q	表示出境动植物、动植物产品检疫
R	表示进口食品卫生监督检验
S	表示出口食品卫生监督检验
V	表示进境卫生检疫
W	表示出境卫生检疫
L	表示民用商品入境验证

海关监管证件代码表

代码	监管证件名称	代码	监管证件名称
1*	进口许可证	2	两用物项和技术进口许可证
3	两用物项和技术出口许可证	4*	出口许可证
6	旧机电产品禁止进口	7*	自动进口许可证
8	禁止出口商品	9	禁止进口商品
A*	入境货物通关单	B*	出境货物通关单
D	出/入境货物通关单（毛坯钻石用）	E	濒危物种允许出口证明书
F	濒危物种允许进口证明书	G	两用物项和技术出口许可证（定向）
H	港澳 OPA 纺织品证明	I	精神药物进（出）口准许证
J	黄金及其制品进出口准许证或批件	L	药品进出口准许证
M	密码产品和设备进口许可证	O*	自动进口许可证（新旧机电产品）

代码	监管证件名称	代码	监管证件名称
P*	固体废物进口许可证	Q	进口药品通关单
R	进口兽药通关单	S	进出口农药登记证明
T	银行调运现钞进出境许可证	U	合法捕捞产品通关证明
W	麻醉药品进出口准许证	X	有毒化学品环境管理放行通知单
Y*	原产地证明	Z	进口音像制品批准单或节目提取单
e	关税配额外优惠税率进口棉花配额证	q	国别关税配额证明
S	适用 ITA 税率的商品用途认定证明	t	关税配额证明
V*	自动进口许可证（加工贸易）	x	出口许可证（加工贸易）
Y	出口许可证（边境小额贸易）		

注：本表格标记有"*"的，表示常见的监管条件。

主要参考文献

［1］张哲. 国际贸易单证实训教程［M］. 大连：东北财经大学出版社，2010.

［2］黎孝先. 国际贸易实务［M］. 北京：对外经济贸易大学出版社，2000.

［3］全国国际商务单证培训认证考试办公室. 国际商务单证理论与实务［M］. 北京：中国商务出版社，2014.

［4］海关总署报关员资格考试教材编写委员会. 报关员资格全国统一考试教材［M］. 北京：中国海关出版社，2013.

［5］徐景霖. 国际贸易实务［M］. 大连：东北财经大学出版社，2006.

［6］祝卫. 出口贸易模拟操作教程［M］. 上海：上海人民出版社，1999.

［7］祝卫，程洁，谈英. 国际贸易操作能力实用教程［M］. 上海：上海人民出版社，2006.